ON THE RIGHT SIDE

Tom Sears

There are many, many people to thank for many reasons.

First of all my brother Bill for convincing me of the importance of writing the column after I initially had serious doubts.

Also, Chuck Pinkey, a strong, true conservative, who filled in for me when I was overseas and unable to get my columns in on time. I am so glad that he was the person who took over the column, and he is doing a superb job.

In addition, I would like to thank the hundreds and hundreds of people, many of whom I never knew before, who wrote and gave me their strong vote of approval all along the way. They were the support I needed to keep going.

Next I owe a big thank you to The Daily Star and especially Sam Pollak, who allowed me to use my columns to create this book. He didn't have to do this since the columns technically belonged to and were the property of the paper.

I have found Sam to be a man of honor and integrity whose word I can trust. He has repeatedly said he doesn't agree with 99 percent of what I say, but he would strongly defend my right to do so. From the beginning he said he would have my back and he was a man 100 percent true to his word.

Lastly, I am so thankful for the family I have been blessed with.

First, my wife, with whom I never discuss politics (she probably agrees with Sam much more than she agrees with me). She has stayed with me and believed in me for a very long time. We have been together for 41 years and are still going strong.

I am so thankful for my two sons, Covar and Ian (and both good conservatives) of whom I am very, very proud, and their wonderful wives Tara and Paige.

Most of all I have been blessed with my first granddaughter, Caroline Josephine Sears. I had no idea at all that being a grandfather could bring such joy.

Table of Contents

Column is Opportunity for Ideas

I want to thank The Daily Star, especially Sam Pollak, for the opportunity to be the paper's local conservative columnist.
I was very apprehensive when I was offered this opportunity because of deadlines and frequency of columns, among other concerns. This was a very serious commitment to be undertaken, along with a high level of responsibility. In discussing this with my brother, he thought I would be crazy to pass up this opportunity, and I received the same opinion from several of my friends.

After giving the matter much thought, I decided to jump in and give an honest
effort.

The Daily Star has told you about my background, but I want to use this first column to tell you about my opinions on a variety of subjects.

I am an unabashed conservative, on both social and fiscal matters. Sam Pollak said the first few columns would flow quite easily, but it would become more and more difficult to come up with topics on a timely basis. I, instead, have a problem with what topic to choose first.

Here are some of the topics I feel strongly about and will be discussing. I am against abortion. I am in favor of lowering tax rates (yes, the rich are paying far more than their fair share). I will certainly have an article on torture versus humiliation and degradation. People shouldn't have a problem distinguishing between the terms but many seem to.

I am a common sense environmentalist. I think the choice between a spotted owl and jobs for 1,000s of people in the lumber industry who are providing for their families is really pretty simple.

We have to reduce our dependence on foreign energy sources. Yes, nuclear energy must be promoted. Hybrid cars, solar, geothermal, wind energy and alternate fuel sources must be advanced immediately but in the meantime we need a bridge to those sources. Drilling in Alaska and off shore is fine with me. It is time to act on a strategy rather than just talk about one.

If I am to be called a member of the Christian right, then I take that as an extreme compliment, even though the person using the term uses it in a derogatory way.

Yes, I am offended when people feel they have to say "happy holidays" instead of "Merry Christmas." People feel Christian symbols, such as the cross, have to be removed from public view because they offend some people. I don't understand this at all.

To a nonbeliever, the cross is simply two pieces of wood attached to each other, whereas, to me it is a very important symbol of my faith. Guess who I think should take the sensitivity classes.

I don't know where the liberals draw the line on morality and other issues. I don't think they have any standards at all. "In God We Trust" stays on our money, "Under God" stays in my Pledge of Allegiance.

I can't wait to take on the topic of extreme left-leaning liberals who have taken over the Democratic Party. Ted Kennedy, Harry Reid, Nancy Pelosi, Pat Leahy, John Kerry, and on and on. Give me a break. This won't even be a challenge.

I read The American Spectator, the Heritage Foundation website, the Cato Institute website, and listen to talk show hosts such as Rush Limbaugh (gasp) and Sean Hannity. I wonder why programs such as these are growing by leaps and bounds. I tried to find some liberal talk show hosts, but I wasn't successful.

I know Bill Clinton had a show, as well as Mario Cuomo, but I guess their programs weren't financially viable. I wonder why. Then I heard about Al Franken, but I couldn't find him on the radio either. Maybe it was because he has an audience of 70 listeners.

I can't wait to talk about the wars in Iraq and Afghanistan and the hypocrisy of the Democrats trying to back away from their original statements. Thank heavens President Bush is finally on the offensive and calling a person who lies a liar. I have very strong opinions on border security and enforcing the strong LEGAL immigration laws already in place.

I have many more issues to touch upon: Supreme Court Justice selections, strict interpretation of our Constitution and its original intent, declining educational standards and our increasing inability to compete on a global basis. Another good topic is our institutions of higher learning and their bias for liberalism.

One thing I don't want to do is get Mr. Pollak mad at me for going over length
limits on my very first column. Like I said originally, I truly appreciate this opportunity.
So, there are some of my opinions in a nutshell. People are going to love me or hate me or agree or disagree with me some of the time. I look forward to the coming weeks to creating discussion and controversy. I have a very thick skin so don't worry about hurting my feelings.

Taking on Cindy Sheehan

About a week ago I attended a presentation by Cindy Sheehan. She is the anti- war camper down at Crawford, Texas. Before I start, Ms. Sheehan, I want you to know that I don't pretend to know the amount of grief you must have for losing a son. It is certainly something no parent should have to go through.

However, for you to make him a political, anti-war issue opens you up to scrutiny and analysis. There are many statements made by you that showed you have a total lack of comprehension of the real world. You seem to be a very naïve person. I hate to waste this column pointing out your mistakes, but I can't ignore them.

You said, regarding the attack on 9/11, "(Americans') reaction to 9/11 was inappropriate to say the least." Also, you said, "Americans attacked two countries in an act of war for what was essentially a criminal act."

That is one of the silliest things I have ever heard. Our response was an act of war, but killing 3,000 innocent people was simply a criminal act?
Also, quote, "I had friends who went to Iraq to stand in front of tanks and airplanes to try to stop the invasion."

I think you are confused. We didn't have tanks and airplanes in Iraq before the invasion. Maybe you were thinking of Tiananmen Square in China in 1989.

I also found it unbelievable for you to quote Tariq Aziz (Iraq's deputy prime minister under Saddam). You would accept as an unbiased statement of fact when he said, "They (Iraq) were trying to comply with everything we told them to do; but you are going to invade us anyway, so why are we even putting up this pretense?"

Your response was very deep. You said, "Wow, he's right."

This probably started out to be a very noble cause. When did your son drop out of the picture? Do you want the attention directed to you? I don't see any Casey coffee mugs or Casey T-shirts. Your name is on these items. You couldn't even put your son's face on the cover of your book!

But enough of this, although I had much more to criticize about your speech. I want to point out a few facts about the other Cindy Sheehan.
Cindy, why do you think you are so special? Did you forget that you already had a meeting with President Bush in June 2004?

Your hometown newspaper ran a story about you. The reporter: "The ten minutes of face time with the president could have given the family a chance to vent their frustration or ask Bush some of the difficult questions they have been asking themselves..."

"...But in the end the family decided against such talk, deferring to how they believed Casey would have wanted them to act. In addition, Pat (Casey's father) noted that Bush wasn't stumping for votes or trying to gain a political edge for the upcoming election."

Another: "We have a lot of respect for the office of the president, and I have a new respect for him because he was sincere and he didn't have to meet with us," Pat said.

Another: "I now know he's sincere about wanting freedom for the Iraqis," Cindy said after their meeting. "I know he's sorry and feels some pain for our loss. And I know he is a man of faith."

One more: "That was the gift the president gave us, the gift of happiness, of being together," Cindy said.

What happened Cindy? I guess your anti-war, leftist friends wouldn't have chosen to use you the way they are using you now had you maintained your original position.

Do you think your credibility will be affected by your association with people and organizations such as: George (Bush hater) Soros, Jesse Jackson, Michael Moore, Al (Tawana Brawley) Sharpton, Maureen Dowd, Maxine Walters and websites such as Socialist Worker on Line, Communist Party USA.upj, and MoveOn.org?

Ms. Sheehan, just remember this. Your adult son volunteered for service and then re-enlisted. I don't know the reason for his doing this, but I am sure it was a noble one. I am sure he fought bravely. I am sure his fellow soldiers trusted him to cover their backs. I'm sure he died a hero's death. I would have been proud to have known him.

Cindy, please think what your son would want. Go back to what you felt in June 2004. You dishonor his good name by your current actions.

Last but certainly not least: I want everyone to have a very MERRY CHRISTMAS. Please, remember what the day truly stands for.

U.S. spying should be supported

Thursday, December 15, was a very historic moment. The Iraqi people turned out in amazing numbers to take part in their first democratic election. It is estimated that up to 70 percent of the eligible population took part, even with the risks of suicide bombings and other dangers. Americans have a poorer turnout for our elections without all the risks. This should put us to shame.

Ignoring this good news, The New York Times chose to publish a story about a highly classified National Security Agency wire-tapping program. In addition, the newspaper strongly insinuated that President Bush used this program illegally and was stepping all over our civil liberties and our right to privacy.

Why did the Times do this? Its intentions are subject to strong suspicions. First of all, it is common knowledge that this rag of a paper is heavily anti-Bush. It is the paper of choice for all the liberals who look for any news, no matter how ridiculous, to use against our president. We will talk about these rabid anti-Bush fools in a later column.

Isn't it strange that the Times had this story for almost a year and withheld it until the Friday when a vote on extending the Patriot Act was to take place? It claims that the government asked it to withhold this story; but remember, this is the newspaper of Jayson Blair and Maureen Dowd. In other words, it is more than willing to lie if it suits its fancy. What a better time to publish a story to guarantee a bombshell than on the day of the Patriot Act vote?

Secondly, the story was written by James Risen, a New York Times reporter who, by coincidence, has a book coming out about this very topic in less than a month. Even a liberal would have a hard time justifying the timing of this article. I take this back. These individuals will stoop to anything, including blatant lying, if it makes our president look bad. Does Dan Rather come to mind?

I think it's time to act tough. James Risen and his "sources" should be tried for treason for aiding and abetting the enemy with these leaks. It is clear that this top- secret, LEGAL program, which has already been proved to have thwarted potential attacks against our country, is now compromised.

The blood of any additional American lives lost through terrorist acts will now be on the hands of these traitors and anyone else who supports the release of this LEGAL spying program.

You liberals have to learn to read beyond the title of an article and study the facts provided by more-reputable newspapers. Contrary to the lie that Bush was using the Patriot Act to spy on American citizens without a warrant, only e-mails and phone calls originating outside the United States and made by known or suspected terrorists were being tapped.

I would like a liberal to tell me how a warrant is supposed to be asked for in time to catch a two-minute phone call that could have catastrophic consequences if not monitored and acted upon immediately.

Also, while you are thinking, make a list of all the "abuses" that have occurred by these actions. Do the same for the Patriot Act abuses. The answer is none in both cases. Don't you think that with all your hate for our president, you could come up with a few?

The last item to point out is that members of both House and Senate Intelligence Committees, as well as other prominent congressional leaders, were repeatedly briefed about this NSA wiretapping policy. We now have Rep. Nancy Pelosi and Sen. Jay Rockefeller claiming to have "discovered" letters in their files that indicated their strong concerns or objections to these policies. Liars!

The Republican chairman of the Senate Intelligence Committee suggested Wednesday that Sen. Rockefeller was suffering from amnesia or selective memory loss given his criticism of the Bush administration's surveillance tactics (Human Events Online, Dec. 21, 2005).

The committee was briefed repeatedly. "There was always time for questions, always time for any point of view, and Senator Rockefeller was always in the end result very supportive," Senator Pat Roberts said.

I am sick and tired of liberal radicals taking the liberty to paint President Bush in a negative light, whether the accusations are intentionally a lie or not. Any American with the smallest amount of common sense should appreciate that President Bush is doing everything within his constitutional power to protect the lives of Americans.

Please wake up. There is an enemy out there who will resort to anything to destroy our way of life. Remember, there are no civil rights if our freedom is lost.

To all you liberals out there, try being more supportive and less negative once in a while. You'll feel better about yourself, and people might start taking you more seriously.

Liberals need to wake up, be patriotic

I've heard enough. It's time to take the gloves off. I am sick and tired of hearing my commander-in-chief and legitimately elected president (twice legally) being belittled, joked about, and especially being called a liar.

It's not that it shouldn't be expected toward a public figure (which we conservatives can take), but rather for the blind hypocrisy on the part of those behind it.

After all, it's not long ago we conservatives were saying the same things about our president's predecessor. One difference though: We were right.

I have a multiple-choice test for you liberals to take. You are either:
(a)   Ignorant of the facts;
(b)   Ignoring the facts;
(c)   Envious
(d)   Unpatriotic
(e)   All of the above.

I can't believe you are still whining about 2000. Grow up and get over it. I would love to have serious, mature discussions with responsible people, but I don't have a bit of time for the uninformed, over-emotional individuals described above.

Some quotes from your leaders:

John Kerry, Jan 23, 2003: "Without question we need to disarm Saddam Hussein. He is a brutal, murderous dictator leading an oppressive regime. He presents a particularly grievous threat because he is so consistently prone to miscalculation. And now he is miscalculating America's response to his continued deceit and his consistent grasp for weapons of mass destruction."

This was your presidential candidate. Did I mention your leader missed 76 percent of Senate Intelligence Committee meetings of which he was a member?

Bill Clinton, Feb. 17, 1998: "If Saddam rejects peace, and we have to use force, our purpose is clear. We want to seriously diminish the threat posed by Iraq's weapons of mass destruction."

Ted Kennedy, Sept 27, 2002: "We have known for many years that Saddam Hussein is seeking and developing weapons of mass destruction."

Al Gore, Sept. 23, 2002: "We know he has stored nuclear supplies, secret supplies of biological and chemical weapons throughout his country."

If you need more, send me an e-mail and I'll get them to you.

Not to let facts get in the way, but what about the 10 times Saddam used WMDs previously, according to Sandy Berger? How about the pictures of weapons inspectors being held up at the front gates while all the trucks were hauling things away out the back? How about all the U.N. resolutions Saddam consistently ignored and violated?

Where are these weapons, you ask? What about the Downing Street memo? I will happily address those issues in a future column.

Now, how about the Democrats' plan for Iraq. Oops, they don't have one. They are getting worried, however. They are trying to come up with one so they can attempt to take credit for a U.S. victory when it happens.

Bush's plan for victory was and still is the most logical and sensible one. He is the one who is most serious about his No. 1 obligation to U.S. citizens. That is our national security.

Notice how he doesn't care about polls? He knows we are on the right course and will continue this strategy to completion. That is a sign of a true leader.

Liberals base all their decisions on which way the political winds are currently blowing without even considering what is best for the country.

You liberals huffed and puffed, exuding patriotism shortly after 9/11 because that is what the public wanted. Now you have completely changed your position and want to bring our troops home, even if it would be disastrous for U.S. security.

"I support the troops but not the war." That is such a hypocritical statement. It might make the person saying it feel good about himself or herself, but it is quite harmful to our troops. Even though all the anti-war talk hurts their morale, you continue to make such idiotic comments.

Even though you hear about all the good, positive things our men and women are accomplishing over there, you don't give them any credit whatsoever as they return home.

They are bravely fighting the global war on terror. It just so happens that this war is currently taking place in Iraq. At least appreciate the fact that they are fighting for you and me, for our country.

Yes, I do question your party leaders' patriotism (and yours if you support them). When was the last time they said something, anything, good about our country that wasn't politically motivated? Can you think of one or two? I doubt it.

We seem to forget the horrors of 9/11 so soon. Remember the innocent men and women who chose to jump to their deaths rather than burn alive? Remember the unbelievable acts of courage and heroism that occurred that day?

How about the vicious beheadings (two to three minutes each with screaming the whole time), the burned bodies and other acts of cruelty that have happened since then? We should all be required to watch those horrible images over and over so we don't forget.

Please wake up and get on the Right side.

Nothing less than a slam dunk.

Samuel Alito made the eight Democrats at the confirmation hearings look overmatched and mean-spirited. The Republicans couldn't have asked for a better process. Their job was quite simple, to sit back and correct the misleading and intentional smear tactics the Democrats were attempting. I am not referring to all the Democrats. Senators Kohl, Feinstein and Feingold were the most professional of the eight.

I must have watched over 90 percent of the hearings, either live, on tape delay that same evening or the video clips that anyone can find on the C-SPAN website.

The first day was a total waste with the Democrat senators taking advantage of the photo opportunities as they strutted and preened for their special-interest groups. The only thing worth watching was the opening statement by Judge Alito.

It was day two when the fireworks began and when the Democrats began to realize how overmatched they were. Republican Senator Jon Kyl of Arizona said it best. He stated that the Democrats were already determined to vote no. They just had to justify their reasons through their questions.

Let me cover some of the most ridiculous statements made by the remaining five Democrat senators:

Patrick Leahy is the ranking Democrat on the committee. Everyone must remember him as having to resign from the Senate Intelligence Committee under allegations of leaking sensitive information to the press. Mr. Ethics himself, second only to Ted Kennedy - his questions centered on all the typical topics: torture, right to privacy and illegal searches (where he insinuated that Judge Alito was in favor of child molestation).

Alito handled his answers so that Leahy had no way to counter with additional questions. Later in the week, Leahy could only think of questions about whether an inmate on death row could be subpoenaed as a witness before the Senate! Even Alito was stumped by that question!

Senator Biden, who actually is an intelligent Democrat, was so caught up in himself that most of his time was spent lecturing, as if getting the answer was unimportant. One newscaster stated that Biden spoke for 26 of his allotted 30 minutes the first day. If I were Alito, I would have asked him, or anyone else whose question went over ten minutes, to please repeat the question

Senator Durbin enjoyed taking one or two sentences out of Alito's rulings and had to be repeatedly corrected and chastised by the Republican members for misstating the facts of each case. He had to be corrected in almost every instance.

Senator Schumer - where do I start? He was the one waving a copy of the Constitution as he questioned the judge about issues that he knew Alito shouldn't answer. I can't believe that he asked if the right to free speech was in the Constitution.

When Alito very diplomatically reminded the senator that it was stated in the first Amendment, Schumer then asked why the judge couldn't answer whether the right to an abortion was in the Constitution. Alito tried to answer the question, but the answer appeared to be over the head of the senator.

Now to Senator Kennedy. You remember him, the swimming champion of Chappaquiddick. It is difficult to understand why he was, of all people, assigned the responsibility of asking questions on ethics. His biggies were a former Vanguard case, where he repeatedly accused the judge of being unethical for not recusing himself, and the judge's membership in an association called Concerned Alumni of Princeton.

The judge answered to everyone's satisfaction, but Kennedy refused to let the facts get in the way. I could just see Judge Alito sitting there, staring at Kennedy with a cartoon bubble over him asking, "Why has this idiot asked me the same question ten times?"

Now to the witnesses. The American Bar Association interviewed more than 2,000 individuals and gave Alito its highest rating for the second time. Every judge he ever worked with and three individuals who clerked for him had nothing but the highest praise for him.

The list of witnesses included people from the entire political spectrum. It is too bad that the Democrat committee members didn't stick around to hear their praise.

Hypocrites all. Why do they question the ethics of Alito and not Senator Byrd of West Virginia, a past Kleagle of the KKK?

What do the Democrats do after having pie thrown in their face? They pout and refuse to honor a previous gentlemen's agreement. They originally stated that if the hearings could be moved to January, they would not delay any committee vote. So much for their integrity.

After Alito is confirmed, there is a bright future ahead. Bush might get to nominate one or two more justices. John Paul Stevens is 85 and Ruth Bader Ginsburg and Steven Breyer are 72 and 68, respectively, each with health problems. Let us conservatives keep our fingers crossed. Janice Roberts Brown, Edith Brown Clement and Emilio Garcia are waiting in the wings.

Two Kinds of Liberals

I can't believe this is my sixth column already. I want to thank everyone who has sent me e-mails as well as the many people who have come up to me on the street, thanking me for writing the column. To date, my e-mails have run 33 positives and 4 negatives.

It is now time to provide some definitions and differences between conservatives and liberals. A good friend of mine, (E.F.), who knows me well suggested that I define my two classes of liberals. Good idea.

I have many friends who would label themselves liberal. They are individuals with whom I enjoy rational, intelligent discussions, and I have a respect for their viewpoints.

They won't change any of my stances, as I won't theirs, about 98 percent of the time. I would call these individuals moderate Democrats. They are good people to associate with, along with my many conservative friends. Fortunately, they are much more numerous than the second class.

The other type of liberal, the one I am usually referring to in my column, is much more dangerous. They are extreme, left-leaning, irrational, radical liberals normally associated with the far left of the Democratic Party. They use as their role models such people as Ted Kennedy, Howard Dean, Pat Leahy, Dick Durbin, Charles Schumer, Hillary Clinton, Harry Reid, Nancy Pelosi and others of their ilk.

Extreme, left-leaning individuals are those people who have one set of rules for themselves and another for those who disagree with them. They are still crying about the 2000 and 2004 elections, and the mention of President Bush causes them to go crazy.

They will blame the President for absolutely everything that has gone wrong, no matter how foolish the association is: Hurricane Katrina, global warming, oil prices, starving children, cutting Social Security for the elderly, any world catastrophe or hardship, even for cutting themselves shaving.

They blame Bush for polluting our air and waters, poisoning our food and allowing our economy to destroy the world. When they state their opinion, they expect you to accept it as fact (Cheney and Halliburton engineered the Iraq war for oil profits being one example of literally hundreds). It matters not that it has no basis in fact.

Their opinions are emotionally driven rather than well-thought-out. If you disagree with them, you hurt their feelings, or they become enraged. In the second case, their faces turn red, their blood pressure shoots up, veins bulge from their temples and small bits of froth appear at the corners of their mouths. You might as well walk away. They will keep ranting and raving and will probably not notice you have left.

Their strategy is to smear or attempt to demean their opponents when they cannot win using facts (the latest confirmation hearings proved this repeatedly). How about their claim that Mrs. Alito staged her crying episode? They believe that the more things they can blame Bush for, the stronger their case.

One of the three negative letters I received, in response to my weapons of mass destruction column, threw in at least eight other issues that Bush was responsible for. They were simple statements of opinion, having nothing to do with my column. These were very shallow statements illustrating no depth of thought.

I think the Democratic Party puts out a tape of these one-liners that all radical extremists memorize and regurgitate on command. It reminds me of a parrot that can be trained to speak a few phrases - a very cute pet, but no one takes it seriously.

This same letter-writer made numerous futile, feeble attempts to insult me. It also displayed a typical level of arrogance commonly found in this radical group. My Manhattan letter-writing friend said, "Most NYC residents—who are among the brightest and best-informed people in the U.S..." Give me a break! Two of the four negative letters were rambling and disjointed diatribes and were actually longer than my column!

So, in conclusion, you can assume that my style will continue to be in the mode of Michelle Malkin, Ann Coulter, Thomas Sowell and David Limbaugh. They pull no punches, back up their statements with fact, and don't worry about political correctness. If you don't want your toes stepped on, don't put them under my big, heavy, conservative foot.

P.S. Three excellent books to read that you won't be able to put down: How to Talk To A Liberal (If You Must), by Ann Coulter; Do As I Say (Not As I Do), Profiles in Liberal Hypocrisy, by Peter Schweitzer; and Unleashed: Exposing Liberals Gone Wild, by Michelle Malkin.

As a matter of fact, here are some of the things Malkin's liberal enemies said about her: "ought to be shot between those Viet Cong eyes!," "an ugly, obnoxious and semi-literate gook," "one hideous-looking and tremendously stupid woman," "some gook out there pandering to the radical right."

Double standards anyone? If anyone thinks I am going to stand by and allow that to go unchallenged, think again.

Louisiana is to Blame For Katrina

I was all set to go with an article about the ACLU (it wasn't a nice one), but I got sick and tired of everyone playing the Washington blame game of who was responsible for the Hurricane Katrina disaster.

First, I want everyone to know that the people of New Orleans and Louisiana have my most profound sympathy. You were the victims of others' incompetence. No, it wasn't the evil President Bush or the slow-moving federal government response. The blame falls squarely on the shoulders of your New Orleans Mayor and your Louisiana Governor.

Yes, the Federal Government (FEMA) was slow to respond, but where the blame truly lies is on the first responders, of which FEMA is not, and the poor planning by the state of Louisiana.

Why do I say this? First, let's compare hurricane Katrina to the 9/11 attack. Even though the 9/11 tragedy was totally unexpected, remember how the firemen, police, and all other emergency departments reacted quickly and effectively? Their swift actions and heroism saved countless lives.

Now look at the first responders of New Orleans. What did the mayor and governor do, even though they had days (actually decades) to prepare for the hurricane's impact? They did absolutely nothing. Where were the bus drivers to assist in the evacuation of New Orleans citizens? Remember the 500 plus buses partially submerged? Where were the police and other emergency personnel? There was no plan, and as a result, many lives were inexcusably lost.

First of all, the mayor didn't even have a plan for response, and he was the one responsible for having one. There is an evacuation order in the Comprehensive Emergency Management Plan that simply says the Mayor is in charge of everything.

Secondly, the governor could have easily called up the National Guard much sooner to protect peoples' abandoned property from looters and to prevent other criminal acts. These actions, or rather lack thereof, are indefensible. It's just easier to blame President Bush, even though he and his administration had zero responsibility.

Not to be overlooked - What about an article in a December 1995 issue of The New Orleans Times-Picayune? It states that the New Orleans Levee Board received federal dollars to protect the region from hurricanes. At this time the board promised the newspaper that the few manageable gaps in the walls would be completely sealed by 1999.

CSNnews.com senior staff writer Jeff Johnson stated that in 1998 Louisiana had a $2 billion dollar construction budget, and less than 1/10 of 1 percent was dedicated to levee improvements in the New Orleans area. As Mr. Johnson stated, "They got the federal money and didn't spend it on what it was supposed to be for."

Here is a novel idea. Since the city of New Orleans had 35 to 50 or more years to prepare for this inevitable tragedy, why didn't it create the necessary programs and funding to provide security for their constituents? This includes development of a long- term plan of levee re-enforcement, using STATE FUNDS to pay for the cost. I know. What a cold-hearted (though many would say practical) thought. But please tell me why do I have to pay for someone else's lack of action. Why is the federal government blamed for the inaction and lack of leadership in Louisiana? It is their state, their responsibility, their cost, and only theirs.

I feel the same way about other costs. I don't want to pay for someone's choice of building on a flood plain, on an earthquake fault line, in a tornado alley, or in a city that is below sea level. The states should bear the responsibility for building the reserves to cover such catastrophes, and those funds should come from the state's citizens.

How were they supposed to do this? Anybody hear of state income taxes and state sales taxes? Louisiana has ridiculously low rates in both areas of taxation compared to other states. It has a three tier income tax structure with the top rate being 6 percent. Its sales tax is 3.97 percent with an additional .03 percent "Louisiana Tourism Promotion District Sales Tax.".

How about a 1 or 2 percent "Let's Include in Our Own Budget The Costs To Protect Our Citizens" tax? This additional tax, collected over 35 or 50 years, would have allowed the entire state to be enclosed in one gigantic dome, to say nothing of strengthening a levee or two. Hey, this could also work for repaying the federal government for funds ADVANCED to Louisiana.

The federal government cannot be a do all – end all solution for everyone. Now, the federal government (that's all of us) is absorbing untold billions of dollars of hurricane relief, and then Bush gets blamed again. What happened to our Founding Fathers' idea of a weak Federal government and strong state powers?

Lawmaker Fabricates Many Issues

I told myself when I began writing my columns that I would not respond to letters to the editor except on rare occasions. This is one of those times.

In the February 24th issue of The Daily Star there was a letter from Congressman Michael R McMcNulty, D-Green Island. When so many (how can I say this in a I restrained way?) fabrications are stated, I can hardly sit by and let them go unchallenged.

First, is the Congressman's, straight-from-the-Democrats' playbook, scare tactics and mis-truths throughout his letter. To mention just a few: "slashes educational spending," "mortgages our grandchildren's future," "unfairness of proposals breathtaking," and finally, "being both fiscally and morally irresponsible."

First of all, Congressman, a slowing of the growth of a budgeted item is not a cut. If one proposes an increase from $10 to $20 but trims it to $18, that is a slowing of growth. If one proposes a cut from the $10 that means the $10 decreases to $8. I know you are mis-using the terms for political gain, but a second grader can see the difference.

Let's take the issues one at a time: There is no one who respects our military men and women more than I do. The Office of Management and Budget says that spending for veterans actually increased by 11 percent to $77.85 billion. The decrease in benefits you are talking about is due to an increase in co-pay for prescription medication from $7 to $15. To demand that the government absorb all of the increase is unreasonable. President Bush cannot control the cost of medication.

You state that 46 million Americans lack health insurance, and that figure is correct. Is it possible that the uncontrolled increases in costs might no longer be affordable to businesses? Don't blame Bush for that, as he cannot control rises in medical costs. Spending for Medicare and Social Security went up 6.7 percent to $980.15 billion, and spending for health programs decreased by 4.9 percent to $280.01 billion, which is still more than half of the amount spent for national defense! I certainly don't agree with the 8.7 percent cut in National Defense to $513.03 billion, but you can see Bush has put healthcare above defense spending.

I agree with you, somewhat, on the new proposals for increases involving the dairy industry. There are no harder-working individuals in the U.S. than our farmers. Remember, however, that these are just proposals. I doubt there will be any cuts in the final plan. Spending for agriculture as a whole increased 9.7 percent to $27.06 billion. A more reasonable approach would be to end paying farmers for not growing certain crops and instead aggressively pursue the opening of other countries' markets for our agricultural products.

We have, for too long, allowed other countries to keep their markets closed to
U.S.   goods while we don't do the same for their goods. Our farmers can compete and
win every time if the playing field is level.

Thank heavens the budget for education is being cut. This is the most wasteful, unproductive agency in the federal government. In 1996, an investigation made by the House of Representatives' Economic and Educational Opportunities Committee "documented 760 unconstitutional federal education programs – 175 from the Department of Education alone – located in 39 separate agencies, departments, commissions and boards!

These combined unconstitutional funds totaled $120 billion. Further, the committee found that only 6 percent of these programs have as their primary function the teaching of math, reading or science!

A study released in 2000 by the (bipartisan) American Legislative Exchange Council showed that there was no correlation between increased spending and student achievement.
I have a column coming up later to address his "tax cuts for the wealthy."

Congressman McNulty, leaders lead. President Bush has provided a budget proposal for negotiation. Your party has offered no plan whatsoever. If you are going to criticize others, tell me what your plan is. Stop whining! Not once in your letter did you suggest alternative strategies. The federal government cannot be all things to all people. The government isn't there to grant our every wish. We can only expect government to provide in a fiscally responsible fashion.

You insist in going in another direction? Unemployment is at 4.9 percent, the lowest since the '70s (Labor Department). There are 4.5 million more workers now than in May 2003, before the Bush tax cuts (The Wall Street Journal). We have an economic growth rate of 3.5 to 4 percent, about twice the rate in Europe (The Journal). States the Journal, this is "especially remarkable given 8 Federal Reserve Board interest rate hikes, oil prices as high as $70 a barrel, and Hurricane Katrina, one of the most devastating natural disasters in American history."

What policies do you want to pursue that will take our country in another direction Mr. Congressman?

Arctic Refuge Has Energy That We Need

As President Bush stated in his State of The Union speech in January, it is Eme to get serious about becoming energy independent. The only thing I disagree with him about is that he wants this accomplished by the year 2025. I feel, with aggressive commitment, it can be accomplished much sooner.

The strategy must be mulE-faceted. I'll list these acEons separately before I discuss each one at length. This will obviously take more than one column.

1.   Immediate opening, leasing and drilling of the ArcEc NaEonal Wildlife refuge (ANWR).

2.   Immediate plans to develop more nuclear power staEons. As in number one above, all environmental groups' stall tacEcs and misinformaEon campaigns should be ignored.

3.   Ethanol producEon should be heavily subsidized, which has already been proposed in the Energy Policy Act of 2005.

4.   Expanded use of our natural coal resources. We have enough for more than 400 years.

5.   Tax incenEves for purchasers of ethanol-driven Flexible Fuel Vehicles (FFVs) as well as tax credits to encourage the manufacture of such vehicles. A total of 600,000 of these vehicles are planned to be produced in 2006 by General Motors, even though they will conEnue to be powered by gasoline because of the lack of availability of fuel-refilling staEons. There are currently only 600 such ethanol staEons in the United States.

6.   Lastly, for now, tax credits for the manufacture of cars with meaningful and measureable increases in miles-per-gallon staEsEcs. This is the one that can be accomplished almost immediately.

Let's start with number one, a drilling strategy for ANWR. The area consists of 19 million acres, of which 1.5 million would be explored, leaving the remaining 17.5 million acres untouched. Of this 1.5 million-acre area, only 2,000 acres would be involved in the actual drilling. This represents a parcel no bigger than Dulles Airport near Washington,

D.C. Give me a break. I'm Ered of hearing about this huge, unspoiled, prisEne area being ruined forever. 99.99 percent of the area remains untouched!

Why bother with all this effort? The U.S. Geological Survey esEmates that ANWR could provide yields of up to 16 billion barrels of oil. There are oil stained sands as well as oil literally bubbling up from the ground! This is roughly equal to all Saudi oil imports for more than 30 years. Saudi Arabia is our third-largest oil supplier, behind Canada and Mexico. As a mazer of fact, it would replace 100 percent of all the oil provided by the Persian Gulf countries for 20 years. Those countries include Bahrain, Iran, Iraq, Kuwait, Qatar, Saudi Arabia and the United Arab Emirates. This is making me feel safer already. It gives us more than enough Eme to fully develop strategies 2 through 6.

The environmentalists have been lying to us long enough. In 1968, they said there wasn't enough oil to make it worthwhile to develop the Prudhoe Bay area. It took the Eme from 1968 to 1977 to create the Alaskan pipeline. Since that Eme, the area has provided more than 13 billion barrels of oil and is sEll producing, albeit at only 50 percent of its capacity. The pipeline is more than 800 miles long and the untapped area of ANWR, where the drilling would take place, is only 60 miles east of Prudhoe Bay.

Did I describe this "prisEne" environment? According to Jonah Goldberg, editor of The NaEonal Review, the area is flat and treeless. Winters on the coastal plain last for nine months. There is complete darkness for 58 straight days, and temperatures can drop to 70 degrees below zero without factoring in wind chill. Summer creates huge puddles and azracts thousands of mosquitoes. No wonder many Congressmen who voted against drilling never even bothered to go and actually inspect the area.

Opponents of drilling also distort the facts by saying drilling would drasEcally affect .the populaEon of the porcupine caribou. Not that I care, but these same groups said the same thing about the caribou if the Prudhoe Bay were to be developed. From 1977, when the development began, to 2002, the caribou populaEon increased from 5,000 to 32,000. Also, the polar bear populaEon conEnues to grow and remain unthreatened.

The Wharton Econometrics Center esEmates that, in full producEon, up to 735,000 decent- paying jobs would be created. Remember, in my first column I said if it was a choice between the spozed owl and jobs for people in the lumber industry providing for their families, the choice would be simple. Replace the words spozed owl with caribou and lumber-industry jobs with oil-producEon jobs. I hear caribou meat is quite tender and tasty. Fire up the grills!

I'll get to steps 2 through 6 in future columns.

Tax Cuts can Benefit Everyone

April 15th is rapidly approaching and the Democratic, leftist, leadership is reinstituting the mantra about the evils of President Bush's tax cuts and how they favor only the rich. Give me a break. It's a great strategy to foment class envy and class warfare, but it is a strategy with no merit whatsoever.

Look up the word "envy" in Webster's Dictionary and you will find it defined as "Discontent or jealousy excited by the sight of another's superiority or success; a feeling that makes a person begrudge another his good fortune; resentment; malice….." Envy is even one of the seven deadly sins in Dante's "Inferno." Is this something to be proud of?

So why is class envy such an effective rallying cry? Simply because 42.5 million Americans who filed a tax return had no tax liability (some had zero taxes owed and still got a refundable check from the government), millions more paid next to nothing, and 15 million individuals and families earned some income last year but not enough to file a return. Therefore the strategy of taxing someone else doesn't affect them at all. It seems easy to rally behind the cry of "tax the rich, they don't deserve their wealth." The liberals promote this attitude even when the top 1 percent of income earners pay 29 percent of all taxes. Extending this further, the top 5 percent pay 50 percent of all taxes and the top 20 percent pay over 79 percent!

Come on! How much should one have to pay to be a citizen of this great country? I know it should be something more than zero. Maybe those not contributing anything shouldn't have a right to vote.

This country is hailed as the land of opportunity. Capitalism is what has made this country great. A large percentage of our economy and employment has been built on the backs of small businesses, in other words, risk takers. These individuals should be rewarded and praised for their efforts, not penalized. Their success benefits all of us.

But still, the rallying cry is a very popular one, even though short-sighted and foolish. If you remember back in the 90's, Congress passed a "luxury tax" on items such as yachts, furs, jewelry, and the like. "Boy, that will sure soak the dirty rich!"

So what happened? These industries were basically destroyed as the "rich" simply postponed their purchases or made them overseas instead. More than 25,000 jobs were lost in the boat building business alone. Way to go. Ask these unemployed boat builders if they feel good about sticking it to the rich.

Yes, billions of dollars are going back to those from whom it was originally taken. Remember, it was not the government's money to begin with. It belonged to the people who earned it in the first place. Most people, other than extreme leftists, would call this fair. As a matter of fact, it is the rich who save and invest which in turn leads to job creation and economic growth. This can be proven time and time again.

It was the tax cuts of 2001 and 2003 that brought us out of the recession that Bush inherited, and in turn is causing the strong growth we are presently experiencing. I wouldn't call 4.5 million new jobs created since the tax cuts of 2003, a 4.9% percent unemployment rate, and a growth rate of 3.5 to 4 percent too bad. But those blind, shortsighted, whining Bush-hating liberals will still find something bad about the figures.

The problem is not tax-revenue generation, it is government spending. And I will agree and blame both Republicans and Democrats for this irresponsibility. In the 1800's, government spending increased from $30 per person annually to $129. In 2004, the federal government was spending $7,100 per person! This is inexcusable!

Article I, Section 8 of the Constitution states exactly the federal authority for taxing and spending. Some of these are national defense, the Post Office, roads, courts, and a few other rather insignificant purposes. James Madison, in Federalist Paper number 45, said, "The powers delegated by the proposed Constitution to the federal government are few and defined. Those which are to remain with the State governments are numerous and indefinite. The former will be exercised principally on external objects, as war, peace, negotiation, and foreign commerce; with which last the power of taxation will, for the most part, be connected."

Thomas Jefferson also said, "Congress has not unlimited powers to provide for the general welfare, but only those specifically enumerated." So where did all these entitlement programs we now have come from? How did we possibly survive without them?

Be proud of the risks others have taken and their resulting rewards. Their successes and wealth accumulation benefit us all.

Israel Shows How to Fight Terrorism

I hope everyone is paying attention to all the terrorist acts of violence against Israel. It could be a glimpse into the future of the United States 10 to 20 years down the line if we do not ruthlessly and relentlessly seek out and destroy terrorists, wherever they are, on non-American soil.

Israel is a tiny nation bordered by enemies whose sole objective is to wipe out their very existence by any means available. No negotiations, no peaceful co-existence, simply total elimination of all Israelis. Anything less than this is unacceptable. Sounds pretty familiar as to how radical Islamists feel about us.

Unfortunately, they are not better protected by two oceans as we are. They have, however, adapted quite nicely, and we could learn many valuable lessons from them. Number one is that we are not fighting individuals who respect the rules of war that were established in past conflicts. These cowards target innocent civilians, especially women and children, and then hide behind their own women and children after carrying out their attacks. They are not human beings, but rather rabid dogs, and should be treated accordingly. Extermination is the only answer.

The Israelis know this quite clearly. No prisons, no courts, no legal rights, no Johnnie Cochran or William Kunstler vermin to defend them. As President Bush has repeatedly said, "they will be brought to justice," but in the severest fashion. We haven't learned this lesson as well as the Israelis have. We must employ more ruthless tactics. Contrary to what John Kerry, Al Gore and other shameless Americans have said, there is a bottom of the barrel for those terrorists who have the ability to plan, coordinate, and carry out attacks against civilians. We have to aggressively seek out this bottom.

I recently read an on-line Associated Press article about recent Israeli airstrikes that killed eight Palestinian militants (a kind word for terrorist cowards). Six were killed when Israeli missles were fired into a terrorist training camp in central Gaza.

Then on Saturday, April 8, two members of Al Aqsa Martyrs' Brigades, which is described as a violent offshoot of the Fatah Party, were killed and a third seriously wounded when an Israeli missle struck their car in Gaza. These terrorists had earlier fired a rocket toward Israel and were getting into their car when the return-fire missle hit them.

Can you believe that a Palestine Authority spokesman said the airstrikes were a "new escalation" and that the Palestinians would appeal to the United Nation's Security Council to pass a resolution condemning the attack?

No innocent civilians killed, only terrorists at a training camp and three terrorists killed after firing a rocket into Israel! What is the problem? I tip my hat to Israel for their resolve and ruthlessness in dealing with these cowardly animals!

Our military is very professional and more than competent to achieve the desired solution. They should be given the clear objective of their mission and be instructed to do everything possible, within reason, to avoid the unnecessary killing of innocent civilians.

Now, let's talk about these "innocent civilians." Are people really innocent when they allow these animals to hide behind their women and children? Were all the people dancing in the streets, celebrating our 9/11 tragedy really innocent? I think not.

Just as during the Vietnam War, our politicians are trying to play general when they have neither the experience nor competence to do so. A politician's unworthy goal is to get face time, and the best way to do this is to degrade our brave fighting men and women and second-guess our military professionals. Remember John Kerry saying "Our troops are terrorizing innocent Iraqi civilians in the middle of the night?"

And yes, you protesting, radical, leftist liberal, you are being disloyal to our troops' noble efforts by aiding and abetting our enemies. Your actions are strengthening their resolve, no matter how much you soothe your own conscience. A good friend and person I respect, W.F., sent me the words to "Just Before The Battle Mother," a popular Civil War Song. The second verse went like this:

O, I long to see you, mother, And the loving ones at home, But I'll never leave our banner, Til in honor I can come,

Tell the traitors all around you, That their cruel words we know, In every battle kill our soldiers, By the help they give the foe.

You liberals should be ashamed of yourselves.

Green Groups Hinder Energy

What's the latest foolish statement from the left? It is now blaming President Bush for the gas price crisis. Well, I have another proposition. It is the radical environmental left that has put us in this crisis, and I blame it for the ridiculously high cost of fuel as well as the severe state of oil dependency we now find ourselves in, which also affects our very national security.

In my column three weeks ago I mentioned energy producing plans we had available (actually I left out wind and bio-mass strategies which good friend G. S. pointed out). Second on my list, after drilling in ANWR, is nuclear energy.

The only nuclear accident ever to happen on U.S. soil was in 1979. From this event there were no measurable radiation releases into the atmosphere and no deaths. The environmental groups used this "disaster" to halt all nuclear plant production for the next 27 years.

They became even more emboldened with the Chernobyl disaster which occurred in 1986. This event shouldn't even count. It was due to an inferior USSR design, no concern for safety, and poorly trained personnel.

To compound this problem, Ronald Reagan was, at the time, bringing this Communist giant to its knees, which halted the ability of this diseased country to provide the resources necessary to prevent such an accident from happening.

Nuclear energy is the best possible option to provide us the protection from fossil fuel blackmail by the Middle Eastern countries (yes, even our Middle Eastern "friends") as well as by the idiotic leaders and possible future leaders of Venezuela and Mexico.

Why have other countries learned this and we haven't? While we provide 20 percent of our electricity from nuclear power, our last nuclear plant was built in 1973. By contrast, other countries have been freeing themselves from energy blackmail at a pace that should embarrass us. Belgium provides 58 percent of its electricity needs through nuclear plants, Sweden 45 percent, South Korea 40 percent and Switzerland 37 percent. It pains me to give the French any credit at all, but they generate 77 percent of their country's electricity in this fashion, and all this with NO accidents.

Why are we so behind and presently dangerously dependent on foreign sources? The answer is simple. The granola bar crowd, with nonsensical groups such as Greenpeace, Friends of the Earth, the Sierra Club, and the Union of Concerned Scientists, is why.

These groups, with others, have prevented us from developing a very promising energy source through lies, mis-representations, unnecessary environmental impact studies, court case after court case, and other obstacles so that it has become foolish for anyone to invest in the construction of nuclear plants. Government intervention and the steamrolling of these obstructionist groups are long overdue.

The facts are these: Nuclear energy is safe, clean (zero carbon dioxide emissions for you greenies) and a cheap energy source; and it, along with Alaskan drilling, will have us no longer dependent on foreign oil sources.

This fact is even being agreed to by such radical environmentalists as Patrick Moore, co-founder of Greenpeace, and Bishop Hugh Montefiore, Britain's long time board member of Friends of the Earth. As a result of their courageous conversions, they have been ostrasized by the very groups they helped to create.

Nuclear waste? Not as big a problem as is being presented. Now that recycling is available, "95 percent of the potential energy that is still contained in the used fuel after the first cycle" is recoverable. Also, "within 40 years, used fuel has less than one thousandth of the radioactivity it had when it was removed from the reactor." All this information came from an article written by Patrick Moore, Greenpeace's co-founder and former poster boy.

But the best news is that eventually gasoline will be replaced with hydrogen. At the present, unfortunately, the most common energy needed to produce hydrogen comes from natural gas and then oil. Nuclear energy is by far a more efficient means to produce hydrogen. In November of 2004 the Department of Energy's Idaho National Engineering and Envoronmental Laboratory proved that a next generation nuclear plant could produce the hydrogen equivalent of 400,000 gallons of gasoline every day!

The solution is to silence the nay-sayers and proceed boldly ahead. The excuse many are saying now is that it will take ten years to implement everything. Unfortunately, these people were saying the same thing 20 years ago.

We would have had energy independence before now if we hadn't listened to them then. Let's not let the same mistake be made now. I, for one, can't wait until the day we have brought the radical Islamic countries, who hate us, to their knees.

From Mexico, Here Illegally? Don't Make the U.S. Your Home

I have to thank the illegal immigrants for their foolish demonstrators last May

1. Your disrespect of our flag by flying it upside-down and under the Mexican flag, along with your demanding rights you are not entitled to and throwing multiple insults at us finally woke up large numbers of people who realize what a problem you are and that you must be dealt with harshly.

For those of you Americans who haven't been convinced yet, how about some
of these quotes:

Richard Alatorre, Los Angeles City Council. *"They're afraid we're going to take over the governmental institutions and other institutions. They're right. We will take them over...We are here to stay."*

Excelsior, the national newspaper of Mexico, *"The American Southwest seems
to be returning to the jurisdiction of Mexico without firing a single shot."*

One more: Professor Jose Angel Gutierrez, University of Texas: *"We have an aging white America. They are not making babies. They are dying. The explosion is in our population...I love it. They are sh...... in their pants with fear. I love it."* (Thanks for the quotes T.B.)

Title 8 Section 1325 of the U. S. Code, under the section entitled "Improper Entry by Alien," states that any citizen of any country other than the United States who: "Enters or attempts to enter the U.S. at any place or time other than designated by immigration officers, or eludes examination or inspection by immigration officers, or attempts to enter or obtains entry to the U.S. by a willfully false or misleading representation, has committed a federal crime. Violations are punishable by criminal fines and imprisonment for up to six months. Repeat offenses can bring up to two years in prison (American Patrol Reference Archive)."

Tough sounding but where is the enforcement? This is just another example of our politicians making decisions based on potential political gain rather than doing what is best for the good and security of our country.

We are supposed to be a law-abiding nation, but do we get to pick and choose which laws we want to obey? Mexico's illegal immigration laws are at least as tough sounding as ours. The difference is they rigorously enforce theirs.

At the same time the government of Mexico publishes comic books instructing how to successfully sneak into the U.S. and avoid later apprehension.

Let's get a few things straight. You are illegal aliens. Your families are illegal aliens. If this hurts your feelings, so what? You are not guest workers or undocumented laborers as the politically correct crowd and the pseudo-intellectual crowd like to call you for fear of hurting your feelings.

I don't care if I hurt your feelings. You and your families are criminals. You have no rights: no right to a job, no right to our public school system, and no right to our welfare system, healthcare system or our police/justice system.

Is this too hard to understand? Sorry, I am not going to print this in Spanish for your convenience. Respect our laws by immigrating legally, learning our language, assimilating peacefully into our culture, and respecting our flag, and you will be welcome.

No, you serve absolutely no useful purpose being here. You are not helping our economy when the vast majority of your "earnings" are sent back to Mexico. There are plenty of willing Americans to do the jobs you are doing as long as they are paid a fair wage.

As an illegal, you have been willing to come in illegally, force the wage levels down (amazing how little one has to make when paying no income taxes), take advantage of government housing subsidies, bleed our welfare system, health care system, and overload our criminal-justice system.

I do agree that the businesses who hire you are as much at fault. There should be stiff penalties for them, also. I also blame our politicians, on both sides of the aisle, who have no backbone but rather drool over the potential of millions of new voters. Hopefully, the 67 percent or more Americans who are finally disgusted with this situation will remember this come November and vote these clowns out of office.

Yes, we need a wall. Yes, we need increased numbers of border guards who can be given more muscle than the present catch-and-release policy. Yes, we need to start deporting those illegals, no matter how daunting the task may seem.

If all else fails, I think a strip of land, two or three hundred yards wide, heavily impregnated with land mines might do the trick. Don't worry, I am not that heartless. I would make sure all the "Danger, no trespassing" signs be printed in Spanish.

Let's Stop the Stalling, Go With Ethanol

A while back I had a column with a six-pronged strategy to achieve energy independence in a short time if we have the resolve to shove the obstructionists aside.

ANWR drilling and nuclear plant construction were the first two. This column will be on the positive potential of ethanol production.

First, I have to scold some of the totally-out-of-it group of environmental/conservation types and their silly ideas. Some examples: They tell us to build smaller homes and drive smaller cars. It's a great idea, but you don't have the right to determine some else's lifestyle (although I am sure you know what is best for the rest of us). My wife designed and we built a relatively large home that is passive solar energy oriented. Does that make me a friend or foe of the "movement"?

Two more "strategies" they have. All of us should walk instead of drive to places, and all of us should have gardens. I can see it now. All those commuters walking/biking to and from work each day covering 10 to 20 miles. How about those large city, high-rise apartment complexes and their row after row of cornstalks growing from their flower boxes? Give me a break!

If that is the best your groups can come up with, then don't expect people to listen to you. Your strategies have to have some modicum of common sense. Remember the comedy series "Green Acres"?

Brazil got it right in the 70's when it was hit hard by the Arab oil embargo as well as war in the Middle East. Because of intensive research involving ethanol production, government subsidies and a lot of vision, Brazil expects to be energy independent in 2006.

It has 29,000 ethanol stations, and 9 out of every 10 vehicles sold are flexible fuel vehicles. These vehicles can be run on gasoline, pure ethanol or a combination of both. Can you imagine us being energy independent? No more having to please the president of Mexico (our second top supplier of crude oil) about illegal immigration.

No more worrying about the socialist wacko down in Venezuela , our fourth top supplier (the one Cindy Sheehan drools over). How about dictating to Saudi Arabia (third top-supplier) what we are willing to pay for a barrel of their crude? Those three countries account for 43 percent of our annual oil imports.

Ethanol production and usage (along with ANWR drilling, off-shore exploration, nuclear energy and wind energy development) can get us to independence in a relatively short period of time.

Ethanol is very easily produced. It is now mostly made from corn but can be made from many other products. The most promising celluosic ethanol will soon come from switchgrass, mentioned earlier in a speech by President Bush.

It is hardy, can be grown on marginal soil and doesn't require heavy fertilizing. There are no waste products from corn-produced ethanol; actually, there are many valuable byproducts, including highly nutritious animal feed.

Other benefits are plenty. It significantly reduces air pollution, and, according to the Department of Energy's Argonne National Laboratory, ethanol blended fuels reduce CO_2 greenhouse emissions by 7.8 million tons. Anything you radical environmentalist want to complain about now? I'm sure you'll find something ridiculous.

More statistics: One acre of maize can produce 300 gallons of ethanol and replace 400 gallons of oil imports. As a matter of fact, if you have two acres of land available, are able to build a still and know how to ferment beer, you are well on your way. You'll need, however, a permit from the U.S. Alcohol and Tobacco Tax and Trade Bureau. With these two acres of maize and a car that gets 35 mpg, you can produce enough ethanol to drive 20,000 miles annually.

What are the economic benefits? One average sized plant (40 million gallons per year) can create up to 700 jobs, add to the local tax base, and strengthen our agricultural sector, to name just a few. We also don't have to keep paying farmers to not grow anything.

Last year the US produced 4 billion gallons of ethanol which represents about 3 percent of our total gasoline needs. With tax credits, government subsidies and strong leadership, we can increase that percentage dramatically.

The only thing we have to overcome is ignorance and stubbornness. Just because President Bush mentioned the topic in a speech, the Bush-haters are automatically against the idea. It's past time to start ignoring those people and start on a path that makes America stronger and safer and independent from foreign interference.

Al-Zarqawi Death is Good News

I went to bed last Wednesday night realizing I had a column to write the next day. I had all the research prepared for that nonsensical Senate bill that just passed allowing amnesty for illegal aliens among other provisions.

The day couldn't have started out any better when my alarm went off at 8:00 (my friends know that is pretty early for me). The very first news I heard was the successful bombing attack that killed that rabid, evil animal Al-Zarqawi, his top "spiritual leader" and one of his top henchmen.

Could the day have started off any better than that? No Saddam Hussein circus of a trial with the strutting and defiant behaving dictator making the court justices look intimidated.

With Al-Zarqawi the capture, judgement, verdict and carrying out of the sentence took place with two 500 pound bombs.

There was more good news when it was announced that a "treasure trove" of information was left behind. If I were a terrorist, I would be worrying whether my name or other information about me was included in those papers.

I ran upstairs and turned on the TV to make sure I wasn't dreaming. Sure enough, the good news was true, and I resented the fact that I had to leave to go to a meeting and run some errands.

Afterwards, I hurried home and tuned in again to Fox News. You know the station. It's the one that all the liberals pooh-pooh. It's also the one that passed CNN, as if it was standing still, in viewership numbers. Oh yes, I also tried ABC, NBC and CBS, but I guess they thought their soaps were more important.

After a few hours of TV and being on the computer, I realized I was being selfish for being so pleased with all the good news. I knew I should get the negative gloom-and-doom spin so I turned to CNN once again.

Sure enough, it didn't let me down. It was having a difficult time accepting the fact that a good thing happened. One CNN reporter said, we were going overboard in celebrating his demise. "In truth, he was a very small part of the insurgency."

A freelance reporter, Nir Rosen, actually said this was a setback. "Death was an advertisement for his success in becoming a martyr. This will only intensify the 'civil' war."

Jack Cafferty, a guest reporter on Wolf Blitzer's comedy hour, read 6 e-mails, all negative, all demeaning the victory. Blitzer even quoted a terrorist website that praised his death. I am praising it also. Right now, Al-Zarqawi is a resident of hell wondering where the 73 virgins are.

Lastly, Wolf had to keep coming back to the Haditha incident to make sure it wasn't overlooked. How about the William Jefferson incident, Wolf? Let's not forget about that bit of news also.

Not to be undone, leftist politicians were desperately seeking out cameras to put their negative spin on the news. Sure enough, there were Barbara Boxer, Nancy Pelosi, and the perfectly coiffured John Kerry; all trying to put a damper on the day by telling the administration to bring the troops home now.

I'm surprised Pelosi didn't suggest that there was a conspiracy involved. I'm sure she thinks the Bush administration had captured Al-Zarqawi months ago and was just waiting for the best time to bring him out. Sorry Nancy, normal people would laugh you right out of the room if they haven't already.

It must have been a particularly sad day for John Murtha. He was the Dem's military "expert" who was sure we were losing the war badly. Sorry John, we are winning, slowly and surely.

With all the scurrying about going on, with liberals looking for cameras, I was sure Al Gore would show up blaming the killing for worsening the global warming situation. Either that or to claim that he was the inventor of 500 pound bombs (W.S.). Sorry Al, no one listens to you anymore. They've probably forgotten you even exist.

So, all in all it was a very good day. We should be very proud of our brave men and women and the job they are doing. We should be impressed with our intelligence- gathering ability and our advanced technology that allowed the bombs to be released miles away and hitting the target with pinpoint accuracy.

We should be pleased that President Bush listens to the military professionals and ignores the questionable polls taken by a suspect media. Every red-blooded, normal, patriotic, common sense American knows this was a good day. Everyone else doesn't matter (W.S.).

President Bush's Plan is Working

I'll be in Romania by the time you read this, and I hope I can get some overseas perspective about our current political debate. I think you will find the Romanians to be much more supportive of President Bush's plan for Iraq. Yes, he has a plan and has been consistent with its implementation from the beginning of the war.

Only the anti-Bush, anti-America, anti-military crowd could be disappointed with the last few weeks' good news coming out of Iraq. But there were plenty of these types to be found in our Congress and the "out-of-the mainstream media."

Since I reported on the good news Abu Musab al-Zarqawi (I wonder? Are you still a martyr if you are simply playing cards with your buddies when the bombs hit?), there is even more to report. The treasure trove of information captured yielded immediate results. How about 452 raids, 104 terrorists killed and 758 captured? Also, there were 28 significant arms stockpiles found and documentation that shows even al- Zarqawi himself stating that they are losing.

More bad news for the antis. Of the 452 raids carried out, 255 were joint operations, and 143 were carried out by Iraqi forces unassisted by us. One of the raids by Iraqi forces in Karbala resulted in the capture of a Sheik Aqeel, "a key terror network commander wanted for assassinating Iraqi citizens and orchestrating attacks against coalition forces." He was one of the top five most-wanted terrorists in Iraq.

This bit of news was hardly even covered. Sorry leftists, we are winning. Patriotic Americans see this as a great step forward. I can't wait to see the spin the naysayers put on this.

Already they've started. They keep trying to refocus all their negativity on Guantanamo, Haditha and Abu Ghraib, all accusations or overdramatized situations. Our soldiers get blamed for prisoners going on a hunger strike and also for force-feeding them afterwards.

Give me a break! If they want to go on a hunger strike, let them. Put food and water in their cells in the morning and afternoon and remove the dishes at night. Then let nature and their own free will take over. End of problem either way.

The Dems are even trying to exploit the horrible, shameful deaths of two young, heroic soldiers when they were captured, tortured and killed recently. The Democrats are insinuating that the abduction wouldn't have happened if we had not made our opponents mad by killing al-Zarqawi. By the way, where are the human rights groups when this unbelievable horror happens to our soldiers?

Then there is John Murtha, the Democrat congressman from Pennsylvania. Be honest. Had you ever heard of this man before he felt he had to stand up to get some of the media attention? He has done nothing of significance his entire time in Congress. Even his website staff has a hard time building a case for him.

He actually wants to re-deploy our troops to Okinawa! Does he even know where it is geographically? Congressman Murtha, which country is north of us (that's up): Mexico, Canada or neither? Thank heavens he has a serious challenger for this November, and if we are lucky, he will go the way of Gephardt and Daschle.

Finally, the Republicans found a backbone and made the Democrats take a stand, an oddity for people who are supposed to represent their constituency. When Mr. Teresa Heinz-Kerry and Sen. Russ Feingold were ranting and raving about the need for a specific date for a total troop pullout, Sen. Mitch McConnell called their bluff and actually made their proposal a resolution to be voted upon by both houses.

Right away, they started complaining about how unfair that tactic was. It's one to be brave when the president's approval rating is sinking, but they chickened out on their beliefs when the issue was to be voted on. Once again, they stuck their finger in the air to see which way the political winds were blowing and voted accordingly. The Senate vote was 93 to 6, rejecting the most restricting proposal and the Dems were left with mud on their faces (again).
Mr. Kerry, this is not a sporting event in which one side wins when the time is up. This Iraq game is won when the other side gives up or is eliminated. Most common- sense people understand this.

President Bush has had a consistent, unwavering plan from the very beginning: Take the fight to our enemies, give the Iraqi people the opportunity to vote for their choice of government, build up the Iraqi police force and army so it can police and defend itself, and only then start drawing down troop levels. Why are you still incapable of understanding this?

Romania is a Growing Democracy

What has been your opinion of Romania during communist times and from 1989? In all likelihood it was a wrong one.

This is my second trip to Romania, and I have found it to be a country with great natural beauty and found its citizens to be as warm, friendly and outgoing as you could imagine.

Hartwick College has provided me with the opportunity to research the evolution of the country's tax system since its beginning in 1989.   My study has been expanded to include other areas, including the political and economic systems they have in place. It has been an eye-opening experience.

Every person who I have interviewed or talked with informally- sometimes with an interpreter- has a very positive attitude towards the United States. I have yet to find a single person who does not, and I have interacted with many individuals and professions. These include doctors, bankers, economists, political scientists, accountants, attorneys, professors, politicians from the major political parties, members of the Financial Guard (their equivalent of our Internal Revenue Service but not nearly as strong), reporters, and the head of the U.S. Consulate in Cluj-Napoca, as well as entrepreneurs and owners of small businesses.

Very importantly, Romania has been our partner in the war on terror right from the beginning. It, along with other former Soviet-bloc countries, understands the need to rid the world of people such as Saddam Hussein and terrorist groups such as the Taliban.

Obviously, the people here have lived under very similar harsh regimes. Sorry Marxists, your ideal utopia is what they overthrew when given the opportunity. They are a country of 20 million and have almost 1,000 soldiers in Iraq and 1,000 in Afghanistan.

Fortunately, I have an English translation of the Bucharest Daily News to keep me informed. Just last Friday, the Liberal Party, one of the five major parties, proposed a resolution to "retreat" (their word, not mine) Romanian troops from Iraq. It was soundly defeated, and even two ministers in their own party voted against the proposal.

Liberal Party Defense Minister Teodor Atanasiu asked these two ministers to resign from the Liberal Party "as an act of honor." Sounds a little arrogant to me but we have the same situation at home when our Democrats vilify Joe Lieberman and Zell Miller for voting their consciences rather than toe the party line.

In response to this resignation request, Democratic Party Vice President Mihai Stanisoara said, "Liberals do not understand that ministers are representatives of the state, not of the party that appointed them. Everything they (Liberals) do is a cheap image game."
There was quite a lot of acrimony in the further debate, and I recognized some close-to-home comments from the speeches. I'll mention only two here.

President Traian Basescu said "When its allies are facing difficulties, Romania
can't take its toys and leave. Romania needs to prove it has a reliable foreign policy."
The best quote came from a Mr. Mircea Geoana, another Parliament member. He said, "The saddest thing is that this proves politicans in the alliance (the ruling alliance is made up of two parties, the Liberal Party and the Democratic Party) have no remorse in using national interest, and foreign policy topics, for a petty purpose with pre-electoral tendencies."

Isn't it easy to list the politicians and individuals in our country to which that statement applies?

I could wonder whether newly forming democracies are falling for the less admirable practices in politics and of politicians found in the Western world. I prefer to understand that this is part of the democratic process, the part that makes constituents of the democratic process stand up and voice their opinions and remind the politicians that we do more than watch the process.

Before I close this column, I have to mention some very special people I have met. All have been indispensable to making my trips and goals successful, doing everything from finding accommodations and translators to setting up interviews.

First there is Miss Ruxandra Baciu, whom I met while she was interning at the Romanian Embassy in Washington last year. Then there are Cristian and Beatrice Aldea, a brother and sister who are attending university in Cluj. They too did so many things for me, both last fall and this trip, so that I could achieve the objectives of my study. They, as is Ruxandra, are very mature, intelligent, pleasant young people.

Most of all I have to mention Mr. Radu Cristea. He is a very successful entrepreneur who I met during an interview last fall. I could not expect to meet a more hardworking, trustworthy, sincere person than Radu. In the very little time we have known each other we have truly become the best of friends.

Democracy Shows Itself at Odd Times

A lot of good experiences have happened to me while in Romania, but two in particular have stood out.

I was taking the bus to my interviews and appointments, just as I do every day. I bought the ticket, perforated it in the machine on the bus, and took a seat.

One stop later an official looking person boarded and waited until the bus started rolling again. He then clipped on some sort of badge and proceeded to ask everyone for their ticket. I handed him mine and waited for him to give it back. Instead, he kept looking at it while shaking his head.

He knew very little English, about as much as I know Romanian, but the words he did know were ominous. He said, "Please, come with me," motioning me to get off the bus.

I tried to ask why, but he kept repeating himself. He wouldn't explain what I had done wrong. He indicated several times that I hadn't punched the ticket, which I knew wasn't true. I was the only American on the bus, and he probably saw me as an easy target. The fine for the 30-cent un-punched ticket, by the way, is 300 Lei or over $100.

He kept getting madder and madder, so I started to get off the bus, but an elderly couple grabbed my shoulder and motioned me to stay in my seat, shaking their heads, indicating not to go with the officer. They had apparently seen me punch the ticket correctly.

As the officer came to grab me and pull me off the bus, others joined in to prevent him from doing so. I estimate that, eventually, about 20 or 30 passengers were on my side, yelling that they too had seen me punch the ticket.

A German on the bus told me in choppy English what was going on. The officer kept pulling me toward the door as the passengers pulled me the other way, each side yelling louder and louder. Eventually, the officer gave up, said something that was probably pretty nasty, threw the ticket back at me and stormed off the bus.

I turned around and told them, "Thank you very much" in my choppy Romanian, and all smiled and nodded their heads at my feeble attempts to express my gratitude.

What impressed me so much about this situation is that in all other situations, older people are usually intimidated by any government authority figure and look to avoid any trouble. All the people who came to my defense were in their 50s, 60s and 70s.

My other memorable experience happened when I went to Kiev, the capital of Ukraine, to visit Elena Myronova, a former student, and her family. I think between Elena and her father I was shown everything I could possibly visit in three days. They, especially Elena, really sacrificed their time, giving me between ten and twelve hours a day.

I had gone there wanting to go to the exclusion zone in Chernobyl, extreme tourism at its best. I found out that I had to submit paperwork first so that they could do a background check.

Why in the heck is it necessary to do a check before letting anyone go to the affected area? What worse danger could I cause? It will take around 20,000 years for the plutonium isotopes to decompose. Was my presence going to add another few thousand?

Anyway, being the 10th anniversary of the accident, the tours were filled, and it would have cost between $150 and $350 if I did have the paperwork filed. A tourist agent told Elena that much of the fee was actually bribes, and the higher the "fee" I was willing to pay, the faster the paperwork could be processed.

However, I was able to attend the Chernobyl museum, a very sobering tour. Pictures of the heroic soldiers who went in first, sacrificing their lives so that others might live, and children, many who will surely die an early death, tell this frightening story.

The real tragedy was the cover-up. The Soviet government initially denied anything was wrong, and then admitted to "minimal" damage that was being taken care of.

The government also encouraged parents and their children to participate in the annual Kiev parade May 1st, a mere 5 days after the accident with Kiev only 48 miles away! I only wish the Michael Moores, Sean Penns and their Communist, Socialist, Marxist friends could visit the museum and see the huge cracks in their Utopian paradise. Maybe they should actually listen to the people who lived through these times and are only now free to speak of its horrors. But then, I guess they wouldn't get all the press they now receive by bashing America.

As Elena's father said, "I don't have to go to the museum. I have the Chernobyl
experience inside me."

In The Middle East, Israel Isn't The Bully

Can you believe the audacity of those Israelis? They actually think they have the right to protect their citizens from repeated attacks from Hezbollah and Hamas terrorist thugs and cowards.

Can you believe they actually have the nerve to act in their long-term strategic interests (survival), rather than pay attention to public opinion polls? Several things should be clarified. First, Israel has never initiated aggressive action against her neighbors. On the other hand, its Arab neighbors have initiated five wars against Israel and lost each one decisively.

Yes, Israel kept lands captured as a result of the war. That's what the winner of
a conflict usually does, especially if it wasn't the one who initiated the aggression. The Golan Heights, in particular, were critical in protecting Israel from further attacks. Twice this area was used by the Syrians to set up military fortifications to shell Israeli villages.

I have no idea why these captured lands should ever be given up. Do you really think Israel's Arab neighbors, especially the Syrians, can be trusted after five wars? Remember, it was Arab actions that caused the loss of these lands.

Second, let's make geographic comparisons. It should be obvious when you look at a regional map but here are some statistics. Israel is slightly smaller than New Jersey, with approximately 8,100 square miles and a population of 6,352,117.

On the other hand, its neighbors, Jordan, Syria, Egypt and Lebanon, have a total area of 501,705 square miles and a total population of 90,548,115. Throw in Iran, another avowed enemy of Israel, and you add an additional area of 642,720 square miles and another 68,688,433 people.

Yes sir, those Israelis sure are bullies. If you can't see why Israel is a little nervous about protecting its citizens and can't understand why they lash out aggressively when attacked, then you will never be convinced of anything factual.

Now let's look at the latest aggression begun by Hezbollah. I think the terrorists are rethinking the intelligence of their latest attack. I can hear a giant "oops" coming from them. Those on the left say Israel's response has been "disproportionate." How can anyone look at the above statistics and claim that?

The Israelis' actions are entirely appropriate and, if anything, they have under- responded to date. They will not have responded appropriately until Hezbollah is totally disarmed and fatally crippled strength-wise.

An acceptance of a ceasefire on the part of Israel would also be a huge mistake. It will only give the terrorists time to allow their sponsor nations, Iran and Syria, to rearm them. An effective cease fire will be when Hezbollah has been wiped out.

Also, if I were Iran or Syria, I would be getting a little nervous about the future.
I think Israel's tolerance of those terrorist sponsoring countries is wearing thin.

Next, let's look at the "civilian" casualties. Other than the children, I am impressed that the Lebanon health organizations can so easily identify who is a civilian and who isn't. If it were possible to do this, they would be able to identify which man or woman would be the next to strap a bomb around themselves in order to kill as many innocent Israeli citizens as possible.

Wouldn't it be nice if these "innocent" Lebanese would take it upon themselves to take care of the terrorists cowardly hiding among them. As scary as that decision seems, what is the alternative? Either you take a stand against the terrorists or do nothing and let your children die. It's a seemingly no-win situation. You know as well as anyone the Israelis do not intentionally target innocent civilians.

Finally, the loss of innocent lives should be addressed. Every single life is precious from its beginning (that's delivery date minus 9 months) to the very end. And the responsibility for every life lost as a result of this latest conflict falls squarely on the shoulders of Hezbollah.
It's an abomination for the terrorists to hide behind innocent civilians. What is Israel to do? Pictures taken clearly showed rockets being repeatedly fired by Hezbollah from near that building in Qana. Hezbollah knew with certainty who was in that building. How was Israel to know? Lebanese citizens have to take it upon themselves so that this is not allowed to happen in the future.

I'm really getting tired to hear the leftist elites calling for war crimes against Israel and the United States. Why don't these same people rise up in protest of terrorist acts? The terrorist acts are much more barbaric and pre-planned.

Remember the beheadings, the assassinations, the mutilations of people. I find it hard to understand why the most vocal groups against the U.S. and Israel don't show the same disgust with terrorist acts. Some people would call that hypocritical.

Thank heavens for the latest terrorist attempt at mass murder. Why? Plenty of reasons.

First, it has reminded us once again that there is a serious war for survival going on. Many have forgotten the horrors of 9/11 and have to be constantly reminded that the threat is not gone. Hopefully, it will give even less credibility to the kooks who claim 9/11 was a government conspiracy. I'm surprised these idiots never came up with the theory that the pictures were computer generated; and the World Trade Center Towers are really still there, the vast open space being just a grand illusion created by some famous magician.

Second, the event has shown us how treasonous the media can be, with The New York Times being the leader. It has already exposed two government programs that secretly (and legally) monitor terrorist conversations and track their financial activities. It is these kinds of legal strategies that are protecting us. Even with this effort by the Times to derail the Bush anti-terrorist programs, these programs, with the cooperation of Britain and Pakistan, uncovered and prevented this latest massive terrorist attempt at mass murder. Hopefully, the Times will fall even further in credibility and continue to have rapidly decreasing readership numbers.

Third, it has temporarily silenced the Hollywood bubbleheads who constantly blame the Bush administration for everything. They don't know what to say when a plot is successfully thwarted, proving the terrorist threat is real and our prevention strategies are working. Barbra Streisand's web site, a perfect example why she should stick to singing and not comment on things political, is strangely silent. Also, it's so nice not to hear the shrill whining coming from the likes of Alec Baldwin, Michael Moore, Susan Sarandon, Timothy Robbins, Martin Sheen, Sean Penn, George Clooney, ad nauseam. They will eventually realize that they are eye candy or there to entertain us, nothing more.

Fourth, I really don't care that the Muslim community is offended when President Bush uses the term "Islamic fascists" to describe these fanatics. They are claiming that this will only inflame anti-Muslim tensions. Well, why don't they themselves do something about it? I haven't heard of any Muslim community leaders coming out and strongly condemning these animals. Overseas, I don't see any Muslim group doing anything to prevent these terrorists from hijacking their religion. Are you really a responsible parent when you allow these evil people to live and operate within your communities, using your children as shields, as is being done in Lebanon? Where is the outrage? I guess the term fascism, when referring to dictatorship, oppression, and racism is a pretty accurate term. Live with it, or give me a reason to think otherwise.

Fifth, and finally, due to space constraints, is what the Democrats are doing to themselves in regards to their anti-terror strategies. Their rejection of Sen. Joe Lieberman in favor of some no-name rich political neophyte is a disgrace. It proves the radical left wing of their party is taking over. I loved the picture of Ned Lamont surrounded by Jesse Jackson, Al Sharpton and Michael Moore. How do these guys find the cameras so often? I'm surprised Cindy Sheehan wasn't with them. She loves a good photo op whenever she can get one. Regardless, that picture is going to get plenty of airtime from the Republicans during the political races this fall. I can't wait for the campaign season to begin.

Joe Lieberman is an honest, moral man who puts America over politics and votes his conscience. Even though he voted with his party 90 percent of the time, that wasn't good enough for the flakes like Howard Dean. I am so happy to see that Lieberman isn't giving up and has vowed to run as an Independent. I am betting he will win the race for Senator, as well he should.

If the Democrats think they are going to win with their "bring the troops home now" strategy, they are sadly mistaken. Already they are accusing the Republicans of using this latest terror incident for political gain. Good for the Republicans. It will come down to the choice of which party has been and will continue to be tough on terror and continue to make our country as safe as possible. Actually, it's a pretty easy choice.

So congratulations Mr. President, the FBI, CIA, NSA and all the Homeland Security agencies on another successful job of thwarting this last terror attempt, as well as the numerous other ones we don't know about. The silence from the left in refusing to acknowledge these successful strategies only shames them. The fact that they can't show any instances where anyone's civil rights have been violated must irk them terribly.

Oh Yeah, be very careful Syria and Iran.

Switching To A Fair Tax Helps Us All

There is a bill in Congress right now called The Fair Tax Bill (H.R. 25) that was initially introduced in Congress in 1999 by Congressman John Linder, Republican from the state of Georgia (it is S.25, Fair Tax Act of 2005 in the Senate). It is finally getting some serious attention, and in the last Congress it had 54 co-sponsers. It is hoped that it will be an important issue in the upcoming 2006 elections.

The bill's contents are more than intriguing. It starts out with the statement that it will replace our present personal and corporation income taxes with a national consumption tax. I know that sounds pretty dramatic, but give me a little of your time to cover the basic principles.

First of all, corporations pay no taxes anyway. I know it would make us feel good to tax corporations more and more, but we are the ones who eventually pay the tab.

The flat tax rate would be set at 22 or 23 percent. Remember, this is not in addition to the income tax, it totally replaces it. That means no federal tax withholdings as well as no withholdings for Social Security or Medicare. No estate tax, gift tax, or self employment tax either. All these costs are factored into the 22 percent rate. You would get to keep 100 percent of what you earn.

If you think the 23 percent consumption tax rate is too high, there was a study done by a Harvard professor a few years back showing that the tax embedded in all goods and services amounted to an average of 22 percent of those goods or services purchased.

Actually, depending on the product or service, the range of embedded taxes was from 15 percent to 26 percent. An embedded tax is a tax paid by the string of companies that have something to do with the product you eventually acquire.

The taxes these companies pay are simply passed on to the next consumer, with the total of these taxes embedded in the final price. In the end, the final consumer pays all the taxes paid by businesses. If you think corporations won't reduce the price of their products by their tax savings, competition will do it for them.

Look at some of the advantages. First, the complexities of the present Internal Revenue Code and Regulations are completely gone. As a matter of fact IRS would be eliminated.

Second, savings and investing are encouraged. Can you imagine keeping 100 percent of your interest and dividend earnings. These savings, after investing them, will provide a significant fueling for economic expansion and job creation.

Third, think of all the money presently being kept off shore for tax avoidance reasons. A Merrill Lynch consulting study done in 2000 estimated that a third of the wealth of the highest net worth individuals is held offshore. This one-third is estimated to total $11 trillion! Since the applicable tax rate on such funds will now be zero, this money will be kept onshore.

Fourth, what about the underground economy? Since this exists solely to avoid income taxes, there would be no logic for continuing this practice.

Fifth, with businesses no longer saddled with high employment taxes, there is the possibility that the present actions of job outsourcing would be significantly reduced and possibly even reversed. There would no longer be any reason to locate in overseas countries that provide favorable tax treatment to corporations.

Sixth, look at how competitive our products will be in overseas markets once that previously embedded tax rate has been removed. In order for foreign companies to receive the same benefits, they would have to establish a presence in the United States. Translation, more job creation.

There are many more justifications for the Fair Tax, but I want to answer a question on everyone's mind. What about the poor? Since the tax is applied on all new purchases, that means the poor will also pay on food, medicine and all other necessities.

The congressman has addressed this issue with what he calls a prebate. The government would issue a check or electronically transfer 1/12th of the first amounts spent that represent the government's calculated poverty level based on family size. It would be indexed for inflation every year.

The book gives an example. If the poverty level is set at $25,660, 22 percent of that would be $5,902. This amount would be divided by 12 and ALL taxpayers would receive a monthly check of $492.

I apologize for having to be so brief, but there is an excellent book for you to read that goes into much more detail and substantiation than I can in this column. The book is "The Fair Tax Book," by Congressman John Linder and Neal Boortz. You should be able to get through it in one evening, and it will answer most, if not all, of your doubts, concerns and skepticism.

Clinton, Bush Faced the Same Threat

I was actually all set to write about the ways in which President Bush has strayed from
the conservative values that got him elected but Monday's 9/11 speech changed that.

On that night the President gave a solemn, heart-felt speech that I hope resonated among the vast majority of Americans. He once again pointed out the seriousness of the terrorist threat still out there, terrorists rabidly wanting to destroy our way of life and value system.

After 8 years of Clinton and his Cabinet's weak, ineffective strategy, the responsibility fell into the lap of President Bush, and he acted with decisive action in the way of any good leader. The facts are strongly on Bush's side.

But for some reason, the extreme hatred for the president blinds the Democrats and their far left liberal leadership. Name me one time when the Democrats gave Bush credit for doing something positive, other than the war votes (which were politically beneficial), in the first six years of his Presidency.

You can't. Like the whiners they are, they still haven't gotten over the fact that Bush legally, officially and even unofficially won the 2000 election over their inferior candidate, Al Gore.

It's sad that these facts have to be continually brought up. Our legal system worked just the way it should have, and the Democrats still won't accept the decision. By a 7 to 2 vote, the Supreme Court ordered the Florida recount to be stopped due to a lack of a consistent standard being followed. Only Justices Stevens and Ginsberg (the ACLU's poster girl) dissented. Then the court followed up with a 5 to 4 count that determined there was insufficient time for a recount in order to meet Florida's deadline for certifying the state electors.

Remember how the Democrats moaned and groaned, worrying who would replace Sandra Day O'Conner, the courts voice of reason and balance? She voted with the majority on both of the above votes. Oops, I guess she wasn't reasoned and balanced that time. But supposedly the facts don't count.

Even when the unofficial recounts done by independent bodies declared that Bush's margin of victory would have been larger if a recount had been taken, this didn't matter to the Democrats. They still would prefer making up "facts" that suit their purposes.

I will admit Democrats are good at it and are still trying. "Oil for Blood?" That's a very cute saying but totally lacking in truth.

"Karl Rove was responsible for the outing of CIA James Bond super agent Valerie Phlame?" I think the facts found differently. Democrats were so excited about seeing him leave the White House in handcuffs, they forgot to apologize for their stupidity.

I will admit, Democrats almost succeeded with lies (oops, "facts") two months before the 2004 elections when mysterious papers about Bush's military service surfaced.

Do you still believe those proven fraudulent papers weren't created simply to ruin Bush's chance for re-election? Once again, blind hatred prevented Democrats from seeing reality and they forgot to apologize once again.

It was Kerry's record that was questionable, but he refused to release his military records, so I guess Democrats expect us conservative Republicans to accept that version of the "facts."

Also, Democrats' hypocrisy continues to know no bounds. In 1998 Clinton and the Dems went on record warning about the terrible danger of Saddam Hussein. I guess when Bush says it, it is a different story.

Let's see. When the dictator violated 16 UN resolutions, refused to let weapons inspectors oversee the destruction of weapons of mass destruction, is a man who has gassed his own people, invaded Kuwait and brutally murdered thousands of innocents, supported terror - these don't count as facts.

Even the 9/11 Commission report is being used to discredit Bush. However, the report said that there had been numerous contacts between Iraq and al-Qaeda but no confirmable cooperation.

Liberals seem to forget that back in 1998, Clinton warned us about those same ties. But I keep forgetting your blind political leanings.

If your boy Clinton had used the same facts above and acted with the same decisiveness as President Bush, you would have hailed him as a bold and courageous savior of the free world. You would have been climbing over each other for the privilege of touching his feet. You probably would have willingly enrolled your daughters in his intern-training program.

So get over it libs. It is time to swallow your pride and get behind the president and our military and show a united front to these Islamic fascists.
For once, do what is best for our country rather than your shallow political gain. This is a war we simply cannot lose, and only through linked resolve can we expect to win it.

U.N. Needs a New Home

It's time for the UN to pack up and leave. Last week should have shown why they no
longer deserve to be located here.

President Bush gives an excellent speech about democracy, human rights and spreading freedom, and he gets a very light applause.

Then the little tinhorn buffoon of a dictator from Venezuela gets up and tries to be a Robin Williams with his comedic speech; and every time he insults President Bush, our country or Israel, he gets a laugh from the General Assembly.

Then, not to be outdone, the mentally unstable "elected" leader of Iran gets up
and accuses the U.S. of war crimes, among other things.

This mental shrimp is merely a puppet of the Islamofascist mullahs and nothing more. If you look closely, you can see the strings attached to him, being pulled by these religious zealots.

Remember, these are the fools who determined which candidates were to be allowed to run for office, removing hundreds of "undesirable" individuals from the ballot. Then to further rub salt into the wound, the assembly gives them both very loud and sustained ovations.
I'm sick and tired of being insulted by these Third World despots and being their welfare agency.

The United States presently is assessed 22 percent of the entire U.N. budget, in addition to having contributed both the land and the U.N. building upon which it sits.
Do you think we get much of a say in the development of the U.N.'s budget? Think again. Of the 192 countries that make up the general assembly, 85 pay the minimum assessment of .01 percent (yes, that's one one-hundreths of 1 percent) and another 13 countries each pay .02 percent.

That means the majority of the General Assembly votes are made up of those countries that pay slightly more than 1 percent of the entire budget of the U.N.!

And yet, this majority pretty much determines how much and where the finances end up. Basically, the American taxpayer is financing all the little pet projects of third world dictators.
Don't feel sorry for these poor, little Third World countries. Although their people may be poor and we should feel sorry for their condition, their elite

certainly aren't. Most of the U.N. funds dedicated to "projects" end up in the pockets of these privileged few.

Do you think the liberals raise a stink about this inequity? No way. This could be made no clearer than when one of the leaders of the Hollywood Socialists, Danny Glover, made a fool of himself when he publicly and repeatedly embraced little Hugo.

Maybe Glover's reading tutor should read to him all the human-rights abuses going on in his hero's country. Wise up Danny. Go back to school and try again. You obviously failed the first time around. Let's not forget about the anti-Israeli, anti- America bias. Of the over 700 General Assembly resolutions passed, almost 480 condemn Israel.

The same holds true in the Security Council, made up of both permanent and nonpermanent members. From the very beginning, of 135 Security Council resolutions passed, 90 were anti-Israel.

Do you think the U.S. fares any better? Think again. Our Middle East "allies" consistently vote against us. Kuwait 86 percent of the time and UAE, Qatar and Jordan 89 percent of the time.

Remember, we send Jordan $192 million a year. Egypt votes against us 86 percent of the time and we give them $2 billion a year!
And don't forget our Saudi friends. They are against us 90 percent of the time. The list goes on and on.

Israel, on the other hand, consistently votes with us over 90 percent of the
time.

Don't even start about corruption. Type in "U.N. corruption" on your computer
and you get almost 14 million hits.

Everybody knows about the oil for food scandal and Kofi's son's involvement. Remember the United Nations Interim Force in Lebanon? During the latest Israeli retaliation, this group actually posted on their website Israel Defense Forces movements, strength and amount of materiel involved.

All this was posted within 30 minutes of it happening. I'll bet Hezbollah forces found this useful. On the other hand, not one bit of intelligence of terrorist action was reported.

You can't convince me of the economic hardships that the U.S. would go through if the U.N. moved out. U.N. bureaucrats, in addition to their extremely high salaries and low productivity, get unbelievable fringes. Monthly rent subsidies of $3,800, education grants of $13,000 per child and many, many others. Remember, we are paying for 22 percent of these costs.

So, where do we move them to? Downtown Damascus would be nice. How about North Korea or even the area the Palestinians presently occupy?

I can just imagine all of these elite bureaucrats enjoying the many cultural offerings of these places, as long as they don't forget to dodge the suicide/homicide bombers.

54

GOP Strayed From Its Roots

I'm afraid the Republicans might have jeopardized their ability to hold on to a majority
in either the Senate or the House, maybe both.

Don't think it will be because of the Democrats and their uplifting message. They deal in dirt and negativity, reacting to polls rather than putting out positive, upbeat ideas for what is best for the United States. Their majorities, if obtained, will be short- lived if the Republicans can regroup and get their act together.

The reason for the possible failures in November will be because of their straying from conservative roots and the conservative voters they've disillusioned and abandoned.

One only has to look back to the Reagan years to see what works. President Reagan stuck with conservative values and did not stray from these principles. It is obvious that this unwavering, core message, clearly communicated, resonated with the vast majority of Americans, both conservative and moderate, rather than the strategy attempted by the liberal left. They kissed up to every special interest, wacko group and had to tailor their message to each, leaving them with no message at all. The proof is in the pudding.

Reagan, running in 1980 against one of the worst presidents ever, Jimmy Carter, won by a landslide. He won 51percent of the popular vote compared to Carter's
41 percent, 44 states to six, and 489 electoral votes compared to Carter's 49. Republicans also gained 33 House seats and 12 Senate seats, kicking out liberal leaders right and left.

The results in 1984 was even more lopsided. Running against a Minnesota liberal, Walter Mondale, Reagan won 59 percent of the popular vote (unheard of previously), 49 states and 525 electoral votes! Mondale only won his home state of Minnesota and that by only 2,000 votes. The facts were simple. The economy was much improved, our military was rebuilt and strong again, national morale was upbeat, and Soviet influence was stopped in its tracks.

It just goes to show that when a true conservative runs against a liberal, the conservative candidate wins every time. Neither of the Bushes were true conservatives although, George W. was closer than his father.

The platform this time should be simple. First, we should continue to build our military strength, which was severely harmed during both the Carter and Clinton years.

Second, government spending must be reduced. This is where Bush has let conservatives down. If our Founding Fathers could see what the federal government has grown to, they would be ashamed.

Third, make the tax cuts now in place permanent. Even with runaway spending, the costs of the Iraq war, and Katrina, our economy has never been stronger and is growing at record rates. Government revenues are up (lower rates mean more revenues), unemployment is at historic lows (tax cuts create jobs), and more and more people are freed from paying taxes altogether every year. There should be even more cuts made.

The Democrats don't understand that tax cuts are for tax payers. Yes, the evil rich capitalists are having their obscene tax burden reduced. The Democrats' definition of a rich person seems to be anyone with a job.

Fourth, strong illegal immigration policies. Illegals don't deserve to be here. They should be sent home, and others should be prevented from coming here illegally. We have laws that allow people to come here legally, and they should be enforced. Strong border security is a must. Three cheers for a Mexican border fence and the patriotic Minutemen.

Fifth, energy independence. That means more drilling in Alaska and off the Gulf Coast and using coal as a major energy source again. It is estimated that we have over 250 years worth of coal reserves. Also, nuclear energy plants, wind stations and ethanol development are a must. There should be no more delays, and environmentalists should be steamrolled if they get in the way. Research and technology will find ways to dispose of nuclear waste safely, burn coal cleanly, and get the cost of ethanol production down. I am more than willing to pay a little more for ethanol if it means countries in the Middle East, Mexico and Venezuela can no longer blackmail us with oil.

Lastly, but certainly not least, is to hold onto the Christian values that the country founded on and has grown strong on. That means bringing back school prayer, displaying the Ten Commandments and putting the Christ back in Christmas. The Liberals just don't get it. 70 percent of Americans want their president to be a person of faith. No secular candidate has a chance. Democrats talk about organized religion in a negative context. Then they suddenly find religion around campaign time. Pitiful.

Reagan proved it twice, and a strong conservative candidate can prove it again.

Conservative values win every time.

Don't Let Liberals Win Congress

I can't believe that by the time you read this column there will be only seven
more days until Election Tuesday.

I know for sure that I will be staying up late Tuesday night, and I sure won't be
listening to ABC, NBC, CBS and CNN for election analysis.

This will be one of the most important House and Senate votes in recent memory. As for me, I am becoming more and more cautiously optimistic that the Republicans will retain control of both Houses.

Why do I say this? I know there are liberals out there that are gloating right now, and I think that is a sign of overconfidence.

Remember all the noise when Joe Lieberman lost in the primaries to Ned Lamont? Everyone was crowing how it was the end of the pro-war politicians. Where is Lieberman now? I think he is 15 or more points ahead of Lamont in most polls. Oops. Any of you liberals have an explanation for that turnaround?

The same phenomenon is happening in Tennessee, where Republican Bob Corker is making a strong comeback against the Democratic candidate, Harold Ford Jr.

A race that the media has claimed as a Republican loss now has a good chance of the GOP keeping another Senate seat. It's the same momentum taking place in the races in Virginia, Pennsylvania, Missouri, New Jersey, and Montana. Even John Murtha might have a tough fight over his House seat. Better keep the champagne on ice a little longer, Dems.

You can tell the Republicans are staging a comeback by just listening to the rabid ranting and raving coming from the media and the Democrats that the Republicans are failing at all points.

They are desperately trying to convince conservative voters that the election is a done deal, and they might as well sit this one out.

Their behavior is a good sign that liberals, Democrats and the media are scared to death of the Christian conservatives and the traditional-values voters coming out to vote rather than staying out of the elections as is being (desperately) predicted.

I think they will come out in droves as they begin to realize what a danger it will be for the country if Nancy Pelosi, Ted Kennedy, John Kerry, John Edwards, Howard Dean, Harry Reid, and others of their ilk take control of the Democratic Party and key Congressional committees.

These are the people who were steadfast against the Patriot Act, who have absolutely no plan for the future, and who will roll back the tax cuts that have been responsible for the strong economy we are now experiencing.

And don't forget about all the activist judges that will be appointed under their reign. You can count on the ACLU and others pushing their minority agenda through a friendly court system that otherwise wouldn't stand a chance if put to public vote.

Just look at the latest travesty of justice when Judge John Koeltl, a Clinton appointee, ignored prosecution requests and jury verdicts and slapped activist Lynne Stewart on the wrist with a 28 month jail sentence that she probably won't serve for years, if ever.

She could have and should have gotten the full thirty years she deserved. All she did was pass messages on from Sheik Omar Abdel Rahman to his radical terrorist group. Who knows how many lives were lost as a result of her actions?

Even scarier, can you imagine Nancy Pelosi as Speaker of the House? She would actually be next in line to the presidency should fate take the lives of the president and vice president. This is the woman who supports the National American Man/Boy Love Association, which I am assuming she does since she has repeatedly marched with them in their parades. Do you really want a woman who has a 90 percent approval rating from the ACLU as the House leader? Get real. I don't care how blindly you hate Bush, you can't possibly see her promotion as a positive step for the country.

She wants to dismantle the Patriot Act, stop legal wiretapping of terrorists, close down Gitmo, and demand a lawyer be present at all terrorist interrogations!

Whatever happens, it will be over in a week. Conservative voters have absolutely no excuse that would keep them from voting in this very important election. But you must do more than this. For the good of the country, lock a liberal in a closet on Election Day.

Don't be totally unkind. Make sure you leave them a flashlight and an Ann

Coulter book to read.

Finding Optimism in Election Stumbles

I have to admit, I was very disappointed in the election results last Tuesday night. I went to bed thinking how bad the final counts would be, and when I woke up the next morning, the results were even worse.

However, when looking closely at the final figures, listening to several commentaries, and reading what many columnists had to say about the election, I started feeling slightly more optimistic.

First of all, many of the races were extremely close. In 18 of the House races that the Democrats won, the vote spread in each was 8,000 votes or fewer. In one district the spread was only 200 votes.

In those 18 races won by Democrats, 13 beat out Republican incumbents. The new liberal-leading Democrat majority certainly shouldn't count Tuesday as a sweeping mandate.

Also, many of the Democrat wins were by conservative-leaning Democrats, especially in the Midwestern states. I am hoping that they will not blindly follow the liberal left's post election plans for big government, big spending, tax increases, and unending Congressional "oversight" investigations.

If they do go along, then the Republicans should be back in control of both houses in two years.

Let's face it, the Republican Party lost its way. That is what really cost it the election and not because the Democrats had a better vision for the country. Far from it.

Actually, it will be interesting to finally see what their plan for leading the country is.

The real reason why the Republicans lost the election is that they strayed from the conservative values and voter base that got them elected in the first place. They took this block for granted, and this act backfired on them severely.

" We conservatives have been stabbed in the back far too many times." Columnist John Hawkins pointed out the many times this has happened.

At the top of the list is the out-of-control spending by Republicans. We want wasteful spending cut, limited government, and individual responsibility.

The Ted Kennedy partnership, the Harriet Meiers Supreme Court nomination when there were many, far more qualified conservative judges to be nominated, and the failure to let the incompetent, corrupt Louisiana state and local governments off the hook for being responsible for the Katrina fiasco all added up to sufficient disgust and sent an important message.

Believe it or not, this message was more important than the dangerous Pelosi- Reid leadership possibility. Hopefully, these two liberals will be prevented from doing too much damage over the next two years when we can reclaim both houses.

As feared, many conservative voters simply sat this one out. For the first time since the 1990 House and Senate elections, Democrat voters outnumbered Republican voters.

They felt it was important to send a strong message to House and Senate Republicans that they better get back to the conservative values that got them elected in the first place. I have a feeling they got this message a little too late.

One bright note to be optimistic about. Stephen Breyer, age 68, Ruth Bader Ginsberg, age 73, and John Paul Stevens, age 86 might now see it safe to step down from their Supreme Court positions. Anyone who replaces them will be a plus for the country. Bush still has the power to nominate potential replacements.

So stay optimistic, fellow conservatives. The conservative movement is still alive and well and growing all the time. The Republican Party, hopefully, got the message and we will be back in power very soon.

I can't believe this is my 26th column. The time has flown by and I want to once again thank Daily Star Editor Sam Pollak for giving me this opportunity.

I have enjoyed writing the columns and all the positive responses I have received. I've had many good conversations with both conservative and liberal friends, and these discussions have always been spirited, rational, intelligent, and positive.

I must admit, however, that I have also greatly enjoyed getting under the skin of those level 2 liberals I described in one of my earliest columns.

If you remember they were the ones who have one set of rules for themselves and another set for those who disagree with them. When they cannot disprove the facts I present or successfully spin what I say to their advantage, they resort to irrational, unintelligible ranting and raving responses.

No matter what they say, I know they read every word of every column. They can be assured I will be causing their blood pressure to rise for a long time to come.

Thanks everyone, for a fun and rewarding first year.

Well, you'll have to admit, the next two years are going to be fun to watch. Heck, the
next few months are going to be something.
Yes, the Democrats won the election, but now what? They have no agenda with which to govern. They never did. This is what is going to keep them in power for a very short time. Hopefully, the short time will prevent them from doing serious damage to the country and our safety.

All they have had to keep them going was their blind hatred of President Bush. They never forgave him for his legitimate win in 2000 and then again in 2004. It is this hatred that continues to fuel them.

Can you think of one thing the Democrats have given Bush credit for? Bet you can't. A booming economy through tax cuts? Not being hit again from a terrorist attack? Nope, not a thing.

The liberals are fooling themselves if they think the citizens voted for a liberal agenda. The Democrats who did win ran on conservative issues such as lower taxes and accountability. Actually, this should prove to be a relief in that the liberal left won't be able to ram their radical ideas down our throats.

One only has to look towards the House to see the Democratic implosion already starting. Nancy Pelosi, the iron lady of the liberal left, is already having difficulty in reining in her troops.

In her very first show of power, she backed her old friend John Murtha of Abscam fame, and that strategy blew up in her face. Murtha lost 149 to 86 and the new Dems elected Steny Hoyer instead as House Majority Leader.

To say that Pelosi and Hoyer don't get along is a massive understatement. It
will be fun to watch them run Congress as a team.

What does she want to do next? She might appoint Congressman Alcee Hastings to head the House Intelligence Committee!

It doesn't matter that Representative Jane Harman is the ranking Democrat on that committee. Pelosi wants to teach her old foe who's boss.

So what if Hastings is only one of 13 federal judges to ever be impeached and only one of seven to be removed from the bench? It was Democrats, including Nancy Pelosi, who both impeached the man and voted to remove him from office. And now she might appoint him to a very sensitive committee chairmanship!

This lady is either showing her very petty, childish side to get back at her enemies and show who's the boss, or showing everyone that she is totally incompetent and without the ability to make rational decisions that will be good for the country.

As strategist Dick Morris says, Democrats still form their firing squads in a circle. And they haven't even taken over the reins of power yet.

Now, about all the talk of bipartisanship. That will last for about five minutes after they are in charge. It will be their actions, rather than their words that will tell the true story.

Are they going to accept the reappointment of John Bolton as ambassador to the United Nations? He has done a stellar job in representing American interests, and it is said by all who work with him and under him that he is an admirable man with great ability. Will they continue to let the best man for the job keep the position, or will they remove him out of pure political spite?

Will they let the booming economy grow even stronger and joblessness remain low, or will they ruin all the gains achieved by reversing President Bush's tax cuts from 2002 and by adding new taxes of their own?

They have claimed they will do this with no justification for doing so other than believing that whatever Bush does must be bad.

The IRS released a report stating that the healthy economy has produced $521 billion in new tax collections over the past two years. The top 1 percent of wage earners pay 37 percent of the income taxes already. This isn't fair enough? Give me a break. The liberals should have to write this fact on the blackboard 100 times until they get it right. Maybe facts just don't matter to them.

Will Patrick Leahy approve only radical left wing judges when he is chairman of the Senate Judiciary Committee?
Will John Conyers be successful in initiating impeachment proceedings, as he has promised?
How about Charlie Rangel on the House Ways and Means Committee? Will he negate all the successful tax cuts as he has threatened?

Don't forget Rep. Henry Waxman and his threats of endless hearings and investigations.
Immigration, the Patriot Act, legal wiretaps, cut and run policies? We will soon see how the Democrats define bipartisanship. Actions speak louder than words.

We're Winning The 'War on Christmas'

We are well into the Christmas season, the commercial part, at least, and there is good news and sad news.

The good news is that the secularists have ended up not having their way. If everyone remembers, Wal-Mart, Target, Macy's, Kmart, Walgreens, and Kohl's, among other retailers, succumbed to the pressure of this vocal minority.

Holiday trees rather than Christmas trees, Happy Holidays rather than Merry Christmas, no more Nativity scenes, no more Christmas carol music being played, and so on. When you say "Happy Holiday," I ask you, what holiday? Remember, the holiday is Christmas. The law that declared Christmas a national holiday was almost unanimously approved by Congress and signed into law by President Grant in 1870.

Christians, however, didn't have to have a law passed to give one of the two
most important dates in our religion the respect it deserved.

To be honest, I don't think Christians are offended by the statements "Happy Holidays" or "Season's Greetings." We are, however, opposed to the blatant attempts of secularists (led by the ACLU) to remove Christ and Christmas from everywhere.
The intimidation tactics of this very small minority had these stores and others running scared until this year.

Foolishly, these stores that worried about offending a very small minority who opposed Christmas certainly didn't mind offending Christians who celebrate the birth of Jesus.

But thank heavens the boycotts worked. Wal-Mart spokeswoman Marisa Bluestone said it best: "We've learned our lesson. This year we're not afraid to say Merry Christmas."

Wal-Mart, along with the stores listed above and others, is now back in the fold. Also, isn't it nice to have The Salvation Army bell ringers back? Another example of secularist/ACLU failure.

Well secularists, you think you have the right to cause change? Then so do other groups. Ninety-six percent of Americans celebrate Christmas and 86 percent consider themselves Christians. Only 3 percent of Americans are offended by hearing or seeing the words "Merry Christmas."

The formation of the Alliance Defense Fund, an organization formed by dedicated Christian Lawyers, is helping us by striking back against the ACLU and winning victory after victory. Each group has to do what it has to do, so let various organizations decide what it best for them.

Now, to the 3 percent group which has fits when the term "Merry Christmas" is
spoken or written. Just what is the problem?

If someone says "Happy Hanukkah" or "Happy Kwanzaa," I don't tell them I'm insulted or break into a cold sweat and hide in the closet for days. I simply return the greetings. It doesn't bother me, nor does it bother millions of other people.

Either this 3 percent is trying to seek attention or has a very weak self-image. They are the ones who have to adapt. They should take sensitivity training courses or seek therapy.

Also, if these people hate the national holiday so much, then perhaps they shouldn't take the day off when offered. They could stand in for their less fortunate colleagues who couldn't get the day off.

They could volunteer at one of the numerous local nonprofit organizations. To not respect the meaning of Christmas but celebrate it anyway seems to me to be quite hypocritical.
Another giant step forward took place when House Resolution 579 was passed 401 to 22 (all the no's being Democrats) with five representatives simply voting "present."

"Resolution: Expressing the sense of the House of Representatives that the symbols and traditions of Christmas be protected.

" Whereas Christmas is a national holiday celebrated on December 25; and Whereas the Framers intended that the First Amendment to the Constitution of the United States would prohibit the establishment of religion, not prohibit any mention of religion or reference to God in civic dialogue: Now, therefore, be it Resolved, That the House of Representatives (1) Recognizes the importance of the symbols and traditions of Christmas; (2) Strongly disapproves of attempts to ban references to Christmas; and (3) Expresses support for the use of these symbols and traditions."

This information about this resolution came from the book "Culture Warrior" by Bill O'Reilly. You can look it up as I did.

The sad news that I mentioned before is the fact that it took lost sales and profits to convince these stores to do the right thing. I hope that message won't have to be sent again.
After all I've said above, I might be more sensitive about the subject after all.
It's ok for you to not say "Merry Christmas" to me. I prefer "Happy Birthday, Jesus."

PETA Is Bad For Animals

As I was exploring what topics to talk about this week there were plenty to choose from: Sandy Berger and his insulting misdemeanor conviction; Barak Hussein Obama, the present darling of the Democratic Party; the ever-present, laughable ACLU; the numerous environmental terrorist groups; and last but certainly not the least, People for the Ethical Treatment of Animals (PETA). I chose PETA.

If any of you have supported or contributed to this group, shame on you. Do you really know what this organization is all about? There is both a laughable side and a serious side to this group.

Not to be outdone by the ACLU and atheist groups, PETA also now attacks public Nativity scenes that use live animals. It claims that "those animals are subject to all sorts of terrible fates in some cases."

"Animals have been stolen and slaughtered, they've been raped (???), they've escaped and have been struck by cars and killed. Just really unfathomable things have happened to them." I had to check to make sure they weren't talking about humans.

But this group takes it one step further. It sent a stern letter to a church in Alaska warning the minister to immediately stop using live animals or there would be consequences.

The pastor found this demand to be a little ludicrous since the only live creatures in the Nativity scene were humans. The animals were all plastic! Way to go PETA, spend those donations wisely.

A more grisly side of the organization was exposed when two of its members were caught putting 18 dead dogs in plastic bags and dumping them in a trash bin.
More dead dogs were found in their van, along with vials of drugs that were used to kill them. These were perfectly healthy animals.

These two PETA members, according to testimony, promised to find decent homes for the dogs but didn't even take the animals back to PETA headquarters. They killed them while only a short distance from the shelter.

PETA, while claiming to attempt to find homes for animals, in fact killed 86.3 percent of the animals in their care. Its defense is that there just aren't enough homes to place these animals in.

Strange, since the SPCA, located in the same town as PETA, was able to find homes for 73 percent of the animals placed in their care.

PETA's defense is that the only humane thing to do is to kill the animals so that they are not brought into a life of cruelty and mistreatment. (Hmmm, sounds like what some people do to humans.)

Even more scary is the fact that PETA is going after children as young as 8 and giving them propaganda in the form of comic books.

PETA passes them out outside school yards without receiving any permission whatsoever from the parents.

One of the comics shows a man trying to rip a hook out of a fish's mouth while the title is "Your Daddy Kills Animals."

Another one shows a lady, again with a demented glare, viciously stabbing a live rabbit over and over while the caption reads, "Your Mother Kills Animals." I can't imagine what material is on the inside.

It also sends graphic e-mails to children, alerting them to new horrors. PETA even gloats that it reaches more than two million children a year.

PETA is a nonprofit organization founded in 1980. This means that all donations made to it are tax-deductible as long as the funds are spent for the charitable purpose for which they were formed.

Animal welfare is an acceptable charitable purpose as per the Internal Revenue Code. However, the miniscule amount spent for this legal purpose is laughable. Of PETA's $29 million taken in last year, most of it went for public relations and defending criminals.

If the proportions are the same as previous years, the organization should have its tax exempt status taken away.

"PETA spent less than $3,955 of its $12 million budget in fiscal year 1995 and
$6,100 of its $10.9 million in fiscal 1996 for shelter programs."

Instead, It contributes thousands upon thousands to defense funds for organizations and their members who carry out criminal activities, all in the name of animal rights.

Two violent groups it aligns itself with are the Earth Liberation Front (ELF) and the Animal Liberation Front (ALF). These weirdo groups have been involved in firebombing restaurants, burning down research labs, destroying the brakes on seafood delivery trucks, and physically assaulting corporate CEOs and laboratory research workers.

The President of PETA, Ingrid Newkirk stated, "more power to these groups if they can get someone's attention." She has made many similar brainless statements over time.

So folks, do animals a favor. Send your money to local animal shelters or the SPCA. Much more good will be accomplished for animal welfare by these organizations.

U.S. Should Learn From New Zealand

Hello everyone. I just got back from New Zealand, and although it is a beautiful country with great people, it is nice to be home.

I hope all my liberal friends missed me. I'll use this time to touch on numerous
small things before I get back in gear for my next column.

I have never met people so warm and courteous as New Zealanders. They consistently greet others on the street, even strangers. Whenever I had a map out looking up directions, it never failed that I had a Kiwi come up to ask if I needed help.

The political polarization is nowhere near like we have here, and it's nice to
have serious and mature discussions with others of a different culture.

I can say all these nice things even though New Zealand has a socialist leaning government with the Labour Party currently in control. This is true even though it holds only 50 of the 121 total seats. It has formed a coalition with 5 other smaller parties to give it a total of 66 seats.

One extremely interesting agency New Zealand has is the Accident Compensation Corporation, which was created by law in 1974.

As a part of the government, it provides for personal injury claims and covers citizens, residents and temporary visitors. Costs covered include the rehabilitation, financing, transport and treatment of the affected individual.

On the other side of the equation, people don't have the right to sue for
personal injuries sustained.

What a concept! People are actually responsible for their own acts of carelessness. Therefore, if you spill hot coffee on yourself or you trip on someone's sidewalk, your medical bills are paid, and you get reasonable compensation if you have to miss work for any period of time.

You don't immediately sue anyone and everyone to pay for your own mistake. If the injury results in permanent disability, the Corporation will pay for such improvements to your home so that you can live a reasonably normal life. You will also receive a reasonable amount of compensation for as long as the disability is present.

I can't imagine how it was possible to get such an act through when the vast majority of Parliament are lawyers. Can you imagine the Johnny Cochrans of the legal profession in the U.S. going for such an Act?

The funding for the commission is provided by employers (on average $1.21 per $100 of payroll), self employed individuals ($3.50 per $100 of net income) and by a levy on automobiles which is about $200 per vehicle.

They have very severe consequences for those individuals who try to take advantage of the program. There is a range of detection methods, including individual reporting and a zero tolerance level for fraud. People seem to be quite pleased with the program.

One night, I had a nice meal down by the harbor, which had a very pleasant ambiance except for the Greenpeace ship docked there at the time.

At least it was where it should be, tied up to the dock for at least the week I spent in Auckland, rather than out causing trouble on the high seas.

It also seemed that they were having trouble raising funds, for I have never seen such a poorly maintained, rusting vessel.

I don't know if it made the news back here, but a man was actually thrown off a Qantas airplane for wearing a Bush-hating shirt that said, "World's number 1 terrorist." The airline didn't care that the clown's right to free speech was violated but instead cared about upsetting the other 200 or so passengers.

Finally, there seems to be a company that is willing to stand up to these idiots.

Hopefully, more companies and individuals will follow Qantas' lead.

On arrival in Los Angeles, I of course watched the President's State of the Union address and the Democrat's response.

Why wasn't there more coverage about Jim Webb's (freshman Democrat senator) response?

In addition to saying nothing constructive and shooting down the president's proposals for energy and health-care initiatives, he actually said that the majority of U.S. troops don't support the war! What a liar. It is typical of liberals to make such irresponsible statements with no basis in fact and the main stream media giving them a free pass.

If he is an example of the Democrats' efforts to reach across the aisle in a bipartisan way, it's a strange start. Let's see how much bipartisan action they actually initiate.

It will be enjoyable to see the Democrats make an attempt to lead with ideas instead of offering nothing but the whining and nastiness of the last six years.

At least the next two years will be interesting.

A few weeks ago I received an e-mail from one of my fans saying that I was the cause of the GOP downfall the last election.

Wow! I didn't think The Daily Star had that great a subscription base or that my column had that many readers and had such a powerful impact.

Here's some of what was said to me in the e-mail: "It's gratifying to see how much your bellicose right wing ravings did to your beloved GOP in the last election. In fact I'd like to think that your brain dead vitriol and partisan propaganda are precisely why you backward conservatives took such a thumping…." See why I love writing this column so much.

I guess it is necessary for me to say it yet one more time: Republicans lost their majorities simply because they strayed from their conservative voter base and conservative values.

Many of the Democrats who won ran with conservative messages and platforms. The war was only a part of the reason for losing both houses. You just have to look at Joe Lieberman's overwhelming victory and stop listening to CNN interpretations.

All of the evidence points to the fact that conservatives are growing in number
day after day. Let's look at talk radio.

Conservatives dominate. The top 5 talkers and their respective listening audience are conservatives, from No.1 Rush Limbaugh to No.5 Laura Ingraham.
On the other hand, liberal talk show hosts fail miserably time after time. From Clinton to Cuomo and the latest failure, Al Franken, they just can't even hold a small audience.

Ever hear of Randi Rhodes or Thom Hartmann? Of course not. Their liberal listening base is probably 1,000 or fewer.

While conservative radio is expanding rapidly, a whole liberal radio network, Air America, with its entire line up of liberal hosts, has had to file for bankruptcy. Quite an embarrassment wouldn't you say?

Come on liberals, show us conservatives how to start and maintain a successful talk show. I know you have all sorts of excuses for the above failures, and you are quite adept in ignoring hard core facts as a part of your arguments.

Another area of liberal failings is cable TV. I was listening to Wolf Blitzer and CNN leading up to the president's State of the Union speech while I was at the LA Airport.

Blitzer had negative things to say even before the speech was made. He honestly thinks he is an unbiased reporter! His negative, partisan rantings are being listened to less and less.

Once again, I must share the facts with you. Fox News Channel, considered a conservative leaning station but much more unbiased than our friend Wolf, recently became the most watched cable news station in the country.

CNN, on the other hand, went from first to third and is now behind MSNBC. Which one is going in the right direction?

How about newspapers? In 2004 the New York Post, a conservative newspaper, was the seventh largest newspaper in the country. In the 12 month period ending September 2006, it had risen to fifth, leaping over two liberal rags, the New York Daily News and The Washington Post.

The Post is only 70,000 subscribers behind the Los Angeles Times and 380,000 behind The New York Times (as negative and biased a paper as I have ever read). I force myself to read the online versions of both just to get the wrong spin on political events.

Also, the New York Post's subscription base increased by 5.13 percent over the six month period that ended September 30 while the Washington Post, the L.A. Times and the N.Y. Times subscription base declined 3.31 percent, 8.02 percent and 3.50 percent respectively. In addition, the N.Y. Times share price has dropped 25 percent over recent times. Oops, there are those facts getting in the way again.

Lastly, let's look at conservative authors. Whenever conservative authors like Rush Limbaugh, Sean Hannity, Ann Coulter, Bill O'Reilly, and Michelle Malkin - all hated by the liberal left wing - come out with a new book, it automatically hits the best seller lists. I wonder why that is.

So all in all conservatives - don't despair. Two things will happen. First it will be shown that the Democrats are devoid of ideas and will have to settle for harassing committee hearings rather than leading the country in a positive direction.

Secondly, I think the Republicans got the message and will realign themselves with their conservative base. The sad and dangerous fact is that it won't take place until the 2008 elections.

The best part is the Democrat's failures are going to give me plenty of fodder for future columns. Also, my fans, like the one I mentioned above, will get even nastier as they become more and more frustrated with the facts.

Did I mention how much I loved writing this column?

Honor Military, Not Celebs

I bet you thought this column was going to be about Anna Nicole Smith. My column was going to be about global warming, but that will have to wait for now.

It isn't going to be about Anna, but I do have a statement to make. Here is a person who has contributed absolutely nothing positive to humanity except for maybe the pocketbooks of a few plastic surgeons. She died, probably from drugs, on February 8, and there hasn't been a day, or maybe even an hour, where her name has not popped up on one news station or another.

The same fascination holds true for the likes of Paris Hilton and Brittany Spears (now there's a responsible mother, don't you think). You can make your own list of names, but it ends up long and disgusting.

On the other hand, last Monday, President Bush presented the Medal of Honor to a Vietnam War helicopter pilot who made over 22 trips (some said 40) into heavy enemy fire, making sure the troops had the necessary ammunition to fight with, and then returned with the wounded soldiers, two or three at a time.

His actions saved the lives of 71 men, and every flight was a grave risk to himself, a risk that few others would take. Know his name? I'll bet you don't. As a matter of fact I think you should look it up for yourself, or even try to find it.

This individual got one-half hour live coverage in the early afternoon when the presentation was made by President Bush, received a brief mention on the evening news, and he was then forgotten about the very next day.

Who do you think deserves the most recognition and respect? Only the most moronic would say Anna or Paris or Brittany or their ilk.

Everyone should take the time to Google the Medal of Honor winners and read their brief biographies and their acts of heroism. What those men and women risked in the name of our country is beyond imagination.

I hope the readings will give people a different perspective about whom we should be hearing every night. And then, what about all the other thousands of men and women who have also performed acts of extreme valor (not including John Kerry of course, until he opens his military records) who have never received the recognition they so rightfully deserved?

Instead, the media, in ignoring these individuals, would rather highlight the few despicable soldiers who perform shameful acts that are miniscule in number and isolated in occurance.

It would take brave efforts for the news networks and print media to change all
this, but don't expect anything of the like to happen soon, if ever.
They would rather demean and degrade our armed forces than bring the true picture of all the positive things happening in Iraq.

At least the Daily Star has created a "Bright Side" article on a daily basis, giving recognition to positive things people are doing. I wish newspapers and TV/radio stations would do the same for our troops. Can you imagine the leftist rags such as The New York Times, The Washington Post, ABC, NBC and CBS doing such a thing? Don't hold your breath.

There are some really great quotes that I came across while reading about these medal winners. I'll list just three of them here.

"Heroes are people who do what has to be done, when it has to be done, when no one else will, regardless of the consequences." – Author unknown.

"There are two tangible symbols of selfless sacrifice. There are two symbols representing the ultimate offer of one's life for others. One of these symbols is the Cross of Christ and the other is.....the Congressional Medal of Honor." – Paul Harvey.

And lastly, "Any nation that does not honor its heroes will not long endure." –
President Abraham Lincoln.

Don't Get Hysterical About Global Warming

Global Warming? Probably. Caused by man? Maybe a fraction. There are plenty of highly esteemed scientists who are presenting alternative explanations that refute the Chicken Little message of gloom and doom, and the "it's America's fault" group comprised of such esteemed scientific experts as Al Gore, Babs Streisand, Alec Baldwin, Melissa Etheridge and other environmental crazies.

One only has to look back at an April 1975 article in Newsweek to show how much credibility some scientists should have. Thirty years ago, "expert" scientists were warning that the Earth's end would be coming soon because of global COOLING.

There was to be drastically reduced agricultural growing seasons resulting in the destruction of "the world's food-producing system." Huge famines and mass starvations were predicted. Political leaders were called upon to begin such measures of stockpiling massive amounts of food and to implement other drastic economic strategies so that the world could be saved! Another ice age was coming!

Oops. If these environmental crazies of the 70's were so wrong then, why is anyone supposed to give them any credibility now? Simply because they say we should? These "experts" didn't even explain why they were so wrong back then or apologize to those who took them seriously.

Thank heavens no action was taken then and very little should be taken now. Once again it is Mother Nature controlling the environment just as it has forever and will continue to do so in the future.

The only truth that was stated was buried near the end of the article. "Our knowledge of the mechanisms of climatic change is at least as fragmentary as our data," conceded the National Academy of Sciences' report. "Not only are the basic scientific questions largely unanswered, but in many cases we do not yet know enough to pose the key questions."

You still don't think these people are a little off? How about The Weather Channel's climatologist, Dr. Heidi Cullen, who states that the American Meteorological Society should "strip their seal of approval from any TV weatherman expressing skepticism about the predictions of manmade global warming."

A CBS News "60 Minutes "reporter called the global warming skeptics "Holocaust deniers." Other people have said that once we have finally woken up to the fact of global warming, and we are being hit with the results, we should have war crime trials, some sort of "climate Nuremberg" for the skeptics.

I would laugh at these people and their off-the-wall statements, except they are actually serious. No, on second thought, I am still laughing at these people.

You can also expect the same arrogance if you ever question their findings. It is easy to tell when people have a weak leg to stand on and want to stifle any alternative notions. They stoop to insults and other demeaning behavior to intimidate you rather than answer some very real concerns and other scientific evidence that disputes their claims. Don't worry when this happens to you. It simply means that you are standing on much more solid ground. As in most if not all cases, common sense and calmness prevails over hysteria.

I'll probably have to continue with this column at another time. There is so much more yet to be said. For example, the U.S. Department of Energy has previously estimated that if we adhered to the terms of the Kyoto Protocol, gasoline prices would increase by 66 percent, electricity prices by 86 percent, and millions of American jobs would be lost. You could kiss our present standard of living goodbye.

But have you noticed the proposed solutions coming from these environmentalists are almost as crazy as their dire warnings? We are to walk to work (after they realized that horses made dangerous methane emissions), grow our own food, live in the dark (no candles please). I guess they want us to wear loincloths and hunt with arrows.

Rational options have already been repeatedly shot down by the fear mongers. Nuclear energy – too dangerous, wind energy – it causes environmental eyesores, bio- mass plants – too noisy or too dirty, ethanol production – people in Timbuktu will starve, and on and on and on. These extremists don't want solutions; they just want to control everyone elses' behavior. Live your life the best you can and ignore the rantings and ravings of these leftist radicals.

In the meantime you have plenty of support behind you. The environmentalists can have Al Gore, even though he did invent the internet. I'll take Richard Lindzen, a professor of meteorology at MIT or Richard Sherwood, a Nobel Laureate for atmospheric chemistry and his work concerning the formation and decomposition of ozone. Pretty impressive credentials and there are many more like them on your side.

If you environmentalists want to slow down carbon-dioxide emissions, find a different way to breathe.

Yes, There's Warming, But It's Not Man-made

I'll try to wrap up my thoughts about global warming before a future column gets into the inevitable military showdown with Iran.

Have faith, common sense people. More and more responsible scientific experts, with distinguished credentials to back them up, are speaking out against the man-made global warming hoax being shoved down our throats.

In addition, there are plenty of good books out on the market, two of which I found to be very informative.

The first is "Unstoppable Global Warming: Every 1500 Years," by Fred Singer and Dennis Avery. The book includes some essays by those scientists who are not part of the group claiming to be the "entire scientific community." They disagree with the end-of-the-world-as-we-know-it groupies who attempt to stifle any debate to the contrary. The other is "Meltdown: The Predictable Distortion of Global Warming by

Scientists, Politicians, and the Media," by Patrick Michaels (too bad he didn't add the Hollywoodites). This book presents tons of scientific evidence that debunks Al Gore's sensationalism and fear mongering.

Yes there is global warming. I said this in my previous column. No, it is not caused by man. There is plenty of research out there that shows solar activity as the possible main cause.

Please remember that the sun is about the equivalent of 330,000 earths and emits heat at about 10,000 degrees Fahrenheit. Do we really believe that our miniscule output can in any way match the sun's ability to warm or cool the global temperature?

Other relevant factors include the tilt and inclination of the Earth's axis, ocean circulation and plate tectonic shifts. Darn, we can't blame President Bush for these causes can we?

The current warming trend lies within the range of normal, naturally caused variations. The media, however, wants and thrives on hysteria and alarmism and so do the politicians.

Man causes pollution. But here again, it will be hard for the "hate America crowd" to lay the blame on the United States.

China is expected to overtake the United States as the largest creator of greenhouse gasses sometime during 2008. But at the same time Gore wants us to sign the Kyoto Protocol, which applies only to the most advanced industrial nations (read the U.S.).

Do you really think that Gore has considered the economic impact that will have on America? The U.S. Energy Information Administration estimates that if the United States signed the Kyoto Treaty, it would end up costing us between $100 billion and $400 billion annually in lost Gross Domestic Product.

Oh yes, I forgot to mention that the treaty doesn't apply to the largest greenhouse gas emitters such as China, India and Brazil.

Now let's talk about the esteemed United Nations and its creation, the IPCC - The International Project on Climate Change. First of all, anything to do with the U.N. shouldn't be taken seriously, and second of all, you can't ignore the anti-United States bias evident everywhere within that organization.

The original report claimed that over 2,000 of the world's leading scientists had endorsed the report. However this claim included the names of scientists who did not agree with the commission's conclusions. They neglected to mention this.

As a matter of fact, there was one Professor Reiter who had to threaten a law suit to have his name removed from the report. Really makes you feel comfortable with the integrity of this group, doesn't it? Its latest report is due to be out this May, but anyone can read an advanced summary on the Internet. It is 20 or so pages in length, but there is some significant pull back from its initial findings about the extent of man's responsibility for global warming. Hmmmm.

So what it all boils down to is that Gore and his environmentally wacko friends simply want to control the way you and I live our lives.

He said in his skit to Congress that he really didn't have anything against
nuclear energy. It simply took too long and was too expensive an investment.

That's right Al, and the only reason it takes 20 or more years to construct a nuclear power plant is because of the blocking tactics you and your environmental leftists create to prevent any progress being made.

Would all you negative people stop your whining and do something productive? You know full well that the path to a clean environment is nuclear and wind energy. Why don't you be leaders of that movement? If you can't do something constructive, go live in the woods and leave us alone.

You people out there with a degree of common sense, the facts are on our side. Tune out the imbalanced individuals and stay strong. I want you all to sit back and enjoy all the nasty vitriol about to be spewed my way.

Well, well, well. The three Duke lacrosse players are innocent of all charges.

How could so many forces seem to relish the attack on these three college students?

A lot of people now have egg on their faces, and they should be pursued with equal savagery.

This so-called district attorney, Mike Nifong, should at a minimum be disbarred, and the parents of the players should initiate a civil law suit as soon as possible. This unethical person should be ruined both financially and reputation-wise.

The police that were involved in the case and exhibited unprofessional behavior should be sued and removed from the force at once.

I am talking specifically about the officer(s) who made attempts to intimidate witnesses.

An African American cab driver who signed a sworn affidavit clearing Reade Seligmann was subsequently arrested on a shoplifting charge that occurred more than two years ago.

He wasn't even the shoplifter but was simply accused of driving the shoplifters in his cab. As soon as he said to the police that he had nothing new to say about the lacrosse case, he was taken straight to court.

How about the accusing liar, Crystal Gail Mangum? Quite a model mother, right? It turns out that there was no DNA evidence found on her from the three Duke students, but there was evidence of at least five other males in her.

At a minimum, the child should be taken from her; she should go to jail and the proceeds from any future book or movie deal she subsequently makes should go to offset the legal expenses of the students' families.

Most disturbing of all, to me at least, was the behavior of the Duke faculty. I am referring to the "Group of 88" who, through a signed statement published in the Duke Chronicle, accused, tried and convicted these three young men without any evidence.

Weren't they supposed to be constantly seeking truth in an intellectual, scholarly manner? Give me a break. These individuals are anything but intellectuals. They were simply a lynch mob, stirring the pot and encouraging protests. Now, they cowardly hide behind their right to free speech.

Would you really want these pseudo-intellectuals teaching your child? Dennis Miller said it best when he referred to Duke and other similar colleges as "the last bastion of aging hippies and their radical, leftist agendas. The 'elite' universities are the repositories of the worst of these kinds."

Now, what about targeting and stereotyping student-athletes? Have you ever seen the names of these three students referred to without reference to lacrosse players in general?

I have been asking some student-athletes, male and female, their opinions on this situation, and some have referred to athletes being held to a higher standard than other students.

They also feel that they are looked down upon and even resented in some cases. There is still the "dumb jock" mentality among some professors whose opinion can't be changed.

Why the resentment? Student-athletes are young men and women who have a gift and a talent for a sport and simply want to pursue it beyond high school, nothing more. They put in hundreds of grueling hours to improve themselves and to represent the college in a distinguished fashion.

Still, their cumulative averages exceed that of the college as a whole. Their coaches are underpaid and put in countless selfless hours themselves, helping these individuals become all they are capable of. They are every bit as responsible for an individual's academic maturation as the professor and should be considered as important.

In the case of the Duke athletes, some members of the faculty described them using the words elitist, wealthy, pampered, spoiled and coming from wealthy families. Is this jealousy and resentment speaking? I wonder how they think their salaries are going to be paid unless it is by those who can afford Duke's $50,000 annual costs.

I can only speak from my experience. The Division I students I have had in my classes have been some of the most disciplined, dedicated, respectful, and hardworking individuals I have ever taught.

Many of the Division I and III student-athletes are among my highest achievers, and all, without exception, have worked their hardest to achieve.

They are also fortunate to have dedicated coaches, all of whom I greatly respect. The coaches have backed me 100 percent whenever I came to them with an issue. The students are fortunate to have them as mentors.

My final observation is this: If you show these young men and women respect for all they do on behalf of the college, they will respect you back.

Gun Right's Shouldn't Be Protested

I've often wondered how protesters keep their days and their specific protests in order. There seem to be so many different protests going on all the time. Anti-war, global warming, many environmental issues, President Bush, anti-partial-birth abortion bans, anti-nuclear energy, anti-wind turbines, starving polar bears, and on and on. How do these people get involved in so many issues and still lead productive lives? It must be miserable to be against just about everything.

The latest attempt to exploit a tragedy, and another protest, the Virginia Tech shootings, was the stirring of the gun control movement and their members.

Fortunately, there was no traction, and their protests fizzled before they even began. Simply put, it was a horrifically evil event caused by an evil person. Guns had nothing to do with this other than the fact that they were the weapon of choice to carry out this pre-meditated murderous act.

Students at the college began to worry about this person and reported him to their professors. His professors were also concerned and referred him to school counselors. Even though anti-social behavior was noticed and reported as far back as 2005, no one did anything about it. Had the Blacksburg mental health clinic ordered him hospitalized, which the police had wanted at the time, none of this would have happened.

Virginia gun law said that involuntary hospitalization denies the committed individual the right to later buy any firearms. You are not going to be able to legislate out of existence evil people. We do not need more laws

Instead of blaming everyone up the line who had some responsibility for not doing enough, who does the gun control group look to blame? You got it, the National Rifle Association.

This "evil organization," with over 4 million members, has the nerve to offer programs that teach Americans, young and old, about gun safety, education and responsibilities.

What a dangerous organization. Yes, it is a very powerful organization, a very effective gun rights lobbying group, and this probably drives the gun control groups crazy.

Tough. The right of all individuals to bear arms is fully entrenched in our Bill of Rights. I wonder why it was listed as second out of ten.

It simply states, "A well regulated militia, being necessary to the security of a free State, the right of the people to keep and bear Arms, shall not be infringed." This was the second of the first ten amendments to the

Constitution which contained guarantees of essential individual rights and liberties that were originally omitted in the creation of the original document.

Many different organizations, especially the ACLU, have repeatedly tried to re- interpret what our founding fathers meant.

The ACLU claims that the Second Amendment applies only to the right of states to maintain a militia. The ACLU's claim is that there is no right for an individual to bear

arms. It also doesn't believe that there is a prohibition against reasonable regulations of gun ownership. At the same time, the ACLU declares itself neutral on the issue of gun control. How about some quotes by people who were close to the issue:

"No freeman shall ever be debarred the use of arms," Thomas Jefferson, 1776.

Maybe the ACLU was confused about the term debarred.

"The Constitution preserves the advantage of being armed, which Americans possess over the people of almost every other nation…..where the governments are afraid to trust the people with arms," James Madison, The Federalist Papers, No. 46.

One more of many, many other quotes: This one comes from a Richard Henry Lee, The Pennsylvania Gazette, February 20, 1788: "Whereas, to preserve liberty, it is essential that the whole body of people always possess arms, and be taught alike, especially when young, how to use them….."

People will argue that gun owners shouldn't worry about reasonable regulations against gun ownership. Gun-rights advocates shouldn't worry about regulations that take only a few rights away, leading to a total ban on guns.

These people are probably the same ones who yelled and screamed about the chipping away of abortion "rights" when aspects of partial birth abortion ban was declared unconstitutional.

I can easily find the right to bear arms in our Constitution, but I am having trouble finding the part about abortion rights - especially the right to drill a hole in a baby's head and suck out it's brains as it exits the mother's birth canal.

Back to my original paragraph about protesters and their numerous protests. I was especially pleased with an article in The Daily Star a month or two ago about a bus trip to take protesters to a war protest rally in Washington D.C.

It was cancelled "because not enough people signed up." Maybe even the

protesters are tired of being negative about so many things.

May 1 has come and gone and the much anticipated pro-illegal-immigration demonstrations were a giant bust.

In 2006, Los Angeles, Chicago and Atlanta had demonstration numbers of 650,000, 400,000 and 50,000 respectively. This year the numbers were 25,000 in L.A., 150,000 in Chicago, and there weren't any rallies even planned for Atlanta.

You know what reasons were given for the huge reduction in numbers? Promoters said that illegal aliens were afraid that if they protested they would be picked up and deported.

That might have been a part of it. Why shouldn't it be? The last I knew, people committing illegal acts were supposed to be arrested and punished in some way. Maybe that is why we don't have murderers, thieves, rapists, child and spouse abusers and others protesting and demonstrating.

I think the real reason is that the average American is fed up with the arrogance displayed in last year's marches, and these demonstrations hurt the protesters' causes rather than helped.

Who wanted to see a repeat of illegals demanding all the rights of an American citizen, Mexican flags waving, American flags being burned, and comparing our immigration laws to those of Hitler's against the Jewish population? They even had the nerve to tell us "Anglos" to go back to Europe.

So let's ignore the sob stories promoted by The New York Times and other mainstream media sources. They love for us to see some poor "hard working" illegal being ripped away from his job, his family, begging for compassion and mercy. The fact is this person knowingly committed a crime by coming here illegally and should have to face the consequences when caught. It doesn't matter one iota that he or she has been in the country for 20 years. It just means he or she has been able to bleed our economy for a long time.

The fact is America is not responsible for the conditions of people living in other countries. That is the responsibility of their own government. Mexico has plenty of oil revenues to provide a better life for its own citizens.

Now consider part of America's citizenship oath: "I absolutely and entirely renounce and abjure all allegiance and fidelity to any foreign prince, potentate, state or sovereignty...."

The Coalition Against Illegal Immigration asks some pretty good questions such as: During these demonstrations, do you hear anyone shouting any of the following: "I love this country and want to become a part of her. Becoming an American has been a lifelong dream for me. America is a great country and I would defend and support her. Becoming an American would give me the chance to pay this great country back." Maybe I just missed these statements being made.

These people have absolutely no desire to assimilate into our culture. They simply want to take and take and give nothing back. In 2006, illegal immigrants sent back $23 billion to family members living in Mexico. No wonder the Mexican government acts indignantly when we try to get tough on immigration enforcement. These payments coming into Mexico are a major source of foreign currency, second only to oil exports.

On the other side of the ledger, what are they taking from us? In a study done by the Center for Immigration Studies, it was estimated that if legalization took place, the net cost to the Federal Government would be from $6,000 to $8,000 per household per year.

Considering there are approximately 12 million illegal aliens in our country, it is easy to see that the cost to the U.S. taxpayer would be substantial.

Finally, don't buy into the argument that these illegal aliens are only doing the jobs that Americans won't do. This is just another false assumption.

More than 65 percent of illegals have less than a high school education and another 20 percent have only a high school education.

There are millions of Americans with the same educational background doing exactly the same kind of jobs. The facts show that employers will hire illegal aliens simply because they will work for much less than Americans, and American workers simply can't compete.

The median weekly wage for American high school dropouts who work full- time is $350, compared to the full-time Mexican worker with a similar educational background who makes $326.

So let's get serious about border security and illegal alien deportations. Get the fence up as rapidly as possible. Deny illegal aliens and their families access to our health care, education and welfare programs. Severely punish those employers who hire illegal aliens.

The strategy is simple if you have the resolve to accomplish it. To those who say deportations can't work because of the numbers involved, I say it can be done....one illegal at a time.

Immigration Reform Could Ruin Our Lives

My last column turned out to be quite timely. Three days later the Senate came up with the "Senate's Secure Borders, Economic Opportunity and Immigration Reform Act of 2007." This bill is truly a watershed moment in all of our lives. Significant changes, all mostly terribly negative, will happen in our society if this bill passes.

Innocent sounding bill isn't it? It almost brings tears of compassion as you read through it. Secure Borders? No way. This was a key provision that was put in to garner support but was already enacted last year with the requirement to build 700 miles of fence along our southern border with Mexico. As a matter of fact, the last time we passed an amnesty bill, in 1986, affecting 3 million illegal aliens, we were promised that this act, along with strong border control, would take care of the problem. Well, we now have between 12 and 20 million illegals here. Oh yes, a whole 2 miles of that 700 mile promised fence has actually been completed.

Economic Opportunity? For whom? Certainly there won't be any for middle and low-income individuals who have only a high school education or less. Millions of low education level taxpaying AMERICANS will be denied the only types of jobs that they can hope to get. Proponents of the bill say that these will be jobs that Americans won't take. Nonsense. The job area where most illegal immigrant labor is found is in agriculture. Even here, only 24 percent of the total labor force is made up of illegal immigrants. If this is the case, who makes up the other 76 percent? Construction jobs, service jobs and other opportunities are taken away from American citizens and legal immigrants simply because the illegals will work for far less.

What about middle-class Americans? Maybe they aren't losing jobs to these illegals, but they sure are subsidizing their "economic opportunities." Robert Rector and Christine Kim of the Heritage Foundation, recently wrote an article titled "The Fiscal Cost of Low-Skill Immigrants To The U.S. Taxpayer." Their findings, using conservative figures of 11 million illegal immigrants in the U.S., found that 9.3 million were adults and 60 percent of these adults lacked a high school education. In 2004, these individuals received government benefits totaling $30,160 per household (direct benefits, means- tested benefits, education, and population-based services in 2004, each defined in the article).

On the other side, these households paid only $10,573 per household in federal, state and local taxes. This imbalance totaled $19,587 per household or a total cost to American taxpayers of 89.1 billion dollars per year. Do you think these figures will go up or down as more illegals enter the country?

Lastly, the "Immigration Reform" section of the act. This can be interpreted as amnesty no matter how much our lying politicians deny it. You don't have to believe me about this statement, just read Title VI of the above mentioned act. The entire bunch of illegals, with the issuance of a "Z" visa, converts them immediately into legals as soon as the bill is signed. All they have to do is present two documents proving they were in the country prior to January 1 of this year (there's a toughie) and pay between $3,000 and $5,000 per household in the form of a "fine." This section also allows only one day for the government to do a background check to determine whether the individual is a criminal or a terrorist. ONE DAY!

If you really want to become depressed, read the entire section. Can you imagine the new levels of bureaucracies being created? It would make Hillary's earlier national health care plan look like a form 1040 EZ tax return.

These politicians are clearly not acting on behalf of the American citizens and the United States. Do you really think they are in tune with what the vast majority of Americans want? We sent them to Congress to represent us. Instead of doing this, they are thumbing their noses at us and pursuing what is best for their own selfish, political interests. I hope we remember this come the 2008 elections, but our "representatives" are probably betting that we won't.

To conclude, picture Osama, in some cave or spider hole, laughing his derriere off. All he has to do is get his terrorists across a very porous border (don't count on the fence being even attempted or finished), get them issued two documents showing that they were here prior to January 1 (easier than underage drinkers getting false IDs), come up with $3,000 per jihadist (from Middle East oil money), and get them through the 24-hour background check done by a severely understaffed ICE staff. Comforting thought, isn't it? Who is to be held ultimately responsible?

Huckabee is Complete Conservative

I told myself that I wouldn't take all the political campaigning seriously until the
first of next year.

It bothers me that the candidates can give us only two years of effort before they start putting their interests first on their priority list. I thought we elected these people to give us dedicated service for a full six years.

A classic example is when the New York downstate liberals got Hillary re- elected in 2006. She immediately went into campaign mode and pretty much forgot what her responsibilities really were.

Of course, she only considered New York to be important for her political ambitions from the start. She had no chance of being elected had she run in her legitimate home states of Arkansas and Illinois.

The drooling, left-leaning liberal state of New York welcomed her with open ideological arms. Can anyone tell me what she has done of significance for our state, especially since she got re-elected? Photo-Ops don't count.

To a lesser extent, most candidates of both parties are behaving the same way, putting self-interests first over those of the country.

But I digress. I have to admit I cheated and watched the rerun of the latest Republican debate on the Internet. I tried very hard to avoid all the posturing and positioning of the early campaign process, but I eventually succumbed to the temptation.

As I expected, I learned nothing new listening to Mitt Romney, Rudy Giuliani, John McCain and Tommy Thompson. Giuliani and McCain have some strengths but are too liberal on a lot of social issues. Mitt Romney looks very presidential but he has changed his position on too many issues. I thought the only way we could get a truly conservative candidate was to get Newt Gingrich or Fred Thompson into the race.

But then I got a very pleasant surprise when I listened to and looked into Mike
Huckabee's candidacy.

He is a person with true conservative convictions, both economic and social. He has not been afraid to clearly state and stand by his convictions. He is not a poll- sniffer and does not waiver depending on the audience he is addressing.

As I said earlier, he is a conservative's conservative. He was governor of Arkansas from 1996 to 2007, and prior to that he was a practicing Southern Baptist Minister from 1980 to 1985.

He, as we all shouldn't, makes no apology for his faith. He had a great quote, "My faith does affect my decision process. It explains me." Very refreshing.

Here is something scary for the primordial soup believers, those who think that our forbearers climbed out of this ancient pre-biotic soup, or mud pit and, by accident, turned into the advanced beings we are now. Huckabee does not believe in evolution. Again, very refreshing.

He is a pro-life candidate and thinks public funding of abortions should be eliminated. At the same time, he does support, hesitantly, the death penalty.

Yes, there is no conflict between these two opposing beliefs of life and death.

Yes, there is very logical reasoning to differentiate the two beliefs.

On the domestic front, he favors not more government but more efficient government. A logical extension of this is to respect the 10th Amendment and strengthen the states' powers.

One of my favorites is that he wants to implement the Fair Tax system. It is not even close to the flat tax principle and was a topic of one of my very early columns.

It's great to see support for this concept growing. A great book to read is "The Fair Tax Book" by Neal Boortz and John Linder. After reading the explanations and logic behind its concepts, it would be hard not to become a supporter of the fair tax.

He supports a strong military, private gun ownership, and becoming energy independent through the development of alternative fuels and a more open policy of domestic oil exploration. He is at the same time very environmentally sensitive but not to the point of destroying ourselves economically to achieve impossible (and suspect) goals.

He is critical of President Bush's war strategy and thinks we should have adopted the "Powell Doctrine" of winning through the implementation of overwhelming force.

He thinks that if we had 300,000 troops in-country from the beginning, they all would have been home safe by now after winning and exiting with an honorable conclusion.

There are many other positive qualities about this candidate, but I don't have the space to enumerate them. His biggest disadvantages are the lack of name recognition and fund raising capabilities.

After reading a lot about this candidate, I have sent in my contribution to his campaign; I hope all you fellow conservatives will do the same. He gives us all a very positive choice.

Face Facts on Enemy Combatants

Earlier this month, a 4th U.S. Circuit Court of Appeals panel, located in Richmond, Virginia, ruled that the Bush administration couldn't continue to hold Ali al- Marri, a Qatari citizen and a legal U.S. resident, in military detention indefinitely without charging him with a crime.

As expected, the hate-Bush crowd had a field day. "Another sweeping repudiation of the administration's strategy of treating suspected terrorists like enemy soldiers rather than like criminals," stated an ACLU representative.

"A major setback," "a severe rebuke," "a victory for the Constitution," and on
and on, ad nauseam.

First, these people shouldn't start partying quite yet. As I said above it was a
panel of three judges making this decision, and the decision was only 2-1.

The U.S. attorney general has already asked the full 4th Circuit Court to review the decision. This means 15 judges, rather than 3, will be looking at the facts of the case. Legal authorities predict that it will end up in the Supreme Court.

Also, let's look at the false accusations that President Bush has misused his power to declare a U.S. citizen an enemy combatant.

Remember how after the Patriot Act was passed, all those Chicken Littles cried how armed men in black suits, wearing black sunglasses, and driving black limos were going to break into citizens' homes by the thousands, tearing them from their crying families and that they would disappear forever?

How many times has it happened? Maybe four, no more than five times. Wow, what blatant disregard for our Constitution. And who were these innocent victims?

First came little Johnny Walker Lindh. He was an easy one. He was the U.S. citizen captured on the battlefield in Afghanistan while attempting to kill Americans.

Briefly (unfortunately) held by the military, he was luckily (for him) convicted in federal district court and sentenced to 20 years. He should have been held by the military, bled for information and then, under the Unified Code of Military Justice, hung for treason.

Next came Yaser Eser Hamdi who was born in Louisiana (his only claim to U.S. citizenship) but grew up in Saudi Arabia. He was another one captured in Afghanistan, held at Guantanamo until his citizenship was discovered, and then transferred to a navy brig in South Carolina.

He lost all of his appeals. The case went to the Supreme Court, which agreed he could be held by the military but only if the administration gave him a fair opportunity to challenge its claims.

After we got all the valuable information from him, he had to renounce his American citizenship and was deported to Saudi Arabia. I'm sure his right to due process will be allowed there.

Then came Jose Padilla, a reputed gang member who was arrested in Chicago in 2004. All he did was train at a terror camp and for a while served at a Taliban camp in Afghanistan. He was accused of being part of a plan by Al Qaeda to explode a dirty bomb in an American city.

The same 4th Circuit Court mentioned above upheld Bush's decision that he be labeled an enemy combatant and held by the military. Since the defense was ready to appeal to the Supreme Court, Bush had him transferred back to civilian control where he is on trial for aiding terrorism, costing us taxpayers much more money.

The civilian trial is still underway, and as of June 21 it was ruled that the prosecution could play a videotape of Padilla being interviewed by bin Laden.

Lastly, we have Ali al-Marri, the person mentioned at the beginning of this column. This gentleman was a trainee in one of bin Laden's Afghanistan terror camps and even met with Khalid Shaikh Mohammed.

So there is the extent of Bush's alleged misuse of constitutional authority.

Pretty reckless handling of the above "innocent civilians and residents."

The reason for declaring an individual an enemy combatant is pretty clear: to keep the individual from performing additional acts of terror and to deny access to an attorney, which would severely limit the ability to acquire valuable information.

In one case an attorney was allowed for Sheikh Omar Abdell-Rahman-Lynne Stewart, a radical American activist attorney. She used her right to see the accused to pass along secret messages to his followers.

She was convicted of such charges, was disbarred, and is serving only a 28 month prison term. She could have, and should have, gotten life.

I wish I had more space to provide you with more facts. Maybe my next column will be used to give you more facts, not opinion. It all depends on what comes up between now and my next column deadline.

'Fairness Doctrine' Just Unfair

I almost had a column completed about the ongoing evolution debate but then the Democrat led Congress once again illustrated its total inability to lead.

In the first five-plus months of their leadership, Democrats have succeeded in bringing only 26 bills to the president. Of this number, 13 represented the naming of federal buildings and five simply extended existing laws that were expiring. The other 8 were bills that wouldn't have passed without having to work in a bipartisan fashion.

The only way they got a major piece of legislation through, the minimum wage increase proposal, was by tacking it on to the bill that fully funded the troops fighting in Iraq and Afghanistan. Even then the heavy-hitting Democrat leadership (Kennedy, Clinton, Boxer, Pelosi, Obama, et al.) put politics over principles and voted against the bill. As a matter of fact, 140 Democrats voted against one of their most important political promises. So much for their caring about the poor and the middle class.

What can they do? They can't provide leadership because they have no vision for the country, and their constant harassment of the Bush administration is going nowhere.

So they started talking about reviving something called the "Fairness Doctrine." Actually I have to take some of that statement back. There were enough sensible Democrats (equally split in the House) who pretty forcefully put this foolish issue back in the garbage can where it belonged.

This doctrine was originally enacted in 1949 to ensure that both sides of a controversial issue were guaranteed to be covered equally in the broadcast media. In 1949, there was not nearly the wide choice of media outlets to turn to as there is today, and radio dominated. Although a seemingly noble idea back then, it stifled political discussion and went against the constitutional right of free speech. The FCC finally recognized this when it abolished the doctrine in 1987. Actually, various related Supreme Court rulings caused them to make this decision.

So why is it even being considered again? After the crushing defeat of the immigration bill, influenced heavily by the public on their elected representatives (Democrat and Republican), the liberal, left-leaning Democrat leadership saw the impact that talk radio, overwhelmingly conservative, had in the arena of public debate. In a word, they were simply scared. Being used to having the liberal main stream media (print and major broadcasting networks) in their back pockets, they now had to confront the success talk radio was having in getting the conservative viewpoint across.

All the facts were against them. The top five talk shows were conservative and overwhelmingly successful. Their liberal counterparts, including Air America, were falling flat on their faces (and declaring bankruptcy). It simply proved that you had to have positive ideas people could relate to in order to succeed. The liberal left was only good at spewing negativity and defeatism, hence a minimum audience.

If a snobbish elitism approach is going to be taken, saying that talk radio listeners aren't as politically astute, that strategy will fall on its face. According to a Pew Research survey taken in 2006, it was found that Rush Limbaugh's audience came in second as far as having the most informed listeners. Only readers of politically related magazines were ranked higher.

So the only strategy left to the liberals is the one they seem to always fall back
on. If they can't win in the marketplace of ideas, regulate the marketplace.

I've got some more good news. We are not only winning the talk radio battle. We are also winning in other fields. Fox News gets consistently higher ratings than the liberal leaning cable news network alternatives. Katie Couric is continuing the fine job Dan Rather did, and CBS News is being taken less and less seriously as time goes on.

There is more good news that I briefly touched upon in an earlier column. There were only 4 major newspapers that grew in readership from 2002 to 2006. Three were conservative op-ed dailies (The Wall Street Journal, New York Post and the Washington Times) and the fourth, USA Today, was labeled neutral. All seven of the leading liberal papers declined in readership, in some cases by 10 or more percentage points (The New York Times, Los Angeles Times, The Washington Post, Chicago Tribune, New York Daily News, Houston Chronicle, and Newsday).

So my conservative friends, even though George W. Bush is unfortunately looking less like Ronald Reagan and more like Jimmy Carter every day, and some of our Republican friends are disappointing us, the facts and trends are on our side. We are winning. We have to work especially hard to make sure that the 2008 elections put us and our country back on the right track.

Well, it looks like Valerie Plame's 15 minutes of fame is just about up. A U.S. District Court judge simply dismissed her lawsuit against Bush, Cheney, Rove and Libby.

Unfortunately, we will probably have to suffer through one more appeal from her, but if she wants to spend more money on legal fees, go for it.

Joe and Valerie Wilson are mere political hacks. They were used by the Bush haters to desperately sling enough mud at the Bush administration to get something, anything, to stick, and all they were able to do was to defame an innocent man. They must be proud.

I only hope that Scooter Libby has a chance to go on the offense once his successful appeal is concluded.

Valerie gave conflicting stories when testifying before the Senate Intelligence Committee. When asked if she, and not Dick Cheney, suggested that her husband be sent on a fact-finding mission to Niger, she first said she didn't, then she said she couldn't recall, and then there was the inconvenient internal CIA e-mail that quoted her as saying her husband "may be able to assist."

Her husband, Joe, has plenty of conflicting statements also. As a matter of fact, he is even lower than she is.

So after all this wasted taxpayer money, what came out of the process? Scooter Libby was convicted of obstructing justice and lying to a grand jury for allegedly leaking the identity of Valerie Plame.

I agree they were serious offenses, but the penalty certainly didn't fit the crime. He was assessed a $250,000 fine, received 2 years probation, will probably be disbarred, and got a 30 MONTH prison sentence.

Give me a break. Sandy Berger, former national security advisor, removed sensitive classified documents from the National Archives by stuffing them in his pants and socks, hid them at a nearby construction site, later took them home, and even destroyed some of them.

He admitted to doing so after first denying that he did in fact steal the documents. His penalty? A plea bargained $50,000 fine, 100 hours of community service, and having his security clearance lifted for three years!

If someone can't see the inconsistency here, they should seek out a mental
health care provider immediately.

So Scooter, former chief of staff for Vice President Cheney, was prosecuted for what? No crime was committed since Valerie was no longer classified as being covert. How can you lie about something and obstruct justice when no crime took place?

His "lie" was his version of when a conversation took place and what was said differed from two key witnesses, former New York Times reporter Judith Miller and former Time Magazine reporter Matthew Cooper.

Remember, this testimony stated the meetings took place in June or July of 2003. Here's Libby, a very busy person who has multiple meetings every day, being asked to recall what was said in 2007! You or I couldn't do it either. So he is guilty of the inability to recall the exact content of these conversations.

Now, when Judith Miller testified, she stated that she "had conversations with other government officials and could not be absolutely, absolutely certain that she first heard about an outed CIA official from I. 'Scooter' Libby." Pretty damning huh?

Cooper was even more sympathetic. Libby granted him a waiver to testify (I'm
certain a guilty person would do this) when Cooper asked him.

In recalling his version of the testimony, he stated in his Times article dated 10/30/05, "Basically, I asked Libby if he had heard anything about Wilson's wife having been involved in sending him to Niger. Libby responded with words to the effect of 'Yeah, I've heard this too'."

The rest of the article is pretty revealing, and I would recommend you read it. You really want this man to go to jail before his appeal rights are concluded? He should have used the Hillary selective memory strategy and simply said, "I really can't recall." It worked for her.

So, now the Dems are all flustered about the grave miscarriage of justice that took place when President Bush simply commuted the 30 month jail sentence. I will have to do an article in the future about presidential pardons and commutations since I don't have room here. Get over it, Dems.

Scooter Libby will appeal and have the decision reversed. If not he will be pardoned. The Bush administration will win again since once more it has truth on its side.

Best of all, those leftist liberals will have to continue pounding their heads against the wall, causing even more brain damage than they already have, since they lost again.

I think Harry Reid should demand another all-night session of the Senate. He certainly got a lot accomplished in the first one.

Questioning the Theory of Evolution

I had promised some time ago that I would be writing a column about the theory of evolution. That time has come. Actually, with all the reading I've done, it's probably going to be three or four columns.

First of all, I want to say that I have the greatest respect for all the fields of science and the individuals who have chosen science as a career.
What I can't stand is arrogant science when it comes to talking about evolution. There seems to be an air of elitism or snobbishness against those who hold honest and educated theories that refute the theory of evolution.

In a book by William Dembski, "Uncommon Dissent, Intellectuals Who Find Darwinism Unconvincing," he quoted Richard Dawkins, a prominent name in the field of evolution, or Darwinism, saying that those who resist Darwin's explanation are "ignorant, insane or wicked."

Isaac Constantine quotes Dawkins as saying, "If people lived according to rationalism, there would be less waste of time. People would concentrate on really worthwhile things, instead of wasting time on religion, astrology, crystal-gazing, fortune- telling, things like that."

Last one by this self-absorbed megalomaniac, from his own book, "The God Delusion." "The God of the Old Testament is arguably the most unpleasant character in all fiction: jealous and proud of it; a petty, unjust, unforgiving control-freak; a vindictive bloodthirsty, ethnic cleanser; a misogynistic, homophobic, racist, infanticidal, genocidal, filicidal, pestilential, megalomanical, sadomasochistic, capriciously malevolent bully. A naïf blessed with the perspective of innocence has a clearer perception."

These are just a few quotes of this maniacal, irrational fool. Do you really think you could have an intelligent discussion with an individual like this? Unfortunately, he is just one of many who will resort to any means of insult, character assassination, snideness and lies to discredit those who have the nerve to question the myth of Darwinism's invincibility.

Another example of dismissive attitude took place last year when I attended a lecture by a retired biologist who shared the very valid concerns he had about Darwinism and evolution. The lecture was very informative and provoking, the speaker having an excellent ability to communicate difficult issues on a level that was made understandable to the layman.

During the question and answer period a person stood and very arrogantly and insultingly raved on about how wrong the speaker was about almost everything the speaker said earlier.

This person was obviously caught up in his self-importance, not having a question at all but rather trying to give all us unenlightened ones the benefit of his genius.

The speaker took what the man said very graciously, something I don't think I could have done; and finally the disrupter sat down (or left, I didn't pay any attention), and we could benefit further from the knowledge and experience of the speaker.

We Creationists and believers in Intelligent Design can take solace in the fact that more and more prominent scientists and intellectuals are questioning the Darwinism myth of invincibility every day.

In addition, based on a Gallup poll taken of adults in 2007, 87 percent of those polled believed in either the Creationist view or in Theistic evolution compared to 10 percent who believed in evolution. The poll was segmented by age, education level, income, race, and gender. The highest percentage of believers in evolution were among those with a college education, and even then only 16.7 percent believed in Darwin's theory of evolution. So even with its monopoly on today's educational system, science is unable to convey a convincing message to the public.

Yet, any other alternative or conflicting theory is not even allowed to be taught in schools. The ACLU actually sued a school district when the board simply wanted to include a disclaimer in textbooks that mentioned the "biblical version of creation and other teachings on life's origin."

The disclaimer went on to say "It is the basic right and privilege of each student to form his/her own opinion or maintain beliefs taught by parents on this very important matter. ...Students are urged to exercise critical thinking and gather all information possible and closely examine each alternative toward forming an opinion."

Robert C. Koons has said in his article, "Why Darwinism Fails to Inspire Confidence": "We have, therefore, the right and even the duty to compare what Darwinian scientists have actually accomplished with what they still must accomplish if their strong claims of certainty are to be sustained. The evaluation of the arguments of biologists is within the competence of each person, as is the task of assessing the appropriate degree of doubt or certainty that is attached to their conclusions."

Based on the above poll, it seems as if people are doing just that.

Evolution Can't Explain Origin of Life

Most people, if not all, would have no problem with the notion of evolution if used properly.

Evolution simply means change. Changes in existing species as they adapt to changing environmental conditions are observable, testable, and, in many cases reproducible.

Creationists and others refer to this as microevolution. There is certainly scientific evidence to back up the theory of evolution at this restrained level.

It is totally inappropriate to use this scientifically provable process and make the gigantic leap to stating that this change, if traced backwards and given enough time to allow the process to change gradually, would prove that life as we know it originated from some single-celled organisms that in turn crawled out of some primordial soup.

There is absolutely no evidence of evolution that can explain new species' creation. This is no longer science; it becomes an unprovable, rather illogical, ideology.

Yet this is what is being taught today in our schools. No other alternative is allowed to be discussed. This is not science; it is scientistic philosophy.

I'm not even sure if you are allowed to question some of the many holes present in the theory. Thankfully, some very qualified scientists and intellectuals are beginning to question the weaknesses present, and they are becoming more and more in number every day.

If you have been presented with the theory of evolution or Darwinism and were expected to believe it simply because someone told you to believe it, this is certainly not education. It is, in fact, indoctrination.

In a creation evolution article I read recently, it quoted from a biology textbook used in high school biology classes. "Life cannot arise by spontaneous generation from inantimate material today, so far as we know, but conditions were very different when the earth was only a few billion years old." (Campbell, Nell; Biology, 1987, page 504). Isn't it great to be able to use time as an excuse to explain anything and everything as long as God is not allowed to enter the equation.

Let's look at the complexity involved. The entire chain of life is supposed to go like this. First the soup, then amino acids, then protein, then the cell, then the fish, the amphibian, the reptile, the mammal to man. Naturalism, mutation and blind chance is supposed to explain how we evolved.

In the 1950's two scientists put together what they believed to be the major ingredients those billions of years ago (in a lab using test tubes which I don't think existed back then).

This mix supposedly consisted of methane, hydrogen, water, and ammonia; and they then ran a current of electricity through this mixture and created a few amino acids (again in a controlled laboratory environment).

It takes a string of amino acids about 400 in length (and remember there are some 20 different types of amino acids needed) to make up an average protein cell.

These acids must also be in a very specific order or else all you have is a worthless mess of chemicals.

The probability that simple chance will form just one functional protein cell is 20 to the 400th power. That's a 1 followed by 520 zeros! The article points out that it would be the equivalent of winning the lottery every week for 11 years. Oops, I forgot to mention that humans have trillions upon trillions of proteins in them, all functioning together. The article points out that DNA and RNA are also required for life. To date, no one has been able to produce chains of RNA or DNA and can't produce even one cell!

There is certainly a long way to go to believability in Darwin's theory. It sure seems just as rational to believe in creationism with God as the Designer as the above. I don't care how many more billions of years you need to make evolutionary theory feasible.

It seems that science has this little black box of explanations, and anything that doesn't fit with conventional reasoning isn't allowed to be placed inside. It just gets rejected out of hand.

When you are trying to hit a target of truth using your own theory of evolution as your bullet, it sure is a lot easier to shoot first and then paint the target around the spot where it hit.

There is a story going around. Three scientists approached God, saying, "We can produce life using dirt and don't need you anymore." God then asks the scientists to show him, which they proceed to do by starting to scoop up some dirt. Then God stops them saying, "Whoa, hold on guys, use your own dirt."

Ah, the arrogance of man. The last column will talk about irreducible complexity and what the fossil records show.

Speciation Has Never Been Observed

Finally, as promised, my last column on evolution (I think). There is so much more to talk about and three columns can't give the topic adequate coverage. So if you like, if you e-mail me, I will give you a list of all the books I have used as research.

One huge stumbling block for Darwinists is to show how one species evolves into another. Has this most basic building block, called speciation, ever been observed or demonstrated as one would expect as a necessary element for scientific validity? Not once.

Even though there are many definitions of the term species, Jerry Coyne and Allen Orr, both evolutionary biologists, use the following in their book "Speciation": "Species are groups of interbreeding natural populations that are reproductively isolated from other such groups."
In other words, humans can't breed with animals, mammals with fish, goats with birds, etc. However, Darwin said we all come from a single common ancestor.

It must be nice to make such claims but it would be nicer if these claims could be backed up. They obviously can't be. There is a website, talkorigins.org that claims there have been 5 examples of observed speciation. Every one has been either dis- proven or improperly claimed in the first place.

Two quotes are relevant here. Alan H. Linton, a bacteriologist, said in a 2001 article, "Throughout 150 years of the science of bacteriology, there is no evidence that one species of bacteria has changed into another.....Since there is no evidence for species changes between the simplest forms of unicellular life, it is not surprising that there is no evidence for evolution...throughout the whole array of higher multi-cellular organisms."

Also, William Dembski, with doctorates in both mathematics and philosophy, in his book, "Uncommon Dissent," which is a collection of articles denouncing many of the claims Darwinists make, says, in reference to speciation, "That's the problem with Darwinism: In place of detailed, testable accounts of how a complex, biological system could realistically have emerged, Darwinism offers just-so stories about how such systems might have emerged in some idealized conceptual space far removed from biological reality."

Again, where is the evidence for these remarkable transformations? Shouldn't we be able to find in the fossil record proof of one species turning into another?
As B. G. Ranganathan says, in his book "Origins?", "There is no evidence in the fossil record of one kind of creature becoming another kind. No transitional

links or intermediate forms between various kinds of creatures have ever been found."

Also, what about now? Has the evolutionary process stopped just before any observations could be made? If, as the Darwinists say, that continuous evolution is a fact, there should be plenty of examples to point to that are in the stages of transition, now, all around us, as well as proof in the past, in the fossil record. I want to see the half fish/half amphibian example, and, as Ranganathan says, "not a single fossil with part fins….part feet has been found."

I apologize for not being able to properly cover some other important areas of concern relating to Darwinism, but there are a lot of conservative issues out there that need to be addressed.

So, in conclusion, as William Dembski says, "Why does Darwinism's back need to be broken? Because it is no longer merely a scientific theory but an ideology. Darwin's original proposal was actually quite modest: organisms adapt to their environments as a result of random variation and natural selection."

If the Darwinists kept the theory at this level of explanation, there would be no arguments. When they take the giant leap to use this theory to explain the origin of life, with all its incredible complexity, people can rightly question the validity of these claims. Michael Behe, PhD in biochemistry, warns us, properly so, when he says, "Our willingness to accept scientific claims that are against common sense is the key to an understanding of the real struggle between science and the supernatural. We take the side of science in spite of the patent absurdity of its constructs….in spite of the tolerance of the scientific community for unsubstantiated just-so stories because we have a prior commitment a commitment to materialism."

So feel comfortable with the fact that all Darwinists can do is belittle, insult and demean their opponents when challenged. The people mentioned above are only a few of the highly qualified scientists and intellectuals who are on your side. Also, based on the numerous polls taken by Pew, Gallup and others, apparently the general public has a lot of common sense on its side.

Someone said it perfectly when he/she said that Darwinism was the atheist's
creation myth.

Petraeus Shamed His Persecutors

Slam dunk. Total success. That's about all you can say about the Gen. David H. Petraeus Iraq war hearings last week. Once again, the public saw a highly competent, professional man of true integrity staying calm during the vicious, mean-spirited personal attacks of the Democrat leadership.

At the same time, he clearly exposed their hypocrisy, ineptitude and disingenuousness as they tried to strut their stuff before the cameras.

Oliver North did the same thing to them 20 years ago, and they didn't learn their lesson one bit. It was actually kind of laughable the way they both outclassed them.

First of all, Bush should completely ignore Democrats' constant calls to change
course. He replaced Donald Rumsfeld with Robert Gates and that wasn't enough.

Then he put General Petraeus in charge of Iraq operations. That didn't work. Then there was the surge strategy, which was and is operationally successful, but the Dems still weren't happy.

There is nothing at all that Bush could do to appease these radicals and still keep the long-term security of this country intact. They are blinded by their hatred of Bush, still angry that he beat them in two national elections (legally) and they can't get over claiming that we shouldn't have started the war in the first place (wrong again).

What in heaven's name does that have to do with formulating a course of action that will defeat al-Qaeda, win this particular battle in Iraq and continue to do everything possible to keep our country safe?

Most people want leaders who will lead us forward with a vision and not dwell in the past. Unbelievably, you see the die-hards who continually write in and chant the same old shallow and tiresome mantra of Bush hatred.

Remember, this was the Congress that had nothing but praise for Petraeus earlier this year. They called him brave, professional, intelligent, and a hero.
Members of Congress said he was the perfect man for the position and confirmed him unanimously! Boy, did they back off when they saw that his and Bush's surge strategy actually began succeeding.

They care nothing about what is best for America and instead are only concerned about their own political power. America losing the Iraq war is all they want, and they will do anything to keep us from winning.

They started discrediting the general even before he said a word or issued any report at all. They knew the surge was working and all the statistics pointed to that fact. But they really turned up the heat the moment Petraeus and Ambassador Ryan Crocker sat down.

I didn't get to see much of the House battle, but the Senate hearings were sickening enough.

I'm sure there is a website where you can replay the entire hearings, but suffice it to say the process was the same every time a Democrat spoke, especially the Democrat presidential contestants.

They opened their speech by first giving the general brief false praise, then proceeded to huff and puff and declare themselves more patriotic than anyone else in the room.

After that, of course, they stated their unwavering support for our troops (I don't know how they get through that part without choking). And finally, they got down to their real agenda of insulting and demeaning the character and integrity of the leader of these same troops, showing that their actions spoke much truer than the lies they were spouting just before.

Some even came right out and called the general and ambassador liars. He was interrupted repeatedly and in some cases wasn't even given the opportunity to respond. The committee members gave speeches; they didn't ask questions. Barbara Boxer arrogantly used the entire time allotted for her self-aggrandizing opportunity and then insultingly told the general, since they were out of time, that he could provide his response in writing.

She knew his response would only make her look unqualified for her committee position and the general would make her look even more incompetent in front of the viewing public. He did this repeatedly to all the armchair generals.

I hope you more main stream, clearer thinking Democrats will start taking your party back from some of these power-crazed zealots. Do you really want Clinton, Wexler, Biden, Kerry, Reid, Pelosi, Lantos, MoveOn.Org, the Daily Kos and others like them leading this country when they treat honorable men like Petraeus the way they did last week?

If that is the way they treat a heroic, decorated leader of our armed forces, what respect do you think they really have for our troops? I think a potential, future, Commander-in-Chief should show a little more respect and class.

In comparison, all their patriotism, integrity, class and honor combined would easily fit in the little finger of General Petraeus.

Hillary Still Lacks Character

Every once and a while you get to have a glimpse of the true character of an individual. No political speech writers, political advisors or spin doctors are around to tell you what to say. You are on your own.

Such was the case when Hillary was asked the very simple question as to whether she felt the MoveOn.org ad slandering General David Petraeus had gone too far. Here was her chance to display her honor and integrity, her support for the troops and their leader.

Well, she failed miserably. She waffled and wiggled out of a straight answer as good as that funny little dictator from Iran did repeatedly while at Columbia University

She simply does not have the character to be Commander in Chief. She has repeatedly through her life shown her disdain for our military men and women.

She is nothing more than a political hack who only strives for personal power and riches. She cares very little about the country. And the sad part is that the media consistently lets her off the hook.

The first indication of her character challenges was when she smeared the reputations of long time workers at the White House Travel Office so that she could give the very lucrative business to her good friend Linda Thomason.

Then there was the Vince Foster "suicide." Then we had Craig Livingston and the Republican FBI files that mysteriously turned up in her possession and her shock when she discovered this. The same holds true with the Rose law firm's billing records regarding the Whitewater scandal showing up in the White House living quarters after she claimed they must have been lost. Again she was truly shocked and dismayed how this could have possibly happened.

The press has a responsibility to answer why they chose to ignore or downplay these very serious character flaws, as well as others, especially now that she is a serious candidate for the office of the presidency.

The press has failed miserably. I would hate to think that all the press outlets were as dishonorable and blatently biased as the New York Times. We will certainly see whether they are or not as the election looms closer. More publications than we think might have the same integrity issues to deal with.

But the most glaring example of being the hypocrite she truly is was when she and Bill were being interviewed on "60 Minutes." Bill's little (and many) sexcapades were being questioned when Hillary was asked how she felt about all these allegations.

Asked what she would do if they proved to be true, she said, in part, "I'm no Tammy Wynette, 'Stand by your Man' type of wife" indicating she would not tolerate this behavior in her husband. Truth or political strategy?

Unfortunately, this interview was given just before the inconvenient sex tape and stained dress discovery. Still no Tammy Wynette Hillary? I have had for a long time a copy of Tammy's record just for when I can have it blaring out of my office if Hillary ever steps on campus.

Now back to General Petraeus. Most common sense, patriotic people saw him as a man of honor. A brave man and proven hero (repeatedly) and a true leader of men. No political agenda, no purpose other than to lead his men in honorable fashion on behalf of his country.

Hillary clearly showed us the type of person she was when she constantly insulted and berated the general simply to look good in front of her supporters.

She had a chance to give respect to this hero and instead she sided with Michael Moore, George Soros and all the other fringe lunatic groups whose only commonality is their hatred of America and George Bush.

So there you have a picture of another Clinton White House. Instead of Babs Streisand and Linda Thomason romping around in the Lincoln Bedroom after having bought and paid for it (I wonder if Bill was home at the time?) it will be George Soros and Michael Moore and their dates. You can throw the honor and dignity of the White House out the window.

Hillary, how dare you call someone of General Petraeus' character into question and say to his face that he had a "willing suspension of disbelief" regarding his testimony.

You Hillary, who have lied repeatedly, pimped your husband and pimped the White House, should be very familiar with the term "willing suspension of belief" since you practice it on a regular basis.

Book Tells Truth About Duke Event

If anyone wants to read a great book about the true story of the Duke lacrosse non-rape event, you should read "It's Not About The Truth, The Untold Story of the Duke Lacrosse Case and the Lives It Shattered," by Don Yaeger. A Duke Alumni had read my column about the Duke case and student athletes in general and graciously sent me a copy.

It is an amazing story of an honorable coach and three players and the horror they went through, caused by many different parties. It is fact-filled with supporting police records, hospital findings, DNA results, and the extensive criminal records of the two strippers who started this nightmare. There is a documented time line that runs from the night of the alleged rape all the way to April 11 when all charges were dropped by the attorney general and, more importantly, when they were also declared innocent. This one word was all the players and their parents wanted to hear all along.

I'm sure everyone could easily follow the case from the beginning. It was front page news day after day in all the newspapers and was constantly reported on stations such as MSNBC, CNN and other untrustworthy outlets. And the traditional media sources wonder why subscriptions are going down and stations are losing viewers. They are too arrogant to see that fewer and fewer people are finding them not credible or trustworthy and are turning to other more reliable sources. If any news source tells you that this was not the case, have them compare the column inches when they were reporting sensationalized lies to the inches given to retraction of rush to judgment and signs of remorse.

Yes, the young men involved acted very foolishly when they hired two strippers and had a party that involved underage drinking. The young men were on campus for practices when everyone else had left for spring break and were bored with nothing to do. This is absolutely no excuse for their actions. Still, why instantly label them as rich, privileged, lacrosse-playing white kids? As to the rich and privileged characterization, many of them certainly did not fit that description. And even if they were, does the description explain their behavior or just demonstrate the hatred and class envy and petty jealousy of others' lives.

But when the facts came out, it showed they were decent, clean-cut kids from decent hard-working families. Is it a problem for anyone out there that parents want the very best possible for their children? They were put through hell for absolutely no reason for more than a year and could have been sentenced to up to 30 years reach if wrongly found guilty. I would love for all the accusers to go through the same period of fear and uncertainty that these young men went through.

And let's not forget about the coach and his family. Mike Pressler is and honorable decent man. He is a man of great integrity who is loved and respected by his players and others. He had been at Duke for 16 years and could picture himself at no other place. He certainly loved Duke and had planned to finish out his career there. He inherited a losing program, turned it into a national powerhouse, and took the team to the 2005 NCAA Championship game

Detractors shamefully took away his season and forced him to resign, but he never stopped supporting his players and believed in their innocence from the very beginning. His family (wife and 2 daughters ages 14 and 7, I believe) endured threats, insults and humiliation throughout the ordeal, to the point where his daughters had to live elsewhere. Coach Pressler, obviously respected by those in lacrosse, found a job and is now coaching in Rhode Island.

Finally, a faculty committee was convened to investigate the lacrosse program and its results were impressive. The committee said "members of the team are academically and athletically responsible students who were not out of control while at Duke." The committee also pointed out that many players were irresponsible in their drinking, but at the same time the committee found that the "men's golf team had a higher percentage of its members with disciplinary records."

All in all, the Duke administrators, media, police, and the radical leftist faculty who prematurely jumped at the perceived social mistreatment of minority women owe a huge apology to all of those individuals whose lives were affected by these false claims. Think they have gotten them yet? I'm sure you know the answer. If not, I think you'll be interested in the next column and the associated sad facts.

Duke Team Still Lacks Apologies

This column marks my second full year of writing this column for The Daily Star. It's amazing how fast time flies when you're having fun. It looks like the upcoming year is going to provide me with a number of controversial topics, and I certainly look forward to this.

Even though it was tempting to write about the Spitzer debacle or the attacks made on the Senate floor by the pathetic little man, Harry Reid, on a private citizen, Rush Limbaugh, I promised one more column on the Duke lacrosse fiasco and the apologies that have not yet been made.

Everyone knows about the out-of-control district attorney who has fortunately been required to resign and has since been disbarred.

After all the law suits are over, he will probably be reduced to selling pencils on a street corner somewhere. It will be a fitting conclusion to a dishonorable career and it will serve him right.

More worrisome are the three remaining lynch mob characters. These are the media, Duke's president, and the ultra-liberal segment of Duke's faculty, all of whom's behavior was reprehensible.

First the media. Can anyone point out where there has been an apology anywhere nearly as spectacular as their pre-judging the case without waiting for the facts to come out?

Someday, maybe someone will remind them that their job is to simply report the news and keep their liberal biases to themselves.

Say what you might about Fox News and The Wall Street Journal, they consistently pointed out all the facts that contradicted the case being made against the three Duke players even before the DNA results came back.

The New York Times, however, stuck with its theme, as Robert Bliwise, author of "One Year Later," points out, of "privileged whites abusing poor black women." It's sad when liberal agendas take precedence over facts, but, hey, if it sells more copies or draws more readers, it must be ok.

President Brodhead's attempt of an apology? If you want to call it an apology, you can find it in the New York Times October 2 edition. You'll have to look hard for it since it was a very small article on the bottom of page 28, right across from the obituaries.

He apologizes for "not having better supported" the players. Wow, what a man of character. It came 1 ½ years later and after he had cancelled the lacrosse season, pressured the coach into resigning (he would have been fired otherwise) and having to restart his career, uprooting his family from a place he loved for 16 years, and suspending three innocent players, players who could have gone to prison for up to 30 years.

Isn't he just wonderful. He simply caved to the radical wing of Duke's faculty,
the same ilk that forced the Harvard President out of town for simply stating a fact.

The faculty? They are too petty and arrogant to even consider an apology. Not one of the 88 signers have asked to have his/her name removed from the original ad, and one professor said "she would sign the petition again in a heartbeat."

Anyone with a brain could see they had tried and convicted the entire program, yet they feel they were misunderstood.

How about this? One professor issued this statement. "We had a long discussion about what the word 'regret' means (very Clintonesque), and professors weighed in and we had a whole range of very detailed discussions in terms of the etymology of specific words. We were disappointed people did not understand the intention — it was never to rush to judgment, it was about listening to our students who have been trying to make their way in a not only racist and sexist campus, but country."

A year later and this was the best they could come up with? Imagine trying to stay awake in that professor's class. Sorry prof, everyone understood exactly your intentions, which is why you and your gang still have egg on your faces. Fortunately, these professors have few if any majors, and their courses are not required for a degree. One blogger hit the nail on a head when she said, "One of the more depressing, yet enlightening aspects of this case is that the response of the Gang of 88 reflects a mentality of the hard left that is prevalent on many, if not most, university campuses today. The most 'elite' universities also are the repositories of the worst of these kinds."

They pretty much are an example of the moral dry rot of our society. Oops, I bet that is a politically incorrect no-no.

Gang of 88, try reading the Fifth Amendment of the U.S.Constitution, which reads, in part, "No person shall be...deprived of life, liberty or property without due process of law."
It doesn't mention race, gender or class status..

At a Hartwick College tailgate party two Saturdays ago (Hartwick won another huge game that Saturday), a fellow conservative friend and I were talking. After awhile he asked me who I thought would be the candidate chosen from each party for the upcoming 2008 elections.

I tried to weasel out of the answer since I had sworn to myself not to get overly involved in all the campaign rhetoric until early next year. He went to get more food, and I thought I was off the hook. But when he came back he continued to hold my feet to the fire.

After giving a lot of reasons and thinking about the issues, I came up with the tired old conventional choices of Hillary and Rudy. I was actually hoping it would be Hillary on the Democrat side but Rudy was not my desired answer for the Republicans. He just doesn't excite me much, and I think he carries a lot of baggage that will be exploited in the general elections.

I think this election, for the first time in a very long time, will be determined by the selection of each party's running mate. I feel this is particularly true on the Republican side. The conservative base has to be brought back to the voting booths, and I don't think the Rudy nomination has the ability to do this by itself.

Way back in June I wrote an article about Mike Huckabee, a former governor from Arkansas (he was the honest one). I thought he was a pretty impressive option and would make some serious waves before the campaign was over.

Sure enough, that is exactly what he is doing. In Iowa he has risen to second place in the polls behind Romney (27 percent to 19 percent) and is still getting stronger.

Although still significantly behind, he is rising fast in both the New Hampshire and South Carolina primary polls and has cracked 10 percent national support levels in the party for the first time in a recent Rasmussen poll.

The best part about Mike Huckabee is his honesty, integrity and true conservative roots. He lays out his beliefs and stands on the issues and refuses to waiver when speaking to different groups. He is the only true conservative in the field, both socially and fiscally, and is a person who can truly galvanize the Republican base. He is someone we conservatives have been missing for quite some time now.

It seems as though everyone who hears him speak is truly impressed. For example, Newsmax pointed out that "Huckabee finished a close second in the values voter online straw poll conducted during the Family Research Council's conference in Washington, D.C. But among the 952 people who actually attended the conference, Huckabee won in a landside, garnering 51 percent of the votes, while Romney got just 10 percent and Giuliani, 6 percent."

It is only his lack of sufficient campaign funds that is keeping him from getting the exposure he will need in order to stay in the race. Even that is improving. While he raised only $2.1 million in all of last year, he is now raising $1 million or more each month.

He is for the death penalty, against abortion, supports the "surge" in Iraq, insists on the Pledge of Allegiance, is for the "fair tax" (another earlier column), opposes gay marriages, wants border protection to be made a priority, and supports a strong military.

At the same time, he is a social conservative with a conscience. He was very active as the governor of Arkansas setting up child obesity programs.

He increased health insurance coverage to 70,000 Arkansas children, and he believes that the arts are just as important to our national creativity as are the sciences. He believes in the Christian idea of forgiveness and is for the granting of parole to criminals if used wisely. He also was very popular with minorities as he consistently won 48 percent of the African-American vote in his 2002 re-election bid..

In a conversation with Michael Gerson, a Washington Post Writers Group member, Huckabee was pointing out the advantage of his pastoral background. "There isn't a social pathology that I wouldn't be able to put a face to. I've talked with a pregnant 14-year-old who hasn't been able to tell her parents, with a 17-year-old high school student who believes he is gay and doesn't know how to break the news, with parents who have a son on life support after a motorcycle accident...It makes me a different kind of public official, not as rigid, not blind to problems."

Mike Huckabee, President? Maybe too much of an uphill climb. As to Vice President? If the party has an ounce of brains, they will take a very serious look at Mike.

Limbaugh Supports U.S. Troops

A few weeks ago there was a letter to the editor that beat me to the punch regarding that despicable little man, Harry Reid, and his lies about Rush Limbaugh.

The happy ending is worth mentioning again since the liberal press forgot to fulfill their responsibilities of objective reporting. It is still trying, as are the treasonous liberal leaders of the House and Senate, to wipe the egg off their faces and hope once again that the public will forget about their embarrassing actions.

The incident began when, on the Senate floor, individual Senators attacked Rush Limbaugh, a private citizen, about his supposedly calling any veterans who opposed the war in Iraq phony soldiers.

This is Senate business? They knew this was a lie before and during their ranting, but were acting on orders from Moveon.org and trying to appease their ultra- liberal base. They also wanted to show everyone, by huffing and puffing with righteous indignation, how patriotic they were.

No matter that they have been making concerted effort after concerted effort to undermine the ability of our troops to win the war and exit with honor.

No matter that they forgot to denounce the Moveon.org ad insulting General Piraeus. They certainly can't denounce their puppetmaster, George Soros.

No matter that they have repeatedly called our troops baby and women killers and torturers. And, luckily for them, they have the main stream media letting them get away with it.

Now, about the phony soldier claim. Rush was, if you listen to that portion of his monologue, specifically denouncing Jesse MacBeth as a phony soldier, a traitor who claimed to be a past Army Ranger and also claimed to have witnessed unspeakable cruelties committed by our forces in Iraq.

It turns out that, yes, Jesse was in the Army- for exactly 44 days- before being kicked out for not making the grade. He is now in prison for falsifying his Army records.

Rush was also speaking of him and others like him who glorify their non-existent military backgrounds to give credibility to their lies.

Maybe you haven't heard much about them either. They don't exactly help the

agenda of Moveon.org and their media lapdogs.

In his faked outrage, the liar, Harry Reid, wrote a letter to a Mr. Mark Mays, CEO of Clear Channel Communications, to publicly repudiate Rush's statement and force him to issue a public apology.

What hypocrisy! Ever wonder why whenever Rush goes over to visit the troops he gets inundated with affection and admiration from our troops, while the many signers of the infamous letter don't dare go near the troops?

People like Harry Reid, John, the war hero (or so he likes to continually remind us) Kerry, Dick Durbin, Joe Biden....(never mind the lengthy list, just put in the entire Democrat party) are never shown with troops surrounding them?

None of our men and women want to be seen with them, and they know it. Even the ever-startled-looking Nancy Pelosi would rather have her picture taken with a Syrian dictator than be seen with our troops.

Back to the letter. CEO Mays found it quite amusing and gave it to Rush, who offered it up for sale on E-Bay. He also issued a challenge to Democrats to put their patriotism where their mouths were. Before the bidding process began, Rush agreed to match the final bid with both amounts being contributed to the Marine Corps-Law Enforcement Foundation. This is an organization that does charitable work with the children of fallen military men and women.

Rush also challenged the 41 signers of this letter to do the same. The letter sold for $2.1 million and Rush matched the amount as he said he would.

110

Guess how much the huffing and puffing patriotic signers contributed? Zippo. Typical liberal behavior. If you just stand up to them, they slink away into dark corners (probably whining along the way).

So Harry, are you going to continue to be an ineffective, totally impotent leader of the Senate or will you end up in the trash bin of history the next time you are up for re-election? While there, say hello to Tom Daschle and Dick Gephardt, who were also as arrogant as you are.

It sure doesn't look good Harry. You only have a 32 percent (and shrinking) approval rating in your own state. Congress, under the leadership of you and the ever- startled-looking Nancy Pelosi, has shrunk to a new low of an 18 percent approval rating. Rush has an audience in the mid-20 millions and is signed on to more and more radio stations (more than 600) at a time you have a 32 percent in a state with 2.2 million citizens.

Just go over to Iraq, visit our troops, and see how much they appreciate your
"patriotism."

I recently finished a great book that I would highly recommend to everyone, even my liberal friends, as long as they can read it with an open mind. It is "My Grandfather's Son," by Clarence Thomas, Associate Justice of the U. S. Supreme Court.

It is an inspiring, very moving book about a great man that few of us know even little about. This book, along with an interview on "60 Minutes" and various question- and-answer sessions, illustrates clearly what an intelligent, caring, ethical, moral man he truly is.

It is certainly a picture that the numerous left-leaning groups who opposed his nomination didn't want us to see. The same holds true for the liberal media who were agenda-driven rather than ethical in their coverage of the confirmation hearings.

He starts out by describing his early years, which constituted a life of poverty that we can only imagine. His father had abandoned the family when Thomas was only two years old, and his mother, making only $10 a week, couldn't support him or his brother. They both packed their belongings in a paper bag and moved in with their grandparents. It was his grandfather who taught him the importance of honesty, hard work and especially, self-reliance.

These lessons served him well as he went on to graduate from Holy Cross and then Yale Law School and then have a very distinguished life thereafter. This is probably why the radical liberal groups hated him so much (and still do). He succeeded without their help or social program crutches they so often champion.

The libs still refuse to accept the truth. They blindly accept the lies spewed forth by Anita Hill, a simple pawn used by bigoted and racist interest groups. He calmly addresses this process and backs himself up with fact after fact, disproving all that was said against him.

We didn't get to hear the truth the first time around because Hill and her ilk had an entire day to present their testimony during prime time while Justice Thomas' multitude of supporters and witnesses didn't get to address the committee until after midnight, and into the wee hours of the next morning.

Rebecca Hagelin says it best in her column while reviewing the book: "Instead of gloating in sweet victory over his tormentors when he was narrowly confirmed after a bloody perversion of the process, Justice Thomas is mournful over how such an austere institution as the United States Senate could become so corrupt."

Predictably, the liberal rags, which fewer and fewer people are reading, lashed out in their reviews. The Washington Post wrote "Justice Thomas Lashes out in Memoir" and he "settles scores." The closest thing to lashing out is probably making Joe Biden look like a self-centered, hypocritical fool.

The Los Angeles Times' Edward Lazarus did a book review that is a total distortion of the truth throughout. A few quotes: The book "is a furious assault on liberalism generally and on what Thomas calls the liberal political elite that sought to derail his confirmation."
How about one more? "Spewing invective, Thomas depicts Hill as an abrasive, vindictive, politically motivated liar exploited by a liberal mob (including a biased press) that was hell bent on his personal destruction to prevent a more conservative court from overturning Roe v Wade."

Thomas did no such thing in his book, but I personally do agree with Lazarus' unintentional true description of Anita Hill. The New York Times makes similar statements, but that paper isn't even worth quoting anymore.

Left-leaning liberals are simply a dying breed that won't go quietly. It seems that more and more blacks are starting to realize that the Democrat Party is only interested in their votes and not them as individuals. Instead of following the Jesse Jacksons and the Al Sharptons, it seems they are slowly turning to more credible leaders such as the highly regarded economist and columnist Thomas Sowell, Condoleezza Rice and Michael Steele to name but a few. I should mention one more, Bill Cosby, who came out with a book titled Come On People: On The Path from Victims to Victors.

So, simply read the book and judge for yourselves as to which side makes more sense. I know the hard core-libs won't spend the money but they can check the book out of the library when no one is looking and fold their New York Times around it when walking out.

Isn't it great to have the truth and the facts on your side? That's what makes this column so enjoyable to write. It's so easy when you are "On The Right Side."

Well, we survived another Christmas, and the atheists (agnostics, secularists, non-theists, or whatever they want to call themselves) had an even lesser impact than in previous years.

We are witnessing a dying breed, a group whose influence and reason for being is becoming less and less important.

Now, I must separate atheists into two groups. There are those who have personally made a serious decision to not believe in God and go about their everyday lives. I'm sure some of my friends are atheists. They are fine people and lead good lives.

The other group is the militant atheists. They are not content to have merely made a personal decision but also feel the need to demean, degrade and insult religion, Christianity in particular.

They pretend that their decision is based on honest intellectual reasoning, but they really have no more than vacuous explanations. If they were honest with themselves, they would admit the decision was made to escape the Christian laws of morality.

Because their arguments are really quite lightweight intellectually, they resort to nastiness. The fact of the matter is religion is rapidly growing worldwide and Christianity is the fastest growing (Islam is second).

The only real hope they have remaining for survival is the hope that they can indoctrinate students as they pass through secondary education and above.

There are two excellent books I have recently read on the subject. The first is "The Politically Incorrect Guide to the Bible" by Robert Hutchinson, and "What's So Great About Christianity?" by Dinesh D'Souza. It is this second book that will thoroughly convince an open-minded atheist or a person who is struggling with his or her decision of the fallacies behind atheist thought and the very convincing arguments in favor of God.

D'Souza does a pretty convincing job of dismembering the tired, old, recycled reasoning behind atheistic rationale. He has faced the leading atheists of the day in debates and won convincingly every time. He debated a leading atheist, Christopher Hitchens, on C-Span in October and easily took apart Hitchen's "facts" and arguments. You can view this debate on D'Souza's website and decide for yourself who won.

Then he debated another atheist, "intellectual" Daniel Dennett, with the same result. View this one on Tothesource.org.

Another heavyweight, Sam Harris, will only do a written debate; and the biggest atheist blowhard, Richard Dawkins, has turned down numerous invitations to a public debate. I'm sure the last two individuals made their decisions after they saw how Hitchens and Dennett fared.

The book also covers the false facts presented by some atheists in regard to violence and Christianity. It covers the facts about deaths resulting from the Crusades and The Spanish Inquisition that happened centuries ago and resulted in deaths numbering in the thousands.

Comparing that figure to the deaths caused by atheist regimes is foolish. Deaths caused by these regimes over a period of decades number more than 100 million.

The Reverend Paul Messner recently wrote a guest column in The Daily Star and it was well-researched and factually correct.

One person responded quite childishly by taking Reverend Messner to task because he stated Hitler was an atheist. The responder claimed that Hitler was a well- known Christian. This is a common statement made on all atheist websites and totally incorrect.

Instead of basing your argument using such shallow, biased sources, I suggest people read "Hitler and Stalin: Parallel Lives" by Allen Bullock. It is much more intellectually challenging and debunks the "Hitler is a Christian" fallacy. "Hitler also stated in Mein Kampf that his public statements on Christianity should be understood as propaganda that bear no relation to the truth but are designed to sway the masses." So if you want to tear apart atheists' reasoning about religion, this book will offer everything you need. It has particularly good sections on Christianity and science, Christianity and philosophy, and Christianity and morality. It is a very easy to read, accurate, and a very thoroughly researched book.

It is a book that every religious person should read, as well as those having doubts or struggling to make a choice. I honestly hope my atheist friends will give an honest attempt to see if their arguments are addressed and answered intellectually.

It is a book that will make them honestly rethink their positions. It could be the most important rethinking of their lives, here on earth and into eternity.

For those militants who are probably too closed-minded and arrogant to give the book an honest reading, I have a much simpler assignment for you. Just read Psalms, chapter 14 verse 1.

I just received confirmation for my upcoming trip and found that I could assuage my conscience "offsetting my trip's carbon emissions."

I'll have someone plant some trees for me. For $10 I could offset the carbon of a trip that included air travel, a one night stay at a hotel, and a rental car for one person. If I paid $40 I could equalize the effects of air travel, a four night hotel stay, and a rental car for four people. What difference a rental car with one or four people in it makes, I have no idea and I don't dare ask. I would only receive some wacky explanation that would depress me. Since I had no guilt associated with the damage I would be causing, I chose not to throw my money away.

It's getting a little too crazy out there. The global warming cultists (forgive me if the latest politically correct term is climate change) want me to change my entire lifestyle to suit their desires.

They don't care a bit when their false prophet, Al Gore, jets all over world strutting and preening and delivering his message. His 10,000 or so disciples, when they held their climate change conference in Bali, spewed forth an estimated 100,000 tons of carbon including 48,000 tons of it in air travel. Why didn't they video-conference instead? Why didn't they hold their party in Antarctica instead of tropical Bali?

Why don't the big guys and Hollywood characters practice what they preach? They live in their 10,000 square foot homes, drive their limos, fly their private jets, and live an opulent lifestyle while they expect us to drive around cheap little cars, grow our own food and bike or walk to work.

Can you define hypocrisy any better than that? But they have assured us that it's okay for them to continue like this because they have paid to offset their "carbon footprint." Isn't that another neat phrase they have coined? I'll wait until they lead by example. What's wrong with their lessening their carbon footprint by flying tourist class, getting rid of their limos, downsizing their homes, etc., and still planting all the little trees? I guarantee you won't ever see that happening.

Also, some of the potential solutions they have are just plain crazy. Cheryl Crow wants us all to use just one square of toilet tissue when we use the bathroom!

A mayor in the town of Great Barrington, Mass. wants us to turn off all Christmas lights (oops, he said holiday lights) by 10 p.m. Does that equal the carbon emissions from the Hollywood celebrities' private jets flying into Aspen for the weekend?

We're also supposed to raise a cow and have our own garden. It would be fun to see everyone in a NYC apartment with a garden in the living room and a cow in the spare bedroom. Just remember, common sense and practicality don't get in the way of these "thinkers." A great book to read is "Unstoppable Global Warming Every 1,500 Years" by S. Fred Singer. In it, he points out that the science in Gore's movie is shoddy at best and then proceeds to back up his claims.

The global warming advocates and their sophisticated models "can't explain the Medieval Warm Period from 900-1300 and then the Little Ice Age from 1500 – 1800, to say nothing of the countless number of cooling and warming cycles before these two examples.

Then there is a great BBC documentary, The Great Global Warming Swindle. It might still be on YouTube, but it has been on TV and is now on DVD. Maybe all the schools that had their students watch Gore's movie should get to watch this DVD.

I should touch briefly on the emotional strategy that is used when their facts are weak. Everything has been blamed on global warming. Wildfires, Darfur (!), dying polar bears. Barbara Boxer said global warming was to blame for a poor 14-year-old boy who died from "an infection caused after swimming in Lake Havasu" (warmer water you see). Who needs facts?

And because their findings and defenses are weak, they don't allow any debate. They claim consensus. These reasons are always used when an argument can be convincingly attacked.

So listen people. Use common sense. Don't believe all the catastrophic things that might happen. Remember, they have been wrong many times before and will be wrong many more times in the future.

Just remember, you have lots of prominent scientists on your side. You don't have to go on any guilt trip. Be a good steward of the planet, but what you are doing now has in no way a significant impact on global warming. Man is not to blame for global warming.

Today is Big, But Not the End

As you are reading this column, we are in the middle of Super Tuesday primaries; and although important, the races will still be competitive after the day has concluded and the results are known.

I will, sadly, miss voting in the New York primary as I am stuck (?) out in sunny California, presently watching the Giants win. Yes!

The Los Angeles Times has publically backed Obama (no surprise there) and John McCain on the Republican side (no surprise there, either).

Considering all the other liberal Republican supporters he now has backing him, I don't see how he can possibly call himself a conservative. The media are also giving him a free ride and will jump for joy if he beats out the two other principle candidates for the party's nomination.

If we're lucky, the three candidates will split the delegate count. This will hopefully mean that McCain won't be able to go into the Republican convention with a majority of delegates, and we can have a brokered convention. Anything can happen then.

Fortunately, we might have history on our side. In the past 120 years, only two candidates went directly from the Senate to president: Warren Harding and John Kennedy.

During that same period, we have had seven governors elected. The only two past governors still in the race are both Republicans.

So who do we have left standing going into Super Tuesday? On the Democrats' side we have Obama and Hillary Clinton. Obama's experience includes an unsuccessful run for the U.S. House of Representatives in 2000 and a mere three years as a U.S. Senator. The only thing he has to offer voters is being a great orator with no real vision of substance.

I'm getting tired of his promising hope, hope, hope and nothing else. Maybe that's all he has to offer.

Hillary? The candidate of experience? What experience for heaven's sake? Being a First Lady is admirable (at least the position is) but what does that have to do with qualifying you to lead the most powerful country the world has ever known? The only experience she has is knowing how to do whatever is necessary to win.

Forget ethics and appropriate behavior. The only thing the Clintons know how to do is sling mud, tell lies (especially about Obama) and make borderline racist remarks.

At least Bill has dropped out of the campaign picture for the time being after his own inappropriate racist remarks surfaced. Even by the Clinton rule book his behavior has been reprehensible.

And if Hillary has enough blind loyalists to win, how would you like to be her vice president? Bill will be her unofficial VP, and her running mate will be selected simply to get her the most votes and then be shoved aside. Do you really think Al Gore was the real vice president under hubby Bill's reign?

The only experience edge Hillary has over Barack is four more years in the Senate (for a total of seven). Even in those seven years, she has shown absolutely no evidence of leadership.

What has she done of any significance legislatively? All she has done is moan and groan about the Bush administration and play the partisanship game to perfection.

Lastly, you have to compare the Republican and Democrat campaigns and debates. The Republicans have been generally nothing but issue and idea oriented, respectfully pointing out their differences as candidates.

Unfortunately, in the last debate McCain and Mitt Romney departed from that strategy and cheapened themselves as a result.

But they didn't come close to the bitterness and hatred displayed consistently
by the then-three-remaining Democrat candidates, except for last Thursday's lovefest debate between the last two.

The admiration they showed for one another almost brought tears to my eyes. Of course, their pollsters pointed out that their behavior was turning voters off, hence their changed behavior.

CNN has also been tossing softballs questions to the Democrats, allowing them to skirt around significant domestic issues with their responses.

I'll talk about the Republican side of things in the future since it might be inappropriate for me to do so now, my being on the ballot as a delegate for Mike Huckabee.

However, I will say this, leaving Mike Huckabee out of my comments. If it does eventually come down to a two-man competition between McCain and Romney, there is only one clear choice.

McCain would be a disaster for the party and the country, and Romney would be the clear choice for the conservative base (if Huckabee isn't there in the end).

Democrats' Mess Only Helps GOP

Although I am disappointed with the way the Republican race is going, I am in absolute glee when I see what is happening on the Democrat side.

Obama is clearly on a roll and Clinton is getting worried. Without Michigan and Florida delegates counted, he is leading with 1,112 regular and 158 superdelegates for a total of 1,270. Clinton, on the other hand, has only 979 regular delegates and 234 superdelegates in her favor.

Everybody is getting anxious, but there are still about 1,279 delegates and 17 states remaining with votes to be cast. There are also about 400 super delegates left, who will probably decide the eventual outcome during the Democrat Convention this August.

Superdelegates are simply elected officials or party leaders who can vote any way they want, and Hillary has the edge there.

You'll soon be seeing the old tried-and-true dirty politics coming out on the "win at any cost" Clinton team. Already, they are starting to campaign for the Florida and Michigan delegates to be counted. No wonder. She was the only one on the ticket in Michigan, and there was no campaigning in Florida. In Florida, she only got 50 percent of the vote and Obama received 33 percent. It was about the same in Michigan where Hillary got 55 percent of the vote, proudly beating out the uncommitted vote, which received 40 percent.

Florida and Michigan have 27 and 17 delegates, respectively. With these tallies (and also the superdelegates that would then be allowed) included, Hillary would lead by about 63. And yes, every delegate is going to count big time in this race.

Also, the Clintons are going to go after the superdelegates aggressively. You can bet that Billy boy is going to be out there calling in favors, as well as his (and her) attack dogs such as Lanny Davis and James Carville.

Originally, superdelegates were those insiders who were never pledged to one candidate and were supposed to have the power to veto what they considered to be a bad decision by the voters. This strategy is right up the Clintons' alley. Get a minority to nix the desires of the majority when the majority's wishes aren't favorable.

As a matter of fact, I hope this happens. That will cause such an uproar in the Democrat party, and many moderate Dems and most of the independents will vote Republican. They are tired of Slick Willy's deplorable actions and will vote accordingly.

So, that takes care of Hillary. What about Obama? You know, the Rev. Jackson without the rhyming. His speeches, although very well presented, are all fluff and no substance.

He will get ripped apart in the debates if our nominee demands answers rather than cute lines. His oratorical skills will take him only so far. He must address the issues that people care about as well as his plans for solving them.

Finally, what about an Obama/Clinton or a Clinton/Obama ticket? First of all, Hillary will certainly not take a second seat to anyone. She has been drooling to be top dog ever since she got a taste of White House power. She will never accept the offer if one is made.

Secondly, Clinton will never select Obama as a running mate, and I doubt he would accept anyway. He is young and knows he has another shot coming and probably doesn't want to be associated with Clinton's dirty garbage (oops, laundry).

Either way, any nominee or combination of the two will make it very easy for the Republicans to keep the White House. My only worry is Obama heading the party's ticket and who his vice presidential pick could be.

There are a lot of highly popular Dems out there, and this would help keep the moderates voting Democrat as well as draw a majority of Independents. Obama will already have the ultra libs committed.

Whatever happens, we Republicans can sit back and enjoy the show. The campaigns of our candidates have been, for the most part, issue oriented, civil, and lacking the rancor of the Democrats debates. Even though there have been disagreements on issues on our side, there is respect for each other and the other's ideas.

The Democrat primaries of today and March 4 represent six states and 565 more delegates. Let's just hope that after that, the race on the Democrat side is just as muddled as it is now. I'm looking forward to the Clintons' book of dirty tricks to come out again. This time, responsible people won't put up with it.

Sympathy for Money Borrowers Unnecessary

The sky is falling! The sky is falling! What to do, what to do? So goes the mantra of the Bush Administration, all the presidential candidates (except Huckabee) and both houses of Congress, especially those individuals running for re-election.

I am talking about the current subprime, adjustable rate mortgage "crisis." The solution is simple. Just follow the advice of Harvard Professor Gregory Mankiw, who was a former chair of the Council of Economics and do "absolutely nothing." This is a free-market system and will be solved within this system. Sure the economy is going to burp once or twice, and emotionally there will be wailing and gnashing of teeth. But, so what?

Even though the politicians and the bureaucrats are counting on your sympathy and compassion for those poor, innocent, naïve borrowers who were defrauded by those big old, mean lenders, don't let yourself get drawn in.

The real problem is a mix of falling housing prices, greedy lenders making bad business decisions, rising interest rates, easy credit granting policies, and impatient borrowers not willing to live within their means.

It is certainly not solely the fault of the big, bad mortgage companies. Sure, they lent money to people who couldn't pay back the loans, but everyone thought the housing boom would go on forever.

Thus the banks would be covered with property worth more than the mortgage; and the lender, if the payments could not be met, could simply sell the home, pay off the loan and walk away with some equity in his pockets.

The last thing we need is for the federal government to come up with a solution, but that is exactly what it is trying to do. One proposal is for the Federal Housing Administration to refinance these risky mortgages for the low rate of 1 percent. The Bush Administration is for giving defaulters an additional 30 days before foreclosure proceedings begin. Hillary trumps that by suggesting a 90 day reprieve from foreclosure and also wants to freeze the rates of these mortgages for 5 years. These are only a few of the solutions being offered. Unfortunately, of the 535 members of Congress, not a single one is a trained economist.

However, as congressmen, they should all know these efforts would be unconstitutional. These mortgages represent private contracts between borrower and lender. What right does the government have to just jump in and change the terms?

It is up to these two parties to solve the issues of refinancing, providing moratoriums or initiating foreclosure steps.

Yes, the lenders got greedy and made poor business decisions. They are the ones who will have to absorb the losses and be careful not to make the same mistakes again.

Economics 101 and the law of supply and demand apply here. The mortgage companies, not wanting to be in the housing business, are simply going to have to keep lowering the prices of the homes until there are willing buyers - perhaps investors or young couples who have been saving responsibly and are looking forward to their first homes.

Now, regarding the borrowers. They aren't necessarily the innocent victims the media makes them out to be. Many banks claim that these borrowers are at fault by intentionally misstating incomes or lying about net assets. This was done so often that phrases have been coined for this behavior: "liar's loans" or "no doc loans." These borrowers simply got in over their heads and will have to adjust their lifestyles accordingly. Renting might be an option.

Also, some borrowers are pretty nonchalant in their behavior. Michelle Malkin gives an example in one of her columns of a story that was in the Los Angeles Times. It was about Californians simply living in their homes for 12 months, awaiting foreclosure, saving their mortgage payments, and then just walking away. Does Washington really want to come to the rescue of these people?

Whatever the solution eventually turns out to be, hard working, patient taxpayers who handle their finances responsibly shouldn't have to pay with their taxes to bail out people who made irresponsible decisions.

An economics professor at Temple University pointed out that 96 percent of all mortgages are being paid on a timely basis. He further points out that only 2 percent to 3 percent of all mortgage loans are in foreclosure and that the delinquency rates were higher in the 1980s than they are now.

Should the government come to the rescue of people taking irresponsible risks at the expense of responsible citizens? I hope these responsible citizens who represent the vast majority of the electorate will make their dissatisfaction known in the voting booth.

Pelosi's Acts Bordering On Treason

Shameful. Just when you thought the Democrat controlled House couldn't sink any lower in being a do-nothing, incompetent Congress, nearing a historical single digit public approval rating, it has proceeded in accomplishing just that. The ever startled looking Nancy Pelosi has allowed the Protect America Act of 2007 to expire.

Her defiance and blocking maneuvers are inexcusable, and I would say bordering on treason.

Here is a horror story that is sure to be repeated if action is not taken now. Texas Republican Sen. John Cornyn pointed out in an article that three U.S. troops were kidnapped in Iraq last year and a search-and-save mission was immediately undertaken. "Within hours, a new source of information was discovered that required electronic surveillance of phone conversations," he wrote. Because of existing laws, it took more than 10 hours to get permission to proceed. Later, one of the soldiers was found floating in the Euphrates River, and the terrorists claimed to have executed the
other two.

The Protect America Act, if in place at that time, would have allowed our forces to act immediately on the information. Do you think the 10 hours of delay may have saved the soldiers lives? I do.

By preventing the Protect America Act to be extended, the ever shocked looking Pelosi will be solely responsible for tragedies like the above happening again. Ms Pelosi, the blood of these possible future tragedies will be directly related to your inaction. How could any patriotic American allow something like this to happen?

The bill to extend the act's provisions was handily passed by the Senate by a
vote of 68 to 29. It came to a standstill when the bill reached the House.
Nancy knew that the bill would pass with bipartisan support if it were brought to the floor, so she simply did not allow that to happen. She also lied about her reasons for doing so. As per the Congress Daily publication, aides said the reason for not bringing the bill to the floor was "a very tight floor schedule."

Yet, as the article pointed out, the House found time to pass a bill labeled H.R. 1143, which was all about approving a lease agreement between the Interior Department and a luxury beach resort that is located in the Virgin Islands. Remember, the House had more than six months to responsibly debate the matter.

The only reason the bill will not be presented is that Pelosi wants the telecom companies not to have immunity from prosecution.

Jay Rockefeller, Democrat chair of the Senate Intelligence Committee, has said, "The quality of the intelligence that we are going to be receiving is going to be degraded if this bill does not become law before the interim measure expires."

On January 28, 21 House Democrats signed a letter urging the leadership to pass Rockefeller's bill. As many as 40 House Democrats would vote for the bill if presented for vote.

The real reason Pelosi is behaving this way is the American Trial Lawyers Association has bought and paid for her. They have her in their front pocket. There are presently almost 40 lawsuits pending against the telecommunications companies that responded when intelligence officials asked for their cooperation in helping to track down foreign intelligence targets located in foreign lands.

Again, the Senate Intelligence Committee concluded, "Electronic communication service providers acted on a good-faith belief that the President's program, and their assistance, was lawful." Jay Rockefeller also asked "What is the big payoff for the telephone companies? They get paid a lot of money? No, they get paid nothing. What do they get for their cooperation? They get $40 billion worth of lawsuits, grief, trashing, but they do it."
But Nancy thinks the trial lawyers come first over yours and my safety. After all, 66 trial lawyers involved in these suits have contributed more than $1.5 million to congressional Democrats.

Also, their extreme left-wing special interest groups like the ACLU demand allegiance to their anti-American cause.

As Adam Putnam, R-Fla., wrote, ""They've put the interests of trial lawyers and
special interest groups before a bipartisan bill to effectively combat terrorism."

Unfortunately for America, Nancy Pelosi represents the 8th Congressional District covering most of the county and city of San Francisco, one of the most liberal bastions with the most liberal judges in the U.S.

She is solidly entrenched with all the America-haters she represents. It would be very difficult to have her voted out of office. We have to find a way for our own future safety.

Dementia. The dictionary defines it as "the usually progressive deterioration of intellectual functions such as memory that can occur while other brain functions such as those controlling movement and senses are retained."

Maybe those die-hard Hillary supporters can use this as an excuse for her most recent lie. In a very detailed fashion, she described how she landed under fire in Bosnia and had to run with her head down to the waiting cars, skipping the welcoming ceremony planned for her at the airport.

She continued to support this claim through several questionings until, oops; the video came out proving her wrong.

It was not an embellishment, not an exaggeration, not her claim that she "misspoke", but a simple, bald-faced lie. Maybe she thought that because the tearing up act won her New Hampshire, the sleep deprivation excuse would work this time.

Who knows? It sure didn't work this time, as her approval rating plummeted to her lowest ever. A Wall Street Journal poll showed her approval rating at a mere 37 percent; even more damaging she was at 24 percent among independents.

Shouldn't we be used to the Clinton lie machine by now? Hillary herself has been caught lying at least a half dozen times and suspected in another dozen or so other incidents.

We don't even have to talk about Bill and his numerous "mis-truths." I think it is impossible for the Clintons to distinguish between a truth and a lie anymore. They simply pick the one that gives them the best chance of enhancing their position.

But, alas, this might be my last column concerning Hillary. Obama has the nomination won unless the Clinton attack machine can uncover or manufacture some dirt on him. If I were you Obama, I wouldn't put it past them.

Now, a little about the latest Obama fiasco. Last week we were down in Virginia backcountry where unfortunately, there are people still displaying the confederate flag from a pole or using it as a curtain or art.

Also, a few years ago, when I was driving the country roads of southern Louisiana, I came across posters still promoting the white supremacist, David Duke. It's scary to find so many bigots and racists stuck in the past. We've got Al Sharpton, Jesse Jackson, Louis Farrakhan, Duke, and the hundreds of KKK members, to name only some. Our latest hate monger is the venom spewing racist, none other than Barak

Obama's spiritual mentor, the not-so-reverend Jeremiah Wright.

Bigots like this man are a dime a dozen, so the real focus is on how Obama allowed this type of person to stay in his life for more than twenty years.

Does it say anything about his own character? His judgment? Of course it does. Also, his continually changing explanations make you wonder just how much they think alike.

African American minister Harry Jackson said that Obama should certainly be judged because of the acts of his pastor. "Pastor Wright's worldview and his understanding of race, culture, and religion of the Bible will in some measure affect how Barak views the world," Jackson said.

Did Barak know what was going on? Of course he did. Everyone else seemed to. Another pretty famous Chicagoan, Oprah Winfrey, attended Wright's church in 1984. Last year it was reported by Newsweek that she stopped attending years ago and said that she did so "to distance herself from Wright's inflammatory rhetoric."

Why Obama's changing story? In 2004, he said his book was inspired by one of Wright's sermons. He again praised the man in 2007. Then, when the controversy first came to the surface, he told reporters that he didn't think there was "anything particularly controversial" about the man.

Next, he said he was never present at any of the fiery sermons. Soon after, he said he was uncomfortable a few times but always told the pastor he was uncomfortable about some of the things he said. In his latest spin he said he would have quit the church if Rev. Wright hadn't resigned. Which story are we to believe?

And it wasn't just Wright. The entire congregation was standing, clapping, and
shouting approval.

Another black Pastor who leads a church in Everest, Washington said that this church doesn't reflect the typical minority congregation. He said, "The way the congregation responds lets us know that the philosophy is not just the pastor's, but the churches."

He added, "If Obama didn't know the pastor's philosophy after being a member of the church for over 20 years...it speaks to the lack of judgment he has."

Better be careful, Barak. You're starting to catch the Clinton disease.

It was fun watching the Democrats leave another televised hearing with egg on their faces. I'm talking about the congressional hearings last week involving Gen. David Petraeus and Ambassador Ryan Crocker. They withstood the nasty barrage from the Democrats, while calmly, professionally, and repeatedly restating the facts to these rather thick headed Senators, although probably unsuccessfully.

However, they weren't unsuccessful with the Americans who watched the proceedings. Most of them had the common sense and ability to distill the information and see clearly which side was presenting the facts correctly.

Let's see, on one side we have Sen. John McCain, a veteran who served for 23 years in the U.S. Navy and spent 5 1/2 years of them in a North Vietnamese prison camp, never abandoning his fellow soldiers even when he was given the chance to do so. In other words, an American hero.

Then you have Petraeus, who has been serving in the U.S. military since 1974 and has a very distinguished career. He graduated from West Point in 1974 in the top 5 percent of his class. He was the top graduate in the U.S. Army Command and General Staff College. He is a four star general with a masters degree in public administration and a PhD in international relations from Princeton University. He was confirmed unanimously by the Senate to be the commanding general in Iraq. His list of achievements goes on and on.

On the other side you have Hillary Clinton, who has zero military service or experience and an utter disdain for our military, with the same being true of the fourth year Senator from Illinois. They have a lot in common in that they simply want to bring everyone home without considering the consequences. They don't seem to care about the security of our country, nor the honorable service put in by our brave men and women in the military. They will instead do whatever is politically expedient for their own self aggrandizement.

The facts that were presented by General Petraeus and Ambassador Crocker were numerous and impossible to refute. Basically, the surge is working. As Republican Congressman John Boehner points out, "the rate of civilian and coalition deaths has declined by 70 percent since last June, security incidents in the once dangerous Anbar province have decreased approximately 90 percent."

On top of this, the Iraqi government has made substantial strides. It has met 12 of the 18 benchmarks set for it and has made impressive progress on 5 others. What more does the Democrat leadership want? The Democrat leadership can't come close to the number of accomplishments made by the Iraqi government. Can someone on the Democrat's side please tell me what accomplishments have been made since taking power in 2006? Naming of bridges and buildings as well as harassment of Bush administrative officials don't count.

David Bellavia, a soldier who won both the Bronze and Silver Stars for his service in Fallujah, said it quite clearly. "No one sober can look at the progress in Diyala and Anbar and argue that the surge is not working. All the evidence points to many good things happening in Iraq."

Yes, progress is slow and sometimes unsteady, but it is still progress. Yet, what does the Commander-In-Chief wannabe Hillary say? Rather than listen to what the people who are doing the actual fighting are saying, in other words, the trained professionals, she listens to her pollsters and says what she erroneously thinks the people want to hear. On ABC's "Good Morning America" last week that "clearly, the surge hasn't worked." Is this another lie Hillary, or just plain ignorance?

Obviously, people want the war to end. Of course we want our troops out of harm's way. But most responsible thinking people want our troops to win with honor and to come home with pride-that they were called on by their country and that they and their fallen comrades answered that call and accomplished something honorable and important for their country. Hillary, Obama, Nancy Pelosi, and Harry Reid, and their ilk don't care one bit for our troops or our country, no matter what they say. All they care about are votes and staying in office.

So libs, let me educate you a little. Webster defines a fact as "something that has really happened, or is actually the case, as distinguished from something merely believed to be so; a truth known by actual observation or authentic testimony."

Instead, you seem to think that facts are Democrat talking points or MoveOn.org sound bites. So wake up. Think for yourselves for a change, take off your blinders, and be proud of your country and our military. You might stop being so bitter and negative and even start to feel better about yourself.

Carter is Humiliating Once More

Just when you thought that Jimmy Carter couldn't possibly embarrass himself or the country once again, he manages to do exactly that. He recently allowed himself to be a useful idiot to yet another terrorist group, this time Hamas.

First he met with Nasser al-Shaer, head of the Palestinian education system. This is the guy who teaches Palestinian children that Jews descended from pigs and dogs.

Then he lays a wreath on Yasser Arafat's grave. Arafat was simply the father of terrorism as we know it today, but Jimmy still considers him a "very dear friend." If that wasn't enough, he went on to visit, with hugs, kisses, and handshakes, Khaled Mashaal, the head of Hamas and now the guest of Syria. This monster proudly claims responsibility for the organizing of numerous suicide bombings, killing many innocent Israeli and American civilians.

While he is causing this mess, he claims to be simply a private citizen concerned only about peace between the Israelis and the Palestinians. It doesn't matter to him that Hamas is considered an international terrorist organization by the United States, Israel, and the European Union. Carter, in his self-righteous, ego driven, morally superior image of himself, ignores all State Department requests not proceed with the trip and does what he pleases. He is utterly clueless when it comes to being used as a tool by our enemies and claims he does only good and causes no harm.

This is not how our enemy sees it. Instead of keeping Hamas and other terrorist groups isolated, his visit gives these goons legitimacy. Immediately after his meetings, Hamas declared, "Political isolation by the American administration has begun to crumble." Carter is still bitter that the American people weren't smart enough to re-elect him to another 4 years. He still can't accept the fact that he is probably one of the worst presidents in American history and his constant efforts to polish his legacy only makes him look worse.

This column can't begin to list all his failings but I must mention a few. He was only elected in the first place because people wanted change. He barely won over Gerald Ford in 1976 by 50.1 to 48.0 percent and 297 electoral votes to Ford's 240. If only people knew what they were in for over the next four years of his "leadership," they would have elected Ford by the same huge margin that they elected Ronald Reagan. Reagan won 91 percent of the electoral vote while Carter won only six states and the District of Columbia.

During his term, he decimated our military readiness. In his first month alone he cut the defense budget by $6 billion and continued to cut throughout his tenure. We had to live through double digit inflation, 7+ percent unemployment, high interest rates with the prime rate hitting 21.5 percent and mortgage rates hitting 18 percent.

We had fuel shortages, unprecedented Soviet expansion with no fear of any consequence, and he saw fit to punish the Soviets for their invasion of Afghanistan by choosing not to participate in the 1980 Olympics. The only people who were punished by this act were our athletes, who had sacrificed and trained for years to represent our country.

Oh yes, he turned his back on our most solid ally in the Middle East, the Shah of Iran, allowing a bunch of crazed Mullahs to take over the country.

We were rewarded by having our embassy seized, our citizens held as hostages for over 14 months and our embarrassing rescue attempt that killed several of our soldiers. We were the laughing stock of the world.

There were, however, some presidential firsts. He was the first and only president interviewed by Playboy. He was the first president attacked by a rabbit. This happened in April 1979. The only good thing that happened during his reign was that he was unable to appoint anyone to the Supreme Court.

Remember when we thought the crazy Carter was his brother Billy? Boy, were we wrong.

As for his latest trip, Rep. Sue Myrick, R-N.C. had the right idea when she wanted the State Department to revoke Carter's passport. If only this could have been done while he was still overseas.

White House Spokesman Tony Fratello hit the nail on the head when he said that Carter had become "increasingly irrelevant with these kind of actions." Even the Democrats are embarrassed by him. Rep. Howard Berman (D-Calif.), chairman of the House Foreign Affairs Committee said, "Jimmy Carter's view of the forces at work in the Middle East and how he likes to attribute blame and responsibility is so warped, to my way of thinking, that I'm skeptical of any initiative he undertakes."

So Jimmy, go back to doing the only good thing you ever did; build some more
houses.

Several So-Called Patriots Fall Short

I received a great compliment last week. An organization called Gathering of Eagles, made up of military veterans, wrote me a very nice thank you note regarding my last column, and put it and quite a few of my other columns on their website. Their web site is www.newyork.gatheringofeagles.org. This group is one of many that include the men and women whom I consider to be the real patriots of this country.

There are those who write mindless, angry, often-incoherent diatribes that show their distaste for anyone who is proud of their country.

These are the people who have been fed mind numbing swill, mostly lies, and they truly want to believe it rather than think for themselves. When someone asks them to give one or two examples of their patriotism, they angrily lash out and simply show their fake indignation.

Webster, not I, defines a patriot as "a person who loves his country, and zealously supports and defends it and its interests."

We all know quite a few people who fall far short of this definition. Two big examples who fall short are our media and our left leaning political representatives.
Considering the latter group, isn't it strange that most of them are Democrats, especially the Democrat leadership? Harry "we can't win the war" Reid, Jack "our soldiers are baby killers" Murtha, John Kerry, Ted Kennedy, Nancy Pelosi, Tom "I served in Vietnam liar" Harkin are just a few.

I'm sick of these Democrats who refuse to meet with groups who don't share their beliefs. A group called The Vets for Freedom finished their national bus tour in Washington D. C. in early April, and most of the Democrat leadership refused to meet with them.

However, when anti-war groups request an appointment, they trip over each other to be first in line to greet them. Why do you think six to eight Code Pink members were allowed in the hearing room where General Petraeus was speaking? Do you think the Vets for Peace got the same equal treatment?

Make a list of all the good things the United States has done around the world. As you make it you will feel yourself getting smaller and smaller. Why don't you redirect some of your hate and anger to those regimes that deserve it?

You come up with your cute little chants like "Bush lied, people died" (which isn't even true) and ignore the atrocities going on in Iran, Cuba, North Korea, China, Syria and others of the same ilk. You actually enjoy living in the state of depression, envy, gloom-and-doom misery and get upset when others don't want to come down to your level.

Now you have another spokesperson in Michelle Obama. She's got some great quotes; "America is downright mean," and "for the first time in my adult life I am really proud of my country."

It makes you wonder what kind of indoctrination she went through in those elite, Ivy League colleges she went to. How about a last one: "America is more a source of shame than pride." Makes you feel comfortable knowing people like this actually have a chance to reside in the White House, doesn't it?

Maybe you should listen to the likes of Dan Maloney, NYS Coordinator of the Gathering of Eagles, when he talks about a book called "Moment of Truth in Iraq" by Michael Yon.

Maloney says the author "as an independent journalist, confirms that the counter insurgency program is working better than many had hoped. The beauty of his report is that he tells you how we are doing it and why it is working at the boots on the ground level."

Let's see if your own great leader, Bill Clinton, can shake you up. In a speech given to the graduating class at Michigan State University in 1995, he said, "How dare you suggest that we, in the freest nation on earth, live in tyranny? How dare you call yourselves patriots and heroes? I say to you, all of you, there is nothing patriotic about hating your country or pretending that you can love your country but despise your government. There is nothing heroic about turning your back on America or ignoring your own responsibilities. If you want to preserve your own freedom, you must stand up for the freedom of others with whom you disagree, but you also must stand up for the rule of law. You cannot have one without the other."

Does the shoe fit? If so why are you still here? Oh, I see, you want to greedily take all the good things and opportunities America offers you every day, refuse to recognize that fact and not bother to give anything back.

Doubts about McCain Just Don't Go Away

I'm beginning to wonder why the liberal media is providing unprecedented exposure to the Democrats and the continuing Barack/Hillary debacle and not giving equal time to John McCain. The Democrat opponents are saying nothing of substance and are merely trashing each others' character. Meanwhile, McCain is out on the campaign trail making speeches and explaining his stance on issues, and we conservative Republicans hear very little of it.

For me, hearing more of what John McCain really stands for is absolutely essential. He's going to have to go a lot further to convince me that he is actually sensitive to the party's conservative base. His 20-plus years in the Senate have shown that he is a Republican in name only and not the Reagan conservative that he now professes to be.

Why does the Republican Party want to distance itself from its conservative foundation and instead pander to the independents and the soft Democrats? Reagan twice proved that a conservative agenda and an inspiring leader will win overwhelmingly. It was proven in 1984 with the Republican "Contract With America" and in 1994 when the party took over both houses while running on conservative values and beliefs. We also saw the disastrous results in 2006 when we strayed from those same principles.

Convince me Senator McCain of who you really are. I know you're a patriot and a man of courage and personal integrity. I know you know the importance of a strong military that is the best-trained, best-equipped, and with the best military leaders in the world. I know you want to win in Iraq and leave with honor, turning the fight over to the Iraqi army only when it is ready. Much to the Democrats disgust, that is exactly what is happening when we see the most recent and frequent successes over there.

I think you want conservative justices at all levels of the courts rather than activist judges who desire to legislate from the bench. However, Robert Novak once pointed out that you dissed Samuel Alito as being too conservative or as "wearing his conservatism on his sleeve." Which one is the real John McCain? You have never flip- flopped in your pro-life belief.

But at the same time, I have my concerns about who is the real John McCain. Is he the one who now says he supports the Bush tax cuts that caused unprecedented growth or the one who originally campaigned and voted against them? Is he the one who says he wants to secure the border or the one who supports giving amnesty to some 20 million illegals? To quote you, "By the way, I think the fence is least effective, but I'll build the &*%#$@*& fence if they want it."

Are you the one who wants strong national security and an aggressive in fight against terrorism? Or, is the real you the one who wants to dilute the Patriot Act, close Gitmo, eliminate interrogation techniques (that are mild compared to our enemies' methods) that could save thousands of American lives? I think you are also in favor of giving terrorists caught on the battlefield the same rights as our own citizens have to our non-military justice system. Convince me this isn't true.

You say you want a smaller, more limited government; but you then turn around and sign on with the global warming wackos and their propaganda. There is lots of credible disagreement in the scientific community that deserves to be listened to.

For now, I'm going to sit back and watch the campaign unfold. Obama will be exposed eventually as a good orator with no experience and nothing of any substance to offer.

Bob Barr, the Libertarian candidate, and a true conservative, is beginning to interest me and it would be wise to pick a running mate of his caliber. I want a vice president who carries the conservative banner proudly and is an inspiring leader, one who has a good chance of winning after your one term is up. Twelve years of a Republican president would finally put Hillary's power trip to bed. She would be 73, even older than you are now.

So be very careful Senator McCain. Don't take my vote or those of other conservatives for granted. The only reason you have my vote right now is because I can't conceive the damage that would be caused to the country by the other side's candidate and not because of your track record.

If the Republican Party, led by you, begins to distance itself from conservative
values, I'll have to look elsewhere for a party that I can believe in.

Don't Fault Companies for Oil Crisis

It is unbelievable how blind these environmental radicals are, along with their leftist liberals in Congress and the anti-capitalism crowd, and how willing they all are to place the blame for the current energy crisis on everyone else when the real responsibility and resulting consequences rest squarely on their shoulders.

Let me see if I can pull you, kicking and screaming, into the world of reality for just a short time while I address rational people, and you can then go put your heads back in the sand.

Unless you can offer rational, workable solutions rather than just complain and unless you can talk about the salient issues in an intelligent fashion, then you don't deserve to be part of the discussion.

Like it or not, our economy is fueled by oil, coal, and natural gas, of which there are immense reserves available for extraction. It has been this way for the last 150 years. You can't simply wave a magic wand and make this fact disappear.

Therefore, the only rational solution is to provide a steady and stable domestic supply of these resources until other alternative energy sources and technologies are available as economical substitutes.

First of all, the problem is not the oil companies' fault. Their return on investment to stockholders is totally in line or less than the returns of other industries, and over 30 government agency reports verify that the pricing of gasoline is caused by legitimate market forces.

It is you obstructionists who have prevented the necessary drilling in onshore and offshore areas abundant with oil and gas. You have also prevented the building of refineries so that an adequate supply of gasoline and other energy products can bring prices down rather than having to import supplies at much higher prices.

The last refinery built in the U.S. was in 1976. We have gone from 324 refineries processing 18.6 million barrels a day down to 155 refineries with a maximum capacity of 16.6 million barrels a day, for a difference of 2 million barrels daily.

Remember when Chuck Schumer said a million additional barrels a day (he demands this from the Saudi's naturally) would drop prices by over 50 cents a gallon?

The cost to build a refinery is huge. There is one being built in Arizona at a cost of $3.5 BILLION and is to open in 2011.

It costs $100 million to set up drilling operations at a particular site, and it is not certain that the well will be a producer. There are tremendous risks involved in locating new reserves. No one, you and me included, takes risks unless the potential rewards are greater.

We can't expect the oil companies to behave any differently. Their responsibility is to their shareholders, not to you environmentalists. Hence the necessary government tax credits.

Also, the oil companies are not simply hoarding all the profits or returning them to their shareholders. They have spent $89 billion since 1993 (as of 2006) to strengthen environmental performance.

As reported by Facts on Fuel, "the average new car on the road today runs 97 percent cleaner than the average car built in 1970 thanks to a combination of cleaner gasoline and more efficient engines."

Also, auto-related emissions are down more than 41 percent even though there are a greater number of cars on the road today than in 1970.

The oil companies have also spent close to $4 billion in alternative energy projects, including wind, solar and biofuels.

But of course, none of this matters to the eco-nuts. It's never enough when it isn't their money being spent. Their purpose is to control other people's lives and they don't care whether their impositions destroy the American economy.

There's a lot more ground to cover and a lot of liberal "untruths" to uncover so I'll have to extend this topic into the next column unless something more important comes up in the meantime.

By the way, I wonder if Ted Kennedy is still for nationalized health care. Instead of getting an MRI the day after his seizure, he would have waited in line to see a neurologist and another three months for an MRI to be scheduled.

Think he would have been able to hand-pick his surgical team and have available the latest experimental drugs to fight the cancer?

Yes, he would, since he has the wealth to afford the best care possible. Maybe he will now realize the importance of all of us common folk having the same access.

Bush's Plan to Fix Crisis Makes Sense

My last column took big oil off the list of those possible groups responsible for the present oil crisis. Excessive profits made by them is simply propaganda spewed by the liberal Democrat leadership.

The facts (yes liberals, an inconvenient truth) show that their return on investment is right in line or less than that of other industries.

In fact, between federal, state and local governments, the revenues produced for them exceed the net profits of the oil companies several times over. The liberal Dems certainly don't see this return as excessive and have no intention of reducing these taxes. Remember, they did absolutely nothing for these dollars.

So now the Democrats and their special-interest lobbyists turn to the president and claim he is also the problem. They claim he has no energy plan. What are they, deaf as well as dumb? Since 2003 he has repeatedly brought sound plans before Congress, and these were voted down every time.

His plans make total sense. No 1, he wanted to build refineries at former military bases. Because of our lack of refineries, we have to import refined product that costs twice as much as if it were refined domestically.

No. 2, he proposed lifting the present ban on leasing federal lands and offshore drilling sites where abundant supplies exist.

The Democrats refuse to allow this, claiming the danger of oil spills and negative environmental impact. Valid, except there hasn't been a major oil spill since 1969.

Also, there are thousands of oil rigs in the Gulf of Mexico and hundreds were either destroyed or severely damaged during the hurricane season that included Hurricane Katrina.

Guess what? No oil spills. Stop living in the '60s Dems. There have been very impressive gains made in extraction technologies and safety measures.

A February 2006 study done by the Interior Department's Mineral Management Service estimated potential offshore resources of approximately 85.9 billion barrels and 419.9 trillion cubic feet of natural gas.

Also, the Bureau of Land Management estimated between 18 billion and 53 billion barrels of onshore resources. While on the topic of onshore resources, has anyone questioned the "pristine" area of ANWR?

You can be certain that there have been no congressional fact-finding trips to the area. They prefer the warmer climes when they take their families along on such treks.

You can also assume that less than 1 percent of the environmental loudmouths have been there, either. No one goes there. In the summer, there are constant plagues of mosquitoes and other filthy pests, and as one columnist pointed out, during the winter "it reached 70 degrees below zero (not counting wind chill, which brings it to 120 below) and is in round-the-clock darkness."

There are approximately 20 million acres making up the ANWR region (which I'm sure 90 percent of environmentalists couldn't find on a map if unlabeled), and we are talking about a drilling footprint of an area 1/7th the area of Manhattan.

Third, Bush has proposed that the Department of Energy reduce the length of time and the risks involved in the licensing process associated with the development of new nuclear power plants. Potential investors are scared away by the length of time involved, upward of 20 years, due to repeated fake environmental studies and frivolous lawsuits. Finally, the last major proposal is to remove the prohibitions for oil shale exploration on federal lands. In a 2005 Rand study it was estimated there existed up to 800 billion barrels of oil in the Green River Formation covering areas including Colorado, Utah and Wyoming.

All very practical solutions to use while we are developing alternative energy sources and conserving. Let's let American ingenuity and entrepreneurial activity solve the problem while we are pumping. We are second to none in these areas.

The typical liberal response? It will take years to develop these resources. Five years ago, 2003, when Bush started pointing out the potential problem, gas was $1.43 a gallon. We would have been well on our way if we acted then. As a matter of fact, we would already be processing 1 to 2 million barrels per day if Clinton hadn't vetoed a congressional bill opening up federal lands for exploration and development. Oil was $19 a barrel back then.

Another problem, libs. A Gallup poll showed more than 60 percent of people favored drilling in currently restricted areas. This percent will surely rise over the next few months. So even if you don't care about American families, the U.S. economy and national security, vote drilling through even if only for simply shallow political reasons.

Once again, I'm out of room for this column. The next column will point out the real culprits causing all this pain for normal, average, hard working families. I'm really looking forward to this.

The last two columns, using facts, reasoning and common sense, removed the oil companies and the administration from culpability involving high energy prices. Who's left then? Congress and its environmental radicals, of course.

Nancy, Harry and now Obama simply say, like trained parrots, "We can't drill ourselves out of the problem." You can expect to hear this phrase over and over right up to election time, even though it is blatantly false. After stating this, one might wonder what their plan is.

First, their strategy has been to blame, in addition to the oil companies and Bush, those individuals speculating in oil futures.

What is wrong with this? People speculate in all kinds of commodities. Some win big and some novices lose big (except for Hillary and her earlier cattle futures bonanza).

Don't the Democrats understand that when demand goes up and supply remains constant, prices rise? This is especially true with necessities. People "speculate" in all kinds of investment opportunities. Stocks, bonds, art, and real estate; the list goes on and on.

If you want to prevent speculators from profiting, show them you're serious about increasing supplies through on-and-off-shore drilling and extracting oil from shale in the Bakkan region of the Midwest, where there exists an estimated supply that would dwarf all of Saudi Arabia's known reserves.

As Newt Gingrich said recently, if the government stated today that we would be releasing the oil in our strategic reserves and showed the world we had a serious drilling strategy, prices would drop immediately, taking the lucrativeness out of oil speculation.

I guess I have to say it once more. The strategy should be to implement rational conservation plans, increase the supply of oil as a bridge until we unleash our entrepreneurial spirit, and provide incentives and come up with alternative energy sources so that we may maintain our present standard of living.

Pretty much common sense. I would ride a scooter for transportation, but only because it would be fun and it would save me money. I wouldn't be doing it because of some global warming hoax.

The same is true with wind turbines. They seem to be making great strides in this area, and as soon as they become cost-effective, and for no other reason, you'll see one in my back yard.

Now, to the Democrats' idea of an energy plan. First they want to have a windfall profits tax against the oil companies. Who do you think will end up paying this tax? It will simply be passed down to the final consumer - you and me. We had a tax like this in 1980 and it was a disaster. We lost jobs overseas, energy costs increased, making us even more dependent on foreign oil. That Congress was at least smart enough to repeal it.

Second, Congress wants to impose sanctions and sue Saudi Arabia if it doesn't
increase its output by a million barrels a day or more.

Here we have the Democrats insisting other countries increase their output while at the same time not allowing our reserves to be touched. This really makes a lot of sense, doesn't it?

So who are the groups responsible for our present crisis? The usual ones. The leftist liberals, of whom probably 90 percent are Democrats, and their special-interest groups whose "campaign contributions" have our representatives right in their front pocket. Some of these wacko groups are the eco-terrorists, the environmental radicals, and the anti-capitalist crowd.

This winter is going to be a watershed moment in history. Already you have people spending anywhere from $60 to $100 simply to fill up their cars. Do you really think that families who are already struggling to make ends meet will be able to afford
$1,300 to $1,400 for heating oil when they fill their 275 gallon tanks two and maybe three times this winter?

So you people in the above-mentioned groups remember this: You are the ones responsible for parents and their children going to bed cold and hungry this winter.
You are responsible for all the jobs being lost and the companies that have gone under, which will continue, especially in the trucking industry.

You are the ones responsible for the rapidly rising costs for food and other necessities. You are the ones responsible for all the personal bankruptcies, the continuing trade imbalances and the exportation of high paying jobs overseas.

You are the ones responsible for parents not being able to provide for their children and give them all the things they should be able to.

Don't you dare try to blame anyone else. You are simply self-labeled elitist intelligentsia and self-appointed do-gooders who are thinking only of yourselves and of controlling other peoples' lives. I hope you're proud.

Traveling Helps Open Our Eyes

By the time you're reading this column I'll be in Romania, continuing my research into the evolution of their tax system, including related investment, evasion, compliance, and corruption issues. It's truly amazing to watch their relatively young tax code change and develop as well as look at the impact it has on employer and taxpayer lives.

However, an additional benefit of being there (and Bulgaria) is to have an opportunity to talk with people from all walks of life about their perceptions of us and other issues including politics, poverty, energy concerns, pollution, and so on.

You want to talk about pollution? Although vastly improved from 1989, some situations are still appalling. In the northeast industrial area you have towns like Baia Mare and Copsa Mica that still have pollution you can see, smell and taste.

The residents of some towns in the area have a life expectancy of 50 years. Lead in the soil is close to 100 times the permitted levels with vegetation lead levels close to 25 times accepted levels.

No meats or crops are sold outside the area; and the residents, being so poor, have no choice but to eat home grown crops. Also, there are hundreds of miles of polluted rivers from metal poisoning and cyanide spills from gold mines. And we complain about our industrial pollution?

As to poverty, how about living on less than $400 a month which is what the vast majority of the population does.

Three years ago, a friend took me to a peasant village where he was negotiating the purchase of land. We went three miles overland since there were no roads and basically no contact with the outside world, save marketplaces where they sold their produce.

Some of these people live on less than $5 a day. Their homes consist of one large, dirt floor room where chickens, pigs and ducks run in and out all day.

Obviously they have no electricity, no heat except for wood and coal, and bathing takes place in the nearby creek. There are no endless government handouts, but the people don't complain a bit. Everyone was friendly, and they were even going to slaughter a lamb on my behalf until I begged them not to. All in all, an eye-opening experience. Our poor in contrast would be their upper middle class.

But enough on that topic. How about the oil situation last week, where the price of a barrel dropped almost $15 in three days. I'm sure we'll hear Congress praising those dastardly futures speculators for selling short and saving the day. Didn't they blame the same investors for causing the price to run up and for making "obscene" profits? Speculators/investors don't care if the markets are rising or falling. They can profit either way as long as they GUESS right.

Most logical people will continue to see it as an economics result. Supply stays the same, demand decreases (people making painful choices) and the price goes down.

Also, the news of President Bush lifting an 18-year-old presidential ban on offshore drilling helped. All the world has to see is that we are serious about increasing our readily available supply, continue to conserve sensibly, and release some our strategic petroleum reserves; and OPEC and other suppliers will start sweating profusely. Your move, Congress.

Are you going to do what over 70 percent of the population desires, which is to start drilling where the oil is abundant, or do you want to continue your partisan whining?

Are you going to bring the issue up before your August recess, or are you going to let the pain continue for many people? I guess you can't expect much from a Congress that has a 9 percent approval rating, according to recent polls. Even Bush is still at a 34 percent approval rating.

I don't know whether logistics will prevent me from getting another column sent next time, so I would encourage you to go to an impressive website referred to me by a conservative friend.

It was a response by a person rebutting Howard Dean, teachers, professors, and the media's description of a Republican as "a rich, greedy, egotistical individual, motivated only by money and the desire to accumulate more and more of it, at the expense of the government, the working poor and all whom they exploit..."

The person's response, in a paid advertisement in the Washington Post, certainly was a slap in the face to the above groups and made them look pretty foolish. Since it's hard to distinguish between a Republican and a Democrat, I choose to read it as conservative versus liberal. You'll find a reprint of the ad at www.whatiam.net. I hope you enjoy it.

Pretty soon all the attention will be on the final 75 or so days until Election Day and I certainly have a lot of ammunition to fire at Saint Obama, but I also am having a tough time supporting John McCain.

If he pulls another stunt that ignores his conservative base and instead shamelessly panders for the independents and left of center Democrats not in love with Barack, maybe I and a lot of other conservatives will sit out this election (at least at the presidential level).

Barack, Harry and Queen Nancy will run the country disastrously and wake people up when their incompetence is revealed. That will give us four years to come up with a conservative candidate with a backbone, along with other conservative congressional candidates to take back both houses.

But, focusing on the congressional races, the Republicans have been served a golden opportunity through the actions of the Dems' exalted leader, the power hungry, incompetent, autocratic, and ineffective leader of the House, Nancy Pelosi.

In addition to leading Congress to a historically low approval rating of 9 percent, she has now closed down the House, showing total disdain for the average American who is struggling to make ends meet because of the current energy crisis. If voters, other than those in Pelosi's congressional district, could express their approval of Nancy and only Nancy, I guarantee her approval rating would be even less than the 9 percent.

All the Republicans wanted to do was introduce the American Energy Act and have a public up-or-down vote in the house. The legislation simply called for the development of domestic energy resources (making us more independent from Saudi princes, terrorists, and despots and creating good paying jobs for Americans) and using this oil resource as a bridge to the development of efficient alternative energy sources.

That's it. Very simple. Yes or no, up or down. Don't you think the voters should know where their respective representatives stand on the issue? Seventy-five percent of Americans want domestic oil sources to be tapped, 71 percent are in favor of off shore sources and 54 percent favor drilling in the ANWR region. What are the Dems afraid of if they are confident of their stance?

Queen Nancy and her minions, however, ignored the polls and voters' wishes and simply closed up shop and went on a five week vacation. I seem to remember her promising change by stating "Democrats are offering a new direction, putting the common good of all Americans first for a change, and will make health care more affordable, lower gas prices, help working families, cut college costs, ensure dignified retirement – and do it all in a fiscally sound way."

At the time gasoline was selling for $2.32 per gallon. How does going on her book tour, which by the way is another dismal failure, help solve the problems facing us ordinary Americans? Especially since after coming back tanned and fit and spending only three weeks in session, they will adjourn again and focus on the elections. How do you define hypocrisy?
If the Republicans can't take this issue and run with it aggressively during their campaigns, they shouldn't be elected to office anyway.

The Democrats are in a pickle also. If they change their mind and vote for the energy issue, it reveals their hypocrisy by proving they are only interested in votes rather than standing up for what the voter wants. This is happening already, as Nancy has given her regal okay to those Dems up for tough re-election bids this year to not vote their consciences but rather vote for political expediency.

If, on the other hand, those Dems allow themselves to be led by the nose and stay in lockstep with Her Majesty, the always shocked-looking, unblinking Pelosi, they are going to have a lot of explaining to do when they get home to their constituencies.
Either way, this race will be fun to watch. I think if events continue down this path, the Republicans have a chance to pick up seats in both Houses. It might be wishful thinking at this point however.

We Republicans are now on the right side of most, if not all, of the issues important to Americans. These are energy relief, lower taxes and national security. It should be very difficult to blow the elections with this fact in mind. McCain should also win if he re-attracts the conservative base. After all, he is running against a candidate with no experience, an energy plan based on inflating our tires (remind you of Carter?) and only vacuous rhetoric.

Obama Should Throw In The Towel

Ballgame over! Sarah Palin, govenor of Alaska, was absolutely the best pick McCain could have made for a VP running mate. She is young, conservative, a leader, the only one of the four candidates who has executive experience, pro-gun, pro-life, and on and on.

After she spoke Friday afternoon, it was obvious she is going to be too much for Joe, the mouth, Biden to take on. I can't wait for the debates. We might as well have the inauguration now and save the public a lot of taxpayer dollars.

As a matter of fact, my liberal friend who bet me a lunch over the winner of the election might as well buy it for me now and start licking his wounds. I seem to remember his calling or e-mailing me and reminding me how much he was going to enjoy his free meal. I can't wait to pull that e-mail out for future use.

It was amazing (and showed how scared the Democrats are) how the Obama campaign came out immediately to disparage her background. They described her background as simply being a mayor of a small town of 9,000. Other than being petty and childish it was extremely stupid. I hope all the small towns across the US see how much saint Barack really thinks of them and remember his statement in November.

Also, she has more executive experience and a longer record of accomplishment than Barack Obama and Little Joe Biden combined. As a matter of fact, as a conservative friend just pointed out, even Cindy McCain has more executive experience than the both of them.

I hope The Daily Star and other media have the courage to tell the public of her background. But, nevertheless, keep it up, Barack. I certainly don't want to silence you. Whenever you don't have a pre-written script to read, you keep putting your foot in your mouth.

But I have plenty of time in the future to talk about our Republican team. I can't wait until this week's Republican convention, since I know it will be run in a more adult-like fashion, avoiding the rock-star gimmickry and proceeding to put holes in every non-policy, liberal, nonsensical idea Obama and his ilk talked about this last week.

It's our turn now, guys, and you ultra-libs better not watch because it will be painful. However, just as a reminder, you have to hear both sides in order to be informed and to carry on an intelligent discussion.

Yes, as a matter of fact, I did go through pain and suffering and watched the circus of a convention the Dems put on last week. It was very hard, but I watched at least 20 hours of the dog-and-pony show and all the related commentary from both Republican and Democrat spin doctors. I think I deserve a medal for this heroic act. I listened to Nancy, Teddy K, Harry, Michelle, Joe the mouth Biden, Billy C., Hillary, and others perform their special acts, and like I said, it was quite a circus they put on.

I do, however, think Hillary showed what a mistake the party made, first for selecting lord Obama over her and then ignoring her as a VP pick. Thank you so much, Democrat strategists. You just handed us the election.

As I said, I watched a lot of the Democrat convention and have a bookful of thoughts and comments to use for my next columns. They won't be pretty for you libs, so I have rated them for mature audiences only. That lets you off the hook. The column will go over the Democrat convention unless the Republican convention is so good that I can ignore yours.

What is important now are the House and Senate races. I think the McCain/Palin ticket will have a positive impact on those also.

Just a final note. One of the statements made by Barack was a challenge to debate Senator McCain anytime, anywhere. If you remember Barack, he already offered to debate you 10 times in a town hall setting. You originally accepted and then mysteriously backed out. Probably because you remembered that you had to think on your feet and offer specifics rather than read from a prepared speech. You aren't very good in that environment, are you?

However, if I remember correctly, the offer is still out there. All you have to do is call and accept.

Dems, Media Using Lies To Paint Palin

Can you believe how scared the cowardly left is about Sarah Palin? Their petty, immature attempts to insult and demean her and her family seem to know no boundaries, and worse, their lackeys, the mainstream media, continue the lies.

It's getting harder and harder to distinguish between the wacko extreme leftist groups like The Daily Kos and the Huffington Post and the media. They are more than happy to perpetuate the lies. And to all you Democrats and liberals out there who don't speak out against this viciousness, you are just as bad as the wackos. Do you guys have any sense of fair play and integrity at all?

There are lots of examples to point out. They have tried to besmirch her by calling her "the beauty queen" and "the stewardess." Then there are the outrageous lies. They have claimed that Sarah faked a pregnancy to protect her 17-year-old daughter and claim that Trig is really the daughter's child. They have even gone so far as to demand DNA testing. Where's the outrage?

And how about some more? The left have claimed that she has banned library books, speaks in tongues, said that the Iraq war was God's will, cut spending for mentally disabled children, cut funding for pregnant teens, and on and on.

All have since been proven to be either taken out of context (Iraq war and God's will) or bald-faced lies. The New York Times had to run an apology. How about the rest of you?

Don't forget the insult thrown at her when South Carolina's Democrat Party Chair, Carol Fowler, said, "Her primary qualification seems to be that she hasn't had an abortion." Pretty classy, huh? She's one of yours and had to issue an apology only when the opinion polls found that it had backfired. Thank you Carol. How can a true feminist take that kind of statement sitting down? Are you really for women role models as strong and successful as Sarah Palin in both her family and career as you have repeatedly said you are, or only for those who are liberal?

Even the Obama campaign isn't immune to throwing around insults. Obama himself has a hard time referring to her as other than the "mayor" of a small town. When you get a presidential candidate going after the other party's VP candidate, you know he is in trouble. Isn't that Joe Biden's role?

His worst gaffe yet? The time he insulted both the Republican candidates with his "You can put lipstick on a pig, but its still a pig" and "You can wrap an old fish in a piece of paper called 'change;' it's still going to stink after eight years." Barack, don't deny that you meant it the way over 90 percent of Americans interpreted it. Your crowd ate it up and you reveled in their cheers.

Now, their latest feeble attempt to destroy her. Alaskan Democrats are conducting an ethics campaign regarding their claim that she pressured the state's Public Safety Commissioner to fire state trooper Mike Wooten, who went through a bitter divorce with her sister.

Remember, Democrats have set up this witch hunt and a Democrat, Kim Elton, appointed a Democrat, Hollis, to lead the investigation. The McCain campaign has referred to the OBAMA website that identifies members of this committee, including French and Elton, as strong Obama supporters. Already this commission, not very far into their "investigation," has promised a potential "October" surprise, with their report coming out October 31, a convenient 4 days before the elections.

Oh, I forgot to mention, as Amanda Carpenter, a columnist, points out, "Police investigations against Wooten found, (not claimed to have found) he had used a Taser on his stepson, illegally shot a moose, drank beer in his patrol car (while on duty), and threatened his father-in-law with death." It's called

148

Sarah Palin standing up to the Trooper's Association, a powerful union. Once again showing her willingness to not back down from what she thinks is right.

But keep it up, Obama. We know you are orchestrating this smear campaign behind the scenes, or at least approving of it. But the more you, your minions (30 of your lawyers and PI's looking for or creating dirt), and your lackeys in the press keep it up, Sarah Palin draws more and more supporters. You are way out of touch with ordinary Americans.

I've got three more columns devoted entirely about you Obama, loaded with facts, before the next election. I wish I had more columns.

Sarah Palin is more than qualified to be the vice president. She is a poised, intelligent, more than competent, experienced, and a tough woman. She is just what conservatives, Republicans and America need. She will make us proud.

All we can do this November 4 is hope that the voting public looks beyond the Obama-praising media and honestly looks at the real credentials of all four candidates. I honestly think that when the voter steps inside the booth, closes the curtain, and pulls the lever, it will be for the team so much more qualified to lead America.

First of all, since the Obama campaign would rather focus on Gov. Palin rather than John McCain we should briefly list her credentials as I will later list his. I already discussed Palin in my last column, but there a few more points I should bring up.

She ran a successful fishing business before leaving that to serve on her city council. She was a city mayor for ten years and then the Governor of Alaska. While governor, she managed 17,000 personnel and was responsible for a $9 billion budget. She was commander in chief of the Alaska National Guard. She planned, promoted and successfully pushed through a project that represented the largest natural-gas line project ever approved in this country. She has shown courage in standing up to senior politicians of both sides, lobbyists, and big corporations.

One final note. As Governor, Palin has actually visited our wounded troops in Germany. Obama almost did until he found out that Defense Department guidelines didn't allow cameras in so Obama conveniently didn't have time for that part of his trip.

It is kind of amusing when these modern "feminists" write about how their intelligence is insulted if John McCain thought his choice of Palin would sway them. I only have to say their vote is unimportant. I think true feminists of the old school will respect and admire the qualities of being able to balance a very high powered career with a successful family life.

The modern group of "feminists" is simply political hacks with a far left radical agenda. Their hypocrisy knows no bounds, i.e. the treatment of Clarence Thomas vs. their support of Willy Clinton.

But the real issue is Obama vs. McCain. Obama can't even come close to John McCain in terms of integrity, honor, and decades of devotion and service to our country. Military men and women honor and respect him, as McCain does them. McCain is stronger on issues of national security, taxes, trade and energy, which I will compare with Obama's policies next column.

Pretty soon people will realize Obama is the emperor with no clothes. He is an empty suit with no substance and without his teleprompter supported speeches (which I have to admit he does deliver quite eloquently) he stumbles, mumbles and bumbles his way through town hall-like discussions with ordinary Americans.

It is disgusting how the media lets him get away with all his antics. Remember how Chris Matthews of MSNBC gets tingles up and down his legs every time Obama speaks? This is an example of a professional unbiased reporter and journalist?

For Obama, everything is staged. I remember that he had to call for water when a swooning fan fainted during his speech. This happened four times in close succession. When he was called on the obviousness of this staging, all the fainting miraculously went away. How strange. How shallow.

Before I get into Obama's lack of everything I have to get to Joe Biden. Remember when the press went bonkers when Dan Quayle misspelled potato? All he did was add an "e" on the end of the word. In fact, either spelling was accepted in the 19th century. But oh, how the ridicule was heaped upon the hapless Quayle by all the reporters. I can guarantee you that there are far worse spellers coming into the field of journalism now.

Now comes Joe Biden. He actually referred to President Franklin Roosevelt coming on TV in 1929 in a speech regarding the depression. No. 1, Franklin Roosevelt wasn't president in 1929 and No. 2, the TV hadn't been invented yet. Honestly, which gaffe do you think is more important? But enough on poor old Joe.

With only two columns to go before the election, I will be listing Obama's "extensive" resume relating to his experience, his questionable associations with dubious characters, his lack of good judgment, and, most importantly, his very scary policy proposals and his vision for our country.

Do we really want this man to be the most powerful man in the world as our next president? I can only hope good sense and judgment prevails in the voting booth.

Since the media has already appointed Barack Obama as their choice, you can expect not to see any objective, professional journalism coming from them. The burden is on the individual voter to do the research him/herself.

Notice how Obama and his faithful always talk in general terms? It's because he has nothing of accomplishment to brag about and no feasible plan for the country, especially if you price out the cost of his proposals. His background doesn't even qualify him for a CEO position, let alone president of the United States.

What does his life look like to date? He graduated from college in 1983. He then went to work as a "community organizer" at age 23, from 1985 to 1988. This is the time period he brags about, so much, so we'll have to talk more about that experience later. For now, he brags about how he gave up high paying jobs to accept a job paying
$12,000 a year. Barack, that was minimum wage. You get paid minimum wage because you have minimal responsibility, and your inexperience means you weren't worth more than that.

Then he went on to law school and graduated in May 1991. I think he briefly worked for a law firm, but in April 1992 he ran a program named Project Voter Registration Drive for an organization known as ACORN (Association of Community Organizations for Reform Now). He trained their workers how to use tactics in voter registration drives. You have to Google "ACORN," "Barack Obama", and "Madeline Talbott" to do your research. You won't find it in any of the Obama-loving press.

ACORN has been indicted or under investigation in thirteen states so far. One subpoenaed witness, Lateala Goins, age 21, said, "You can tell them you're registered as many times as you want – they don't care. They will follow you to the buses, they will follow you home, it doesn't matter." She simply signed her name to numerous registration forms; the ACORN people filled in everything else. Freddie Jones, also subpoenaed, filled out 72 registration forms. And these are only a few of the hundreds of stories out there.

The point of all this is that ACORN is actively participating in (and found guilty of) voter fraud, a felony, and other criminal activity. Obama trained these people, made sure they were funded with taxpayer dollars and benefited from campaign donations in return.

Don't you also expect that since Obama impacted so many lives (his claim), at least one or two of these individuals would come forward and offer testimonials on his behalf?

After this honorable exercise in radical, left-wing activism, he went on to serve seven years as an Illinois state senator. During this time he accomplished nothing noteworthy except for not voting up or down on critical issues but merely voting "present" over 130 times.

In November 2004, he was elected U.S. senator and has served a mere three- plus years, two of which have been campaigning for the presidency. He has not been the leader on even one signature issue during this time. He misses critical votes and waits to determine which way the political (radical left) winds are blowing before he votes on the others. Again, nothing accomplished.

This lack of accomplishment has forced him to enhance (lie about) his claims of accomplishments. During his visit to Israel, The Jerusalem Post has quoted him as saying, "Just this past week, we passed out of the U.S. Senate Banking Committee – which is my committee – a bill to call for divestiture." CNN, hardly a critic, had to point out that Obama wasn't even on that committee.

One more claim, pointed out by The Jerusalem Post, "We're told that Obama 'passed laws' that 'extended healthcare for wounded troops who'd been neglected.'" As the Post pointed out, the bill passed the Senate by a vote of 91 to 3. Six Senators did not vote-including Obama.

And yes, even though his supporters try to discount the facts, there are his associations with the convicted Tony Rezco, William Ayres, the domestic terrorist and killer (lots of proven contacts, and not just a man he knows who lives in his neighborhood), his racist minister Jeremiah Wright (twenty years), and more. Either he is stupid and naïve about the backgrounds of these despicable people, or he is lying about his relationships with them. I choose the latter explanation.

I know the Kool-Aid group of Obama fans won't do their own research. They wouldn't know a fact if it hit them in the face. I am appealing to the independents and the common sense-crowd. This is an extremely important election coming up, and Obama's record just doesn't cut it.

Just as his running mate, Joe Biden, has said about Obama, "The presidency doesn't lend itself to on-the-job-training."

Finally, we have only a week to go before the elections. McCain/Palin have pulled close in the polls but still have an uphill fight.

What compounds the problem is that John McCain originally accepted public fund raising limits and stuck to his word while Obama, just to illustrate another character flaw, lying, originally made the same pledge but then reneged.

The consequence? Obama has raised more than $600 million, has $134 million on hand and $700,000 in campaign debts. McCain has been allowed to spend $84 million over the last two months of the campaign. You can bet Obama will be swamping the airwaves with lies and smears about McCain's economic and foreign policy issues.

But maybe help is on the way. Barack hurt his cause when a simple question made by an ordinary citizen exposed his socialist beliefs.

Barack said yes, Joe (the plumber) Wurzelbacher, would pay more taxes if he went ahead and bought a business that generated more than $250,000 a year. He said he really didn't want to punish the rich. He simply wanted to spread the wealth around! If that's not socialism (along with his national health care plan) I don't know what is.

He enforced this strategy when he stated that he is going to lower taxes on 95 percent of taxpayers. That will be a great trick since 38 percent of Americans already don't pay any tax at all. What he really meant was he would expand the welfare state. Admit it, Obama. You want to take from those who produce and give it to those who don't. Makes you want to run out and work harder, doesn't it? So much for his sound economic policies.

Then, Joe "the gaffer" Biden, the person who is supposed to shore up the foreign policy weaknesses of his running mate, actually told the truth this time. In his own words he said, "Mark my words. It will not be six months before the world tests Barack Obama like they did John Kennedy. Watch, we're going to have an international crisis, a generated crisis, to test the mettle of this guy."

He then went on to say, "And he is going to need help....to stand with him. Because it's not going to be apparent initially, it's not going to be apparent that we're right."

That's just great Joe. You want us to vote for someone who is going to cause an international crisis for the United States and then stand by the same person who, as you say, will fail?

I thought Obama, the miracle worker, could just sit down with the world's most
evil people and smooth out all our problems. Why would they want to test us? If you listen closely, you can hear Putin, the mullahs of Iran, Osama, Ahmadinejad, Kim Jong Il, al-Qaida, Chavez, and on and on, laughing and rolling in the aisles. Even Hamas has endorsed Obama for president! They all are probably some of the mysterious international donors to Obama's campaign. It's an evil world out there, and just as Biden has said, "The presidency isn't the place for on-the-job training."

So, he is going to fail on the economy and put us at risk on the international scene. Only those blind, irrational, Bush-haters will be willing to support these strategies.

Obama is simply a cheap copy of Jimmy Carter. As columnist Amir Taheri points out, the world also perceived Carter as weak and inexperienced, and we had Iran taken over by mullahs, the Soviets brazenly invading Afghanistan, the first oil embargo, double-digit inflation and high unemployment. He seriously weakened our military and we became the laughingstock of most of the world. Get ready for part two.

With a naïve presidential candidate and a phony foreign-policy mentor, the pundits are already starting to make excuses for the failures their team is about to cause. As expected, all the trouble that will happen in the early days of his presidency (if that happens) will be and already has been blamed on Bush.

Sorry, guys. Don't you remember? Obama is transformational and will bring us change. Whatever happens starting from day one of his potential presidency rests squarely on his shoulders.

One final note. Please vote for Jim Seward this coming Tuesday. He has served this area faithfully for over 20 years, and his many accomplishments and good deeds have earned him another two years. Also, his length of service has won him important party positions, an advantage that our area would lose should he not be re-elected.

There is not room here to list his many accomplishments, so please go to his campaign website and see that impressive list yourself. He has earned and deserves our support and our vote.

It has sure been a depressing seven days for me and my fellow conservatives, and I fear it will be the beginning of a depressing four years for our country.

Isn't it amazing what $650 million can buy? It can buy you the presidency of the United States. It can take a man with no executive experience, questionable associations (Ayers, Wright, Rezco, et al.) and no accomplishments of any significance and make him the most powerful man in the free world.

The money can trick people into voting for a person with the most liberal voting record in the Senate, a man who chooses the third most liberal for a vice president. A person who promises bipartisanship but has reached across the aisle only once, when he co-sponsored a bill with Republican Sen. Richard Lugar which eventually failed.

In contrast, John McCain pledged to accept public financing and had "only"

$280 million to spend. How can you not win when you can more than double the spending of your opponent? I hope people will remember how both candidates pledged to accept public financing, and only one acted honorably and kept his promise.

What can we now expect? How about: a reduced and weakened military; terrorism flourishing; higher taxes, reducing productivity, job creation and wealth- building; diminished quality of health care through a national health care program; and no nuclear, clean coal, or on/offshore drilling initiatives.

Want more? How about three new radical Supreme Court nominations and a government with Nancy Pelosi, Harry Reid and the most liberal senator in the senate, Barack Obama. How about a president who thinks the U.S. Constitution is flawed and who thinks the Supreme Court didn't go far enough in not considering the issue of wealth distribution.

Depressed yet? I haven't even mentioned the $1 trillion of proposed new spending, which represents a one-third increase in the size of our government. Oh, I forgot, "change" is going to pay for these new programs.

I think I better stop with the list now before it gets to be too much to take. I will say that 57 million voters got it right, and the future will prove just that. It's sad that our country will have to go through so much hardship before we can get it right again. But Ronald Reagan righted a worse predicament that our country was in with the bumbling Jimmy Carter, and that's what we now have, another Jimmy Carter.

How about Obama's ridiculous proposal to redistribute the wealth? I wanted to see the reaction of my students when I told them that the next exam would be graded a little differently. I said I would be taking points from the high achievers, the ones who worked hard and prepared properly and give these points to the lower- achieving students so that we would have a fairer redistribution and a kinder class. You can guess how that idea went over. But how is that different from Obama's proposal? I want to make it perfectly clear that I don't bring politics into the classroom, but the students who came early to class wanted to know my feelings about the election. They, too, saw the depressed state I was in.

But yes Barack, you won the election and deserve to be supported as long as your path is in alignment with mine. I will not compromise my principles just to get along. Your flowery speeches won't count; it will be your actions that resonate. I think you are soon going to feel the tremendous burden that has been placed on your shoulders. You can't vote present; you can't run away from difficult votes (which you have a history of doing); and you are going to have to deal with some very evil people that only want to harm us and destroy our way of life. In other words, you will have to grow up very fast.

What are we conservatives to do in the meantime? We have to start right now and choose leaders who have true conservative principles and don't compromise values just to get more votes. We have recently seen the results of that strategy. Polls show the country still has a large majority of conservative-leaning individuals who want a leader who doesn't compromise.

Reagan swept his elections, one of which resulted in a 49-state victory, and Newt Gingrich took control of the House with his "Contract with America," promoting pure conservative values. We have to find those individuals now instead of waiting until the next election. And yes, control of the Senate and the House is just as important, if not more important, as the presidency. Let's not give up quite yet.

I can't believe that today's column comes after two years of writing for The Daily Star. It has honestly been a lot of work, but the enjoyment I get from the experience makes it well worthwhile. I'll try to give it another year if Sam Pollak allows it. He has been true to his word and covered my back, never changed any of the column's content, and I am sure he gets plenty of grief because of it. More on Sam later.

I can't believe how the paper reaches such a number of readers from all over the United States. My e-mail responses impress the heck out of me. I have heard from people in 38 different states (also three countries, Romania, Bulgaria, and the Ukraine but they probably shouldn't count since I know those individuals personally) totaling 286 responses.

Of these responses, 242 have been positive and 44 negative. The November 11 alone column got 21 responses, 17 for and 4 against.

Among the negatives, some of which seem like threats, I have two special ones. One man loves to send postcards about my column to The Star, which then get forwarded on to me. I have no idea why he doesn't just send it to me. Maybe he wants a lot of people to read it along the way. I have kept them all and have accumulated quite a few.

My favorite is one on which he has a man with a club about to hit a baby seal. He has circled the man and labeled him "Tom Sears" and the title he gives to the circled baby seal is "The Truth." I got a kick out of that one and once in a while he expresses his anger quite creatively.

The other is my first and only e-mail stalker. He sent the first one in the middle of September stating a few nasty things and went on to insult the paper by saying "Thankfully, you write for a small-town rag with a very limited circulation." As you might guess, I wrote back a very diplomatic response questioning his sanity. Wow, did this set him off. For about two weeks he wrote almost daily, and on some days I received three or four letters.

This continued even though I only responded to him that one time. Finally, I had his e-mail go directly to my spam file so I don't know if he is still sending me any more. I hope when he reads this (and he will), he will save himself a lot of time and find something more constructive to pursue.

I want to tell my supporters out there that I very much appreciate your feedback, either by e-mail or just coming up to me with a few kind words. I have tried to respond to each of your notes and apologize if I have missed anyone. Your positive feedback makes it much easier for me to keep writing the column. Thank you very, very much.

I must admit, however, that I get a kick out of the negative ones, also. I do read them, but so many of them write so much and say so little. More than a few are two or more pages in length, but I keep them, and, knowing that my columns get under their skins in an irritating way makes it easier for me to keep on writing too.

As for the negative ones sent to the editor, I enjoy them also. It's just that most of them are too far gone, and any attempts to have a conversation with the writers would be futile. Their anger simply shows their fear and how afraid they are of a conservative viewpoint. Emotional responses are the only way an ultra-lib knows how to respond when confronted with factual statements.

Now, back to Sam. Yes, I did lose two bets to him and yes, I will be taking him to lunch (just not where he wants to go). However, before meeting Sam I always told myself I would never take a liberal to lunch and be seen publicly with him or her.
Now, after getting to know Sam and realizing he is one of the sanest liberals I have met and a pretty good guy, I have changed my policy and now will take a liberal to lunch once every two years.

If he continues to cover my back and keeps getting grief which I know must be hard to do, I might even change my policy to a once-a-year lunching with a liberal (and maybe even to a place of his choosing).

Election Process in Dire Need Of Changes

Now that the elections are over (as soon as Al Franken admits his defeat), we can all start the recovery process and get back to our normal lives.

It is ridiculous that the primaries and the election campaigning took two years to complete. What do these people do for us? Aren't they supposed to be getting something done on our behalf in Congress? Do you really think they realize their whole purpose of being there is to serve the people and not self-aggrandizement? It's starting to get a little out of hand.

Wouldn't it be nice if the process could be changed? I've got a few suggestions. No. 1 - How about a six-month primary period and a three-month election period? With all the mass communication outlets, shouldn't that be enough time to get a message across?

No. 2 - Each candidate gets one hundred million dollars. That should be more than enough, maybe even too much. Then we wouldn't get a deluge of phone calls, pamphlets, advertisements, and all the other major nuisances that disrupt our lives.

No. 3 - Each candidate issues an upfront statement of his or her stances on a variety of issues, along with his beliefs and value system clearly. No waffling and flip- flopping depending on the audience you are addressing. The issues can be as numerous as they desire but certainly would cover foreign policy, a domestic agenda, and social issues. A leader should be able to stand tall, not be afraid of offending certain groups, and present his beliefs and stances in a clear and cogent fashion.

No. 4 – We, the voters will have to be responsible enough to realize that there will never be a perfect candidate. We must look at the entire package being offered and not be single-issue voters. That is selfish and ignorant. If there are issues that you don't agree with, get more involved in the party and have an impact.

No. 5 - Candidates should have more debates for both the presidential and vice presidential positions. Also, these debates should be led by a strong moderator. If the candidate does not directly address the question being asked, the moderator should interrupt and remind the candidate to stay on topic. If this doesn't work, then the moderator should shut off the microphone, and the candidate loses any remaining time.

All of the debates this year were pretty much ineffective. Presently, the candidates come in with a list of objectives they want to get across and don't seem to care what the question is.

Along with this, the questions should be considered by a bipartisan panel and relevant ones agreed on and chosen. All the wacko ones can be thrown out. Then the questions would be drawn randomly from a drum and simply read. Some of the debates could be in a town hall-like setting, and individual audience members could read the questions.

No. 6 - The candidates have to appear at least once on all the news networks, including cable. They have to be able to face hostile audiences as well as friendly ones. A true, strong leader with a strong belief system shouldn't be afraid to stand up and support what he or she truly believes.

How about this one? News media actually reports, and only reports, the news. I don't give a hoot what some self anointed hot shot has to say. My neighbor's viewpoint means just as much if not more. Don't try to slickly hide your biases in your opinions. Just report.

Finally, give us a clear choice. All politicians are beginning to behave in the same way. They forget all about us when they get elected and are more concerned with what social cocktail parties or what lobbyist they are supposed to meet with this week. Our ballot should have the option available to vote "none of the above." I certainly would have chosen that option this election. Give us a strong candidate with conservative beliefs as well as one with liberal beliefs. If "none of the above" gets the majority, the parties have to go with another choice. They might get the hint that kowtowing to special interest groups and choosing a pabulum candidate won't win the day any more.

Pie in the sky, wishful thinking? Maybe, but a few changes would be welcomed.

People have been coming up to me suggesting that I should find a few good things to say about our president elect. That's going to be hard since he hasn't done anything yet rather than make a few good Cabinet choices. I'll try real hard, however, and include them in my next column.

Merry Christmas everyone!

What Are Atheists Afraid Of?

Christmas is upon us; one of the three most important dates in Christianity. I was hoping to get through the season without any atheistic zaniness, but that didn't happen.

Starting in Olympia, Wash., and spreading to two or three other cities, atheists
couldn't stand by and not attempt to draw attention to themselves.

Olympia originally simply allowed a Nativity scene and a Menorah, two symbols important to Christians and Jews, to be displayed on public property.

The atheists predictably demanded a display themselves. Their wish was granted when city officials caved, but rather than being a statement of their non-religious, unbelieving "faith," they chose to denigrate and insult my religious beliefs. I, and many other Christians, simply won't sit still for this behavior.

I know I have friends who are either self-proclaimed or silent atheists and this column is not about them (even though I can't understand their decision and know they are making the biggest mistake possible). This column is for the radical members of their group.

Why are you so afraid of religion, and Christianity in particular? What do you fear? It's easy to declare yourself an atheist, especially out of laziness, since I'm sure very few of you ever attempted to give religion a serious chance through exploration and introspection. Isn't it also quite egocentric to not acknowledge a supreme being greater than yourself?
Instead of proudly proclaiming your stance and backing it up with research that lead you to your ultimate decision, you choose to exhibit nastiness and hate towards my religious faith.

You post a sign next to the above-mentioned displays that says, "There are no gods, no devils, no angels, no heaven or hell. There is only our natural world. Religion is but a myth and superstition that hardens hearts and enslaves minds."

Christianity has been around for more than 2,000 years. Our country was founded on Christian/Judean principles. I could fill many columns with quotes and speeches from the Founding Fathers to back up this claim.

Christmas has been a national holiday since the late 1800s. Polls show that there are only 3 percent of Americans who consider themselves atheists (still way too many), 92 percent who believe in God, and 84 percent who consider themselves Christians.

Is this why you're afraid? Is this why you feel that you have to remove all references to God and religion from the public square? Are you worried that a child could see a Nativity scene and wonder who this Baby Jesus really was? Of course you are.

Here's what you should do, and I won't protest your right to do so. Pick a day, any day you choose (probably not a workday since it will never be declared a national holiday). Spend it celebrating your atheism. Have an atheist tree, exchange atheist presents, have a nice atheist dinner, wish each other a happy atheist day.

Maybe some of you who believe there is no being more supreme than yourselves can sit on a stool in front of a mirror and praise yourselves all day. Just don't trample, insult or show condescension towards my religious convictions. I promise I won't bother you (but I will still worry about you and pray for you).

The saddest part of all this are your children. I'm sure you won't even give them the opportunity to make an informed decision on their own. Why wouldn't you do this? You're afraid of the choice they might make.

In last weekend's edition of The Daily Star there was an article titled "Israel celebrates Hanukkah tale." It tells of an Israeli village where the re-enactment of the Hanukkah story takes place, which I believe is an annual event.

A person is quoted as saying, "Thousands of Israeli children have visited here. They learn about the Maccabees and understand their nationalism, and their religion becomes stronger."
Is this what you are afraid of? That they might hear the story of Jesus and make a decision different from that of your own?

People, we are on the right side of this issue. We have the numbers to effectively boycott films and stores who pander to this atheistic theme.

A perfect example was Bill Maher's film "Religulous." It was highly promoted and a total flop. Compare that to the movie "The Passion of The Christ." This was produced by Mel Gibson with his own funds since Hollywood rejected it's religious theme. It ended up being twelfth of the top 1,000 grossing films. So we do have some clout and can exercise it if pushed too far.

So let's switch the focus back on Christmas. As Nathan Tabor, a columnist, says, Christmas isn't anything without Christ. On that note, I wish everyone a very Merry Christmas, but more importantly, happy birthday Jesus.

Here we go again. Israel takes the actions necessary to protect its citizens and remove a menace that is intent on exterminating Jews and wiping Israel off the map. Guess who's being held at fault? The propaganda machine of Hamas is proving once again their ability to sway public opinion and sympathy its way.

If you still have a Dec. 29 copy of The Daily Star, take a look at the very dramatic AP picture on Page 1. Tell me it's not posed. I can hear the photographer setting up the scene. "Ok, now, let me get down on the ground so the picture will be looking up at you. Much more effective. Now I want you to look off into the distance and look heroic. That's it, good. Now, I want you pointing off into the distance. No, it doesn't matter what you are pointing at, just point. One last thing. Move over here so that the smoke and dust are much heavier. Good, now hold it." Click, click, click.

Another picture, among many, created for maximum impact. This one comes from the Dec. 31 online copy of the New York Times, the main propaganda arm of Hamas, Hezbollah, Iran, Syria, and any other "hate America" group. This one shows a solitary man, hunched over and attempting to plant a shredded Hamas flag on top of the rubble of a supposed mosque hit by an Israeli bomb.

I can imagine that picture being set up. The photographer says, "Ok, I want you off in the distance, appearing hunched over and exhausted. Wait, does someone have a Hamas flag we can use? Not that one, it's too new. Tear it up first. Now take the flag and move over there so I can get the top part of the destroyed 'mosque' in the picture. That's it, good. Now hold still." Click, click, click.

Give me a break. First of all it is not a mosque if it is being used as an arms depot, thereby making it a military target. And what about these innocent civilian casualties?
Of course it's a tragedy when an innocent civilian is killed. No civilized person wants this to happen. But who bears the responsibility? The blame falls squarely on the shoulders of the despicable terrorists, the ones hiding themselves amongst the civilian population and firing rockets from playgrounds, schools, homes, mosques, and wherever they think they are safe. They know Israel values human life and will do anything to avoid civilians. What cowards!

Now what really is an innocent civilian? A Palestinian spokesperson says 45 innocent civilians were killed, including 25 children, and the reporter's pen streaks across his notepad, treating this as a fact. Who cares where the figures came from.

Also, it's really amazing how they can tell an innocent from a militant. Is it because they aren't wearing a uniform? Smart move for these cowards. They saw what happens when it is Arab coalition armies against Israel's. How long did those wars last? Three days? Six days?

Are they innocent when they dance in the street and celebrate what happened on 9/11 or as they do every time innocent Israelis die due to a suicide bomber?

How about the mothers who allow bombs to be strapped to their children and are proud of them when they kill innocent people and become martyrs? How about the "innocent civilians" who allow Hamas terrorists to roam their streets and are allowed to mingle amongst them? Are they innocent? Who can truly tell the difference?

Also, who can tell whether these "innocents" were killed by Israel or Hamas? It has been documented that Hamas will kill anyone who is suspected of collaborating with the enemy. No jury, no trial, no decision, no proof needed, just a judgment call by these worms.

And talk of cowards. The real cowards are those leaders who have abandoned their people and are safely living in Syria, supposedly out of the reach of Israeli bombs. Can anyone remember a little effective group called the Mossad?

So, now the facts. 9,400 rockets and mortars have been fired from Gaza since 2003. 3,200 fired in 2008 alone. At least 6,500 have been fired since Israel withdrew completely from Gaza in 2005.

Lastly, how about the 543-plus rockets fired during the 6 month "ceasefire" from June 19 to Dec. 19. And do you think Hamas was concentrating on hitting military targets only? If you do, then you are probably a New York Times subscriber.

So keep it up, Israel, until the animals are no longer a threat to your peace- seeking citizens. Egypt, I'd be very careful who you associate with, allowing arms and fighters to get into Gaza from your borders.

And you Palestinians, innocent or not, try to stay out of tunnels for the foreseeable future.

Israel Need Not Give In To Hamas

I'm trying very hard to give Obama a 30-day honeymoon period, but it's getting harder and harder to do so. He sure is giving me plenty to write about in future columns, but first, one more column on Israel and Hamas.

Let me see if I have this right. Israel accomplished most of its goals during its self-defense actions.

They destroyed Hamas' infrastructure and greatly reduced its military capabilities, eliminated 1,000-plus terrorists, destroyed over two-thirds of the smuggling tunnels and caused Hamas' brave leaders to scurry like cockroaches.

The Israelis declared a unilateral cease-fire and pulled back, applying their own time frame. So what did the cowards do?

Hamas crawled back out of their Saddam-like spider holes, peeked warily out from behind the women and children, nervously looked around to make sure it was safe, and then, and only then, did these brave warriors stick out their chests and declare victory!

I'm sure Israel would love to have more losses like this in the future. These terrorists pound their chests and celebrate every rocket launched, hoping to kill Israelis. Any Israeli will do.

Yet they declare to be victims when fire is returned. They sure do know how to play the victim part, don't they? It's amazing how they can cry, producing real tears on cue. Even a lot of Hollywood actors can't do that.

Then the world, seeing Israel respond with force in self-defense, claims Israel has reacted disproportionately. How is it supposed to respond when their very survival is at stake? They should respond until the threat has been removed.

When you walk back and forth to your garden and are harassed daily by wasps or hornets, being stung once in awhile, what do you do? You buy a can of wasp-killing spray and seek out the nest. Once you find the nest, do you wait and try to identify the wasps that stung, eliminating only those, or do you wipe out the whole nest? Most of us know the right answer. And what makes the wasps smarter than Hamas is that the wasps know enough to leave the area and seek out a new home.

Only those of the anti-Israel crowd would answer differently. If it were your home or your town constantly bombed, you living in constant fear, you would be reacting exactly the same way.

Now, what about negotiations? There is really nothing to negotiate. As an article in The Daily Star pointed out, "Israel has only four main demands: an end to Gaza rocket fire, a halt to Palestinian attacks, international supervision of a truce, and an agreement to stop Hamas from rearming."

I would add a fifth. Israel simply wants to live in peace with its neighbors. Aren't these truly fair requests? Israel has already given more than enough. Gaza was created from land seized from Egypt, and the West Bank was land taken from Jordan as a result of the six-day, 1967 war.

At the same time, Jerusalem's old city was recaptured from Jordan. Israel has already given Gaza and The West Bank to the Palestinians. There is nothing more to give.

Also, how can you possibly negotiate with people who want your elimination and have shown no flexibility in that regard?

Israel obviously wants none of its people eliminated. Is the U.N., the European Union, or some other world body supposed to assume that in negotiations an acceptable percent is to be agreed upon? Can you see the negotiations going back and forth with Israel eventually accepting 30 percent as an allowable percentage of its citizens eliminated? Get real.

The fate of Jerusalem? It should remain, undivided, in Israeli hands. Jerusalem has been the Jewish capital for more than 3,300 years. It has never been the capital of any Arab or Muslim entity. It is mentioned hundreds of times in the Bible and not even once in the Koran. All Muslims and other Arabs are welcome to visit peacefully, but not stay.

Yet, all of these peace initiatives are probably a waste of time. Peace will never be achieved when one country wants the other wiped off the face of the Earth and will accept nothing less as satisfactory.

Our objective should be simply to arm Israel sufficiently to defend itself from terrorism and hostile nations.

The Israelis have proven able to protect themselves time and time again. They also seem more capable than we are at solving the growing Syrian and Iranian threats. I say let them.

The Palestinian homeland issue? It's already been settled. When the state of Israel was created, an Arab state was also created with substantially more land. It already is more than 70 percent Palestinian. It's called Jordan.

Obama Well on His Way To Ignominy

Move over, Jimmy Carter. You've got someone on the fast track to replace you as the worst president in the history of our nation. And he's done all this in only 28 days!

First of all, he's arrogant. Going around, still in a campaign mode, blaming Republicans for blocking progress, while, depending on the poll taken, 56 to 60 percent of Americans see the "stimulus" package as a bad solution to our present economic woes.

Then you chide Republicans by saying on one of your campaign stops, "What do you think a stimulus is? It's spending. That's the whole point!" This of course earned him a few chuckles from his "Kool-Aid crowd. But as Lindsey Graham pointed out on a Sunday news show, of the massive $787 billion bill, only $3 billion is going to small business.

Sorry Barack, it's you who doesn't know what a stimulus package is supposed to be. It's not about welfare and pork spending. It's about job creation and economic growth. I wonder if he really knows that jobs come from small businesses.

How about his dishonesty? Even his biggest fan, The New York Times, is starting to get a little antsy with the guy.

On his first day in office, he solemnly pledged to impose the toughest ethics rules of any modern-day president. It was a huge campaign promise and it took about a week for him to break it.

Bill Richardson, commerce secretary nominee, was the first casualty. Then came William Lynn, nominated for the No. 2 position in the Defense Department.

Somehow, Treasury Secretary Tim Geithner slipped through with all his tax cheating, but Nancy Killefer's and Tom Daschle's tax cheating didn't.

Finally (so far) there was Hilda Solis and her husband's problems. It was ver inconvenient for her that she filed a joint return with him.

Remember how he promised transparency in government and the opportunity to allow the public to view any passed proposals for five days before he signed the bill into law? Oops, there goes another promise broken. The Senate had the final bill, 1,073 pages full of vagueness, given to them only hours before the vote was to be taken.

The Republican senators were also, as were the House Republicans, shut completely out of the process. No input, no give-and-take, no negotiations and no consideration of any Republican suggestions.

So much for bipartisanship. Fortunately for Obama, he was able to buy three make-believe Republicans, - Spector, Collins and Snowe - to get his bill passed. Spector was bought for $6.5 billion for "medical research." No details, again, just vagueness.

Now for Obama's radicalism. He is now responsible for the largest pork and welfare spending act in history. This is the largest welfare bill ever.

It will cause the size of government to expand hugely and permanently. Future generations, from both liberal and conservative families, will be hit with a massive federal debt to be paid back with very, very high taxes. People shouldn't forget that he was the most liberal, partisan member of Congress. Did you really expect to get the "change" that was promised?
You 53 percent who voted for him are now responsible for him. You got a youthful, radical, naïve, inexperienced liberal who has no idea how to run a country. Nancy Pelosi and Harry Reid and their radical ilk will be leading him by the nose repeatedly in the future.

As columnist Rich Lowry points out, Ronald Reagan and Newt Gingrich tried to limit the size of government and partially succeeded. From 1983 to 2000 government spending went from 23.5 percent of GDP to 18.4 percent. Newsweek pointed out the percent was 20.9 percent last year and will probably go to 28 percent this year. It also says "In 2010, total U.S. government spending will be 39.9 percent of GDP, only about 8 percent less than the average in the socialistic eurozone countries."

So conservatives, there is a silver lining. With Obama leading the country, our party can only gain in strength. As columnist David Limbaugh rightly says, "President

Barack Obama has done more in the first three weeks of his presidency to validate the
suspicions of his critics than I thought possible."

Republicans had a chance to control spending, and let everyone down when they failed to illustrate the differences between themselves and the Democrats. They dropped the ball that time, but we will have one more chance to lead in the near future. Fortunately, Obama is helping us tremendously in pointing out the distinctions between the parties. Let's just sit back and enjoy the show.

Soon, I want to bring to the fore all the ridiculous spending features of the bill. It might take more than one column to point out all the wasteful spending, and you never know how soon Barack will screw something up again.

Talk about having a love affair with himself. Obama couldn't even wait 11 months to give his first State of the Union-speech. So to massage his overwhelming ego, he decided to give it last Tuesday.

It was certainly full of rhetoric, with lots of efforts for hopefully historically memorable quotes - as if enough attempts were made, some would stick. But was there any substance? Absolutely none.

He is slick, I'll give him that. And he is a skilled orator. Give him a good speech writer and a teleprompter and he's ready to go. A little advice Barack. It takes more than speech-making and glorious promises to be an effective leader. It takes a person who is willing to roll up his sleeves and help manage the process.

So what does he do? Weeks before his speech, he simply tells Congress (actually only half of Congress) to come up with a stimulus bill that he can sign.

He then ducks out of sight and lets the two most radical, irresponsible members take over the process – Sen. Harry Reid and Rep. Nancy Pelosi. The result is the worst possible, pork-filled, non-stimulus bill that could have been created.

This person is going to single-handedly ruin this country, and the press and
Obama's cultists are letting it happen.

George Bush's largest deficit, according to the Congressional Budget Office, was $454.8 billion, and that occurred in fiscal year 2008. Obama's antics, to date only, will result in a $1.3 TRILLION deficit for fiscal year 2009.

Therefore, his promise to cut the deficit in half by the end of his first term in office means we will be saddled with more than a $533 billion deficit for fiscal years 2013 and beyond.

Great job Barack. Your deficit will still be nearly $100 billion larger than Bush's total deficit in 8 years. The problem is he is lying to us once again. He has very optimistic economic projections and he has only begun to spend! You can expect much, much worse to come.

One positive result of this should be that all those over-the-hill lefty hippie
wannabes might finally have to be quiet about the "obscene' Bush deficits.

This might be too much to hope for. They are still obsessed with their hatred for George Bush and will never change. The sad part is that they will continue to use the same old, unoriginal mantras, even when they have no idea

what they are talking about. There is a slight sliver of hope that this out-of-control leftist liberal can be checked. There is a fiscally conservative coalition of 49 Democrats in the House who
claim to be committed to seriously shrinking the federal deficit.

If they are true to their word, Obama's plan for ruining this country can be stopped dead in its tracks. This would make the House count of 178 Republicans and 49 "Blue Dog" Democrats" a majority of 227 to 208.

Also, do you think the 66 million Americans who voted for Obama would have still done so had they known what his real agenda was? I'm guessing at least 20 or more million would not have.

Look up the definition of the word "narcissism." It is defined as "excessive self admiration and self-centeredness. It is a personality disorder characterized by the patient's overestimation of his or her own appearance and abilities and an excessive need for attention and admiration."

You might as well put a picture of Obama there as an example. A conservative friend recently sent me an article by a Sam Vaknin, PhD., who has written many articles about narcissism and is the author of the book "Malignant Self Love."

The article is lengthy but very well supported. To summarize, he says, "Barack Obama appears to be a narcissist." Send me an e-mail and I can forward it to you.

Lastly, another friend sent me a video clip of a news report done by a very reputable television station that lays out the historical time line. It shows who is responsible for the present mess we are in and those who repeatedly tried to warn Congress about it as far back as 2002.

If anyone wants me to forward a copy, again, just send me a quick e-mail and I will attach it and zip it right back. I know how you lefty libs don't like to be frustrated with facts, but I'll send you a copy too, for as long as it stays online.

It looks like Barack is going to give me plenty to write about, for much longer than I had anticipated. I know that has some of you jumping for joy and others looking for the nearest cliff to jump from. Sorry about that.

I guess it should have been predictable. Disagree with Barack about anything and he sics his attack dogs on you. How presidential. First it was the Republicans in Congress, the party of "no" as he described them. All because they voted their consciences not to spend the country into bankruptcy. They simply thought the bill should have been debated first, let alone read, before it was voted on. How dare they.

Maybe it was because they didn't fall for his repeated doom-and-gloom message he loves to preach to convince everyone we are on the brink of something catastrophic and then use his "Trust me, we'll work out the details later" explanation.

So what has he accomplished so far? After the trillion dollar "stimulus" bill filled with pork, which isn't going to stimulate anything except for the special-interest groups that were being paid back, he has moved on a $410 billion (loaded with pork again) spending bill and is proposing a $3.6 trillion budget.

This final little item, by itself, spends more as a percent of gross domestic product than any period since World War II. As Tony Blankley, a columnist, points out, "it's higher than any year during the Bush administration, despite the full costs of 9/11, the Iraq and Afghan wars and the rebuilding of New Orleans after Katrina."

However, Obama is just getting warmed up. He is now using his "Chicken Little, The Sky is Falling" speech to propose disastrous changes in health care, education, energy and tax policy.

I forgot to mention the abolishing of the secret vote process in unionization elections. It's the same old, "if we don't act now it will be the end of the world as we know it.
Maybe he didn't have the child fable "The Boy Who Cried Wolf" read to him as he was growing up. Maybe someone should read it to him now.

Anyway, I think members of his own party are getting a little tired of his worn- out mantra. We can only hope there are some sane members of his party on the other side of the aisle.

Most recently we have the most ridiculous action yet. We have the most powerful person on the face of the Earth worried about a talk-show host. Here is a guy who allows his ego to be bruised so easily and we let him have his hands on the nuclear suitcase. That's a comforting picture.

What Rush Limbaugh did was simply state that he wanted Barack to fail and listed is reasons.

Sure enough, Barack and his minions heard (or wanted to hear) only the first part and then pretended to get all indignant. I guess it makes for some good prime-time viewing, but all it did was make Barack look foolish and Rush's popularity grow even more.

Congratulations, Barack. You have done more to generate excitement and hope among the Republicans' conservative base than George Bush and John McCain could ever hope to achieve.

But I too want to see you fail, Barack. You're taking this country down a Big- Brother, big-government, socialistic path that will lead to the destruction of this great country.

You lie about so many things, I don't think you realize you are doing it any longer. Or you do, but think you are simply above all the rules set for us normal people.

You promised the highest level of ethics in your administration and then appoint criminal after criminal to key positions. You say you don't believe in big government but then go on the biggest spending spree in history. You say you will not sign bills that have any pork in them and then go right ahead and do so. Has anyone said "Mental health check," yet?

The most deceitful one, however, is one taken from the Bill Clinton "How to Lie Convincingly" handbook.

You said in your major speech to the American people how you were going line-by-line through the federal budget to eliminate wasteful and ineffective programs.

You stated, "We have already identified $2 trillion in savings over the next decade." One of your senior officials had to back off that lie on your behalf when confronted by a reporter.

The aide said that rather than there being $2 trillion in spending cuts, the figure actually was Obama's efforts at deficit reduction. One trillion of that total represented future tax increases.

The official also said, "It also includes hundreds of billions of dollars saved by not continuing to spend $170 billion a year in Iraq." So a tax hike represents a spending reduction? Billy C. would be proud.

So yes, Barack, for the good of the future of my country I want you to fail and fail miserably.

New York Could Learn From Other States

What a difference 950 miles makes.

Anita has been researching potential areas for retirement and came up with a pretty intriguing option: Winchester, Tennessee.

To be honest, her search was somewhat biased due to her being such a garden and landscape enthusiast (I would use the term fanatic or addict instead). She was excited by the fact that we would be moving from something called a zone 4 (bad?) to a zone 7 (good?). I think it has something to do with growing seasons.

I admit she did 95 percent of the work (I was more interested in the tax and political environment), and I have learned long ago to trust her judgment. I should qualify that previous statement so as not to include political persuasions, as she is at the other end of the political spectrum. We learned long ago not to discuss politics which is one of the reasons we have been married 38 years.

So, last week we took a trip to Winchester. We were both favorably impressed. The difference between liberal New York and conservative Tennessee is dramatic, but first the weather. While upstate New York was suffering with temperatures ranging from the 40s during the day to the teens at night, Winchester was experiencing temperatures ranging from the 70's to the 50's, a huge plus for me right there.

The cost of living in Tennessee is very low. It is the third lowest-state in that category. In contrast, New York is the 5th highest. As a matter of fact, the 18 out of 21 states with the lowest cost of living statistics were states that voted Republican in the last election.

Tennessee, for example, went 57 percent to 42 percent Republican. In contrast, 24 out of 29 states with the highest cost of living were tax, spend, borrow and waste states who voted Democrat. You could probably list them yourself. As a matter of fact, the top 13 out of 14 states with the most expensive housing markets and the highest cost of food also voted Democrat.

When it comes to spending, Gov. David Patterson could learn a few things. While New York is considering more spending and higher taxes (I guess they call them fees, charges and the like to make them sound less harsh) Tennessee is considering trimming 1.5 percent from the current budget, and the governor (a Democrat, but conservative) has offered up plans to shrink the budget 12 percent in three years.

All this will be accomplished with no increase in income taxes. It should be pointed out that Tennessee's income tax taxes interest and dividends only, not wages. Compare that with New York rates. I sure did.

When it comes to housing, what we found was pretty impressive, also. We looked at quite a few parcels, either by ourselves or with an agent.

One example is a house in a nice, quiet neighborhood, walking distance to downtown, with almost a half-acre of land listed at $123,600!

The agent said it will probably sell for much less. We were thinking of offering
$100,000 and he didn't laugh. If this wasn't good enough, how about annual property
taxes of only $680!

The reason for all this fiscal conservatism is most likely due to the political makeup. Both U.S. Senators are Republicans, split representation in the House, a conservative Democrat for governor and a Republican controlled state House and Senate.

Republicans ran on a conservative agenda, and this platform is what was credited with their making gains in both the House and the Senate, giving them a constitutional majority.

In addition to their conservative spending plan and budget cutbacks, there will be no tax increases, and they will be left with untouched surplus reserves of $1.72 billion. What a unique approach. And one that is very similar to the strategy we ourselves personally have to follow.

Lastly, I have to mention the people. Everyone, without exception, was polite and friendly and went out of his or her way to offer assistance.

We went to the Chamber of Commerce to get statistics on crime and other issues, and we talked with an elderly couple staffing the office at the time. They were from the state of Michigan and had moved to Tennessee 11 years ago.

Unfortunately, the wife was a gardening enthusiast, also, making it difficult to pull my wife away.

But I don't want my "fans" to worry. I'm speaking about all those people whose skin I get under. We're only in the planning stage right now and Obama is giving me a lot to write about. How could I abandon you at this critical time?

Well, according to the Tax Foundation of Washington D.C., Monday is tax freedom day.

This is the date that, on average, we have paid off all levels of government for the year and can start keeping what we work hard for.

Basically we work 103 days for the government and allow it to keep wasting our money; and Obama, not even three months into his reign, is setting records as to the amount he wants to waste. To put it another way, we pay more in taxes than we spend on housing, food and clothing combined.

We New Yorkers even have it worse. We are ranked third-highest of all 50 states. That means all levels of government keep sucking the money out of our wallets until April 25. Only New Jersey and Connecticut are worse than we are (barely).

Great job Governor Patterson. The sooner you're out of office the better off we all are (I hope).

Alaskans had their governments paid the soonest. They're done by March 23, more than a month sooner than we are. Hmmm, now who runs Alaska? Congratulations Governor Palin. Tennessee, my eventual home state, has a freedom day of April 5th.

That makes Wednesday more important than ever. This is the day that over 3,000 towns and cities across the country will be holding their TEA (Taxed Enough Already) parties.

Haven't heard about it? Of course you haven't. Most, if not all, of the main stream media have chosen not to report about this event. Too bad our future budding journalists aren't taught to just report the news, no matter what it is, even when you don't agree with it. A class in Ethics 101 would probably help also.

Fortunately, the conventional media are becoming less and less relevant. Won't it be great when these biased, liberal bastions are out of business? It will be a great day for everyone when the New York Times, the L.A. Times, the Washington Post and others like them have to close their doors for the final time.

Back to Wednesday's TEA parties. The number of parties is growing every minute, even at this late date. You can go to taxdayteaparty.com for the complete list. There are thirty pages of cities and towns! New York state alone has more than 85 sites. Those closest to us include Albany, 11:00 to 2:00, Binghamton, 5:30 to 7:00, and, most recently, Norwich, 9:00 to noon. Many of these 3,000 plus sites are expecting numbers in the thousands.

Remember the Million Man March in 1995? The media swooned and salivated over this event, giving Louis Farrakhan all the free publicity he wanted, months in advance. Even though Louie predicted attendance of three to five million, he had to settle for numbers in the range of 400,000 to 800,000. Let's see how Wednesday's numbers compare.

Go to teapartyday.com to see the issues, in addition to repressive taxes, that will be addressed. Most common sense Americans will agree with most, if not all of them.

To list a few, the site asks, "Are you fed up with a Congress and a president who vote for a $500 billion tax bill without even reading it, are spending trillions of dollars, leaving a debt our great-grandchildren will be paying, and want to take your wealth and redistribute it to others?"

The same fed up question is also applied to social issues. Do you want a Congress and president who "force doctors and other medical workers to perform abortions against their will, want to take away the right to vote with a secret ballot in union elections, want to appoint a defender of child pornography to the No. 2 position in the Justice Department, want to punish those who practice responsible financial behavior and reward those who do not?"

Go to the site to see the other important issues. Let's go and show Barack we aren't going to stand for his version of "ethics" much longer.

So, let's see how big a success tomorrow's parties will be. Better yet, let's see
if the mainstream media report on the event, either before or after they take place.

Will they be professional and unbiased and report the facts or even the events, or will they continue to be the increasingly irrelevant supermarket rags they are becoming? Tomorrow might answer that question.

Obama's continual incompetence is giving me so much material, I think I have enough for my next ten columns.

As much as I would like to begin to write about these weaknesses, I really have to write about the recent TEA (Taxed Enough Already) parties held in all 50 states last April 15.

I attended one in Milford, New York and was truly impressed. It was organized and run by a gentleman who paid for all the costs out of his own pocket.

It was estimated that over 50 people attended, and everyone had the opportunity to express personal concerns about where this country is going and what can be done about it. The whole event was orderly, peaceful and everyone acted responsibly.

The other parties had the same result: unbelievable success. The numbers are still coming in but the latest estimates, as of were over 1 million people at over 2,500 locations.

What makes this amazing is that there was no George Soros, MoveOn.Org or Acorn group to finance and organize the events. It was truly a grass-roots effort made by thousands of normal, patriotic, tradition-believing individuals who really care about this country.

Now, the left, predictably, attempted to use lies and distortions to demean and degrade these events. Normal, intelligent people easily saw through these weak, pitiful attempts.

One of the best outcomes was that young people, the ones who overwhelmingly supported Obama, are beginning to see the real Barack rather than the one who lied and deceived his way into office.

Now that they are seeing their future and their children's futures being mortgaged away by the Obama, Reid, Pelosi cabal, they are realizing what a big mistake they made. The good news is that I am certain most of them won't allow themselves to be duped again.

This is not to say the Republicans came out of this unscathed. The event I attended held contempt for both free-spending parties, and rightfully so.

However, while the Democrats were bashing President Bush for the deficits he was creating, Obama and his cohorts in Congress, in just three months, have managed to more than triple the deficit. They have succeeded in making George W.Bush look like Ebenezer Scrooge.

Why do those on the liberal left always have to use emotion, lies, and distortions when they speak out against people who disagree with them?

The answer is pretty simple. They don't have the facts or truth on their side.

They are either scared, ignorant and most often both.

Why scared? They realize that the majority of the people in this country are center-right or right in their beliefs, and if this majority is awakened the left, and their socialist ideas, will become a thing of the past.

Why are the lefties so afraid of these TEA Parties? Lorie Byrd, in her April 14
column, listed five reasons to attend one. I'll list three.

No.1 - "You don't mind paying reasonable taxes, but you don't believe your
wealth should be spread around."

No. 2 - "You believe the 'Stimulus' bill contained too much pork and not enough stimulus." Remember when Obama promised to reduce earmarks and then permitted thousands of pork items to be signed into law?

No.3 - "You oppose the current bailout mentality and oppose bailouts, both past and future." Why reward the irresponsible actions taken by individuals and then have responsibly behaving people pay for them?

Why do these reasons makes the lefties lash out with such venom?

Now, the ignorant side of the left. Letters to the editor, on the local, state and national level, are all the same. They simply act as parrots and repeat what their leaders tell them to say.

For example, they don't make the effort to see what events, such as the TEA parties, are about. They let others form their opinions for them.

Pretty shallow, huh? There is often little thought involved. Almost all of them are irrational Bush haters, and their letters simply try to get in as many nonfactual accusations possible. It gets rather tiresome. There is no originality involved. I can buy a parrot of my own and teach it to say the foolish things Janeane Garaofolo, Keith Olbermann, CNN, Sean Penn, and many other bottom feeders spout.

What's next? Have patience. 2010 and 2012 aren't that far away, and we must be sure not to burn out before then. We must harness the energy that was created April 15, use it wisely, and talk to as many others as we can.

Rest assured, the youth of this country are tired of being indoctrinated and represent a huge source of energy to make real change happen. They, and the many other people who were fooled once, will make sure the same mistake won't be made again.

SEALs Deserve All of Our Respect

SEALs Deserve All of Our Respect

Last week, a student brought in a book for me to read entitled "Lone Survivor," a No. 1 best seller about the personal story of a U.S. Navy SEAL and his experiences in the mountains of Afghanistan.

I literally couldn't put it down until I finished it. The review that follows will probably take two columns and then I can tie it all in with Janet "from another planet" Napolitano's Department of Homeland Security report that pointedly slanders our military forces and American conservatives in general.

It begins with the author, Marcus Luttrell, sadly making a trip to visit all the families of his fallen comrades to console them and tell of his fellow SEALS' bravery; they died while he and these men carried out a sensitive and dangerous mission in Afghanistan.

It then moves on to tell the reader what the requirements are in order to become a SEAL. It is impossible for you or me to comprehend the intensive training these young men go through. Many, although totally dedicated and fit, don't make it. They don't go through all the pain and suffering of the program for monetary gain or personal recognition. They simply want to be the best of the best and serve their country to the best of their ability, willing to sacrifice their lives, if necessary, to keep you and me free and protected.

And it is not just the SEALS who are willing to go through hell to keep us safe. There are also the Green Berets, Rangers, and Delta Forces. The bravery, heroism, selflessness, and patriotism of these young Americans and other service members make you proud to know we have individuals like these defending the freedoms that we take for granted.

Unfortunately, some Americans don't give back the respect our military deserves. Fortunately, those in the service see right through this and view with disdain the liberal politicians, the liberal press and the "I support the troops but not the war" crowd.

Our soldiers are becoming more and more aware of the growing problem that faces all our forces throughout the world.

As Lattrell puts it, "For me it began in Iraq, the first murmurings from the

liberal part of the U.S.A. that we were somehow in the wrong, brutal killers, bullying other countries; that we who put our lives on the line for our nation at the behest of our government should somehow be charged with murder for shooting our enemy. It has been an insidious progression, the criticisms of the Armed Forces from politicians and from the liberal media (and liberals in general) which know nothing of combat, nothing of our training, and nothing of

180

the mortal dangers we face out there on the front line. We constantly had in the back of our minds the ever-intrusive rules of engagement."

These rules of engagement are drawn up by some air-headed politician sitting safely in his Washington office "a very long way from the battlefield, where the slightest mistake can cost you your life."

SEALS, contrary to what John Kerry and others say, are not stupid individuals; and they, more than most Americans, read the press stories coming from the American media.

Lattrell takes issue with "serving members of the armed forces who have been charged with murder in civilian courts for doing what they thought was their duty, attacking their enemy."

The rules are very straightforward. Don't open fire until being fired upon or have determined who the enemy is and have proof of his intentions. Sounds very noble, doesn't it? The author saw how these rules worked in his specific case, and it resulted in costing the lives "of three of the finest SEALS who have ever served." There is no way you can ever convince me, or them, that all those sign-waving, quote-spieling groups care one bit.

Lastly, for this column, let me tell you what additional fear these men have when they go into combat against the Taliban or al-Qaida.

"The fear of our own, the fear of what our own Navy judge advocate general might rule against us, the fear of the American media and their unfortunate effect on American politicians. We all harbor fears about untrained, half-educated journalists who only want a good story to justify their salaries and expense accounts. Don't think it is just me. We all detest them, partly for their lack of judgment, mostly because of their ignorance and toe-curling opportunism. When the media gets involved, in the United States, that's a war you have a damned good chance of losing, because the restrictions on us are immediately amplified, and that's sensationally good news for our enemy."

Truer words have never been spoken.

The Military Deserves More Respect

Just a little more on the book "Lone Survivor" by Marcus Luttrell, Navy SEAL. He continues to describe what the military are up against.

It gets very discouraging for them to pick up a paper and read about our politicians degrading the military. We all remember the Haditha Marines who were accused of murder. Jack Murtha jumped out front (with Kennedy, Kerry and Reid close behind), and with absolutely no facts, declared them guilty.

It got even worse. He called our military rapists, murderers, and uncontrolled criminals. Predictably, the lapdog media loved it and aggressively ran with it.

Remember, there were no facts known about the incident, there hadn't been any trial, and no evidence had been presented, but that didn't matter to the media and our leftist, anti-American politicians.

Lo and behold, the charges turned out to be false. Seven marines were acquitted, and one had the charges reduced. Egg on the accusers' faces? Of course. The sense of honor to apologize and retract? Of course not. Murtha sure didn't feel any need to.

And the main stream media wonder why more and more people are seeking other outlets to get the truth? If they don't wake up soon, they will simply follow the path of the New York Times into oblivion and irrelevance. Actually, I sort of hope they don't wake up.

Luttrell hits the nail on the head when he says, "In the military, if we don't know something, we say we don't and proceed to shut up until we do. Some highly paid charlatans in the media (and politics) think it's absolutely fine to take a wild guess at the truth and then tell a couple of million people it's a cast-iron fact, just in case they might be right." Do you really believe they have these special undisclosed "sources" that for integrity purposes must remain so? I don't anymore.

Bad things are bound to happen in war. It is not a game where you keep score and have umpires, regardless of what the politicians think. Occasionally the wrong people get killed. But what rules are you to play under when you are facing murderous, monstrous terrorists who will do anything possible to kill as many military and innocent Americans?

When two of Luttrell's comrades were dying, the Taliban emptied clips of ammunition into their faces so they couldn't be recognized. This apparently is a common practice of the Taliban when they find a wounded or dying soldier. Then you say the Geneva Convention rules apply to these monsters? Give me a break. Won't it be nice when we start working as aggressively to protect the rights of our soldiers at least as much as we do these terrorists?

Another quote from the book: "I am hopeful that one day soon, the government will learn that we can be trusted. We know about bad guys, what they do, and, often, who they are. The politicians have chosen to send us into battle, and that's our trade. We do what's necessary. And in my view, once these politicians have elected to send us out to do what 99.9 percent of the country would be terrified to undertake, they should get the hell out of the way and stay there."

Of course the bad things should be reported, but not sensationalized. When the media start reporting the thousands and thousands of good deeds done by our military, the public will see how extremely isolated the actions of a few bad apples are.

So who do you think deserves the higher level of credibility and respect? The combat soldier actually out on the field of battle and experiencing all of the unspeakable horrors that go with it, or the people who legislate and report in the safe little confines protected under the freedoms kept safe by our military?

Marcus Lattrell and others like him deserve our respect. He is a decorated warrior who earned the Navy Cross for combat heroism. He has the right to speak out and be heard. Other people haven't earned our trust and respect quite yet. Unfortunately, the persons who need to read this book the most are those who will be too obstinate to do so. Fortunately, the vast majority of Americans respect men and women like Marcus Lattrell and our military.

A physician friend of mine asked that I point out a piece of history that occurred last week. After the president's weekly radio address, the opposing party is allowed to reply with a rebuttal. The doctor proudly pointed out that for the first time in the history of radio, the opposing party was represented by an orthopedic surgeon, Sen. John Basso, from Wyoming. Now he owes me

Cheney Is In the Right

I think the Democrat's, Barack "shoot from the lip" Obama, and "Queen" Nancy
Pelosi in particular, learned some valuable lessons recently.

They learned the hard way not to go up against a Republican who has a backbone, experience, ethics, a protect-Americans-first philosophy, and the truth on his side. That person is Dick Cheney.

All Cheney did was simply state that America was less safe under Obama than it was under President Bush. He was sick and tired of all the insulting comments made by Barack and the Democrats, attacking Bush and Cheney, and wanting to treat them as criminals. And the Democrats didn't like it when Cheney pushed back.

Obama, in a childish, immature snit, actually put our security in danger simply to make a political point. He irresponsibly caused the release of classified interrogation reports describing the procedures used on terrorists but conveniently forgot to also release the follow-up reports that showed how critical these methods were in obtaining valuable information, information that probably saved thousands of American lives.

Cheney simply demanded these follow-up reports also be released so that the public saw the entire picture, not the less than ethical half truths Obama wanted them to see, letting them decide who was telling the truth and who was lying.

Lo and behold, Obama, like all liberals do when exposed, immediately backed down. This guy is becoming easier and easier to catch deceiving people, and I am having less and less concern that he will last longer than his present four-year reign. I am concerned, however, as to how long it will take for the country to heal itself from his poorly thought out, destructive goals he wants to accomplish.

Now let's us turn to Nancy Pelosi. Talk about an embarrassment to the party. Here is a typical liberal Bush-hater who is so desperate to tarnish the Bush legacy that she will revert to anything that could possibly bring this about.

She willingly took up the Chris Dodd call for "Truth Commissions" to be held in order to prosecute and throw in jail those in the Bush Administration who allowed these enhanced interrogation methods to be used on our enemies.

She (and other radical lefties in the Democrat Party) feigned moral outrage, and manufactured indignity, about these methods of "torture" and her wild stories of CIA lying to her and Congress got her into some pretty hot water during one of her recent weekly press conferences.

I actually enjoyed watching her make a fool of herself by stammering, stuttering and tying herself into knots as she tried to respond to reporters' questions about what she knew and when did she know that water boarding was being used on terrorists.

She claimed that the CIA had lied to her in a September 2002 briefing, saying, "We were told specifically that waterboarding was not being used."

Unfortunately for Nancy, truthfulness is a foreign concept. Also unfortunate for her is that the reporters didn't let her off the hook with her wacky answers.

When her first explanation didn't fly she said "I wasn't briefed. I was informed that someone else had been briefed about it."

It was simply lie after lie, and it eventually caught up to her. Other members of Congress remembered her being there when they were briefed about the methods being used. The CIA released a chart that showed a minimum of 13 briefings at which she had been present, where specific mention about waterboarding took place.

Former CIA Director Porter Goss said the CIA provided truthful information to Pelosi and others. He also stated that during the briefings, the members asked if enough was being done, meaning, should even more harsh techniques than waterboarding be used?

Leon Panetta, the current CIA director, agreed with the Goss version of events. Now you can say that Goss was being partisan because he's a Republican, but Panetta was appointed to the position by Obama and hardly a Bush lover. He has to carry some credibility.

Nancy finally just stormed out and said she was finished with answering questions. In desperation, she flew off to China to discuss global warming. Pretty pathetic.

Hopefully the House Democrats will get a backbone and realize she is a detriment to their party and vote her out of the Speaker's position. She only won the Speakership originally by a 118 to 95 vote and she has to be in a much weaker position now.

Everyone is pretty much laughing at poor Nancy now. From CNN and the Washington Post to the Wall Street Journal, they are all piling on. Even Jay Leno and Jimmy Fallon now have lots of joke material about her on their programs (Google "Nancy Pelosi jokes").

Go away Nancy, just go away.

How Long Till Obama Is Booted

I'm wondering how long it will be before the word "Impeachment" starts being bantered about? The list of reasons to expel Obama keeps getting longer and stronger, and this is only five months into his reign.

Everyone knows about his inexperience. His rhetorical abilities made people overlook this weakness. Even his eligibility to have become president is becoming an issue.

He places personal and party ideologies over what is best for America. I thought when appointing justices it was supposed to be "the best person for the job" and "justice is blind." Affirmative action policies and "empathy" aren't part of the requirements for appointment.

He fits the definition of being a narcissist perfectly. This makes him extremely dangerous for the country. He only cares about what is best for him, and not the country.

He is ashamed of our country (as was his wife until Barack won his party's nomination) even though it has given him immense amounts of opportunity. He constantly feels the need to apologize for our country's history of perceived repressiveness.

Sorry Barack, we are the greatest country in the history of the world. No country has done more for other countries where there has been suppression of human rights, and Americans are unmatched in raising money and necessary supplies for others when natural disasters hit. You have been hanging around the Reverend (?) Wright and Bill Ayers too long.
You have been going around (the Muslim world in particular), speaking of "the promise of a secular nation." How much more arrogant and ignorant can you be!

Even though you think highly of your rhetorical skills, you are not going to change the fact that a vast majority of Americans believe in God. Why do you keep implying to other countries that our country was not founded on Judeo-Christian principles?

Your history of duplicity is unmatched. This was illustrated numerous times throughout the campaign. You carry it forward into your presidency.

You incur the largest-ever budget deficit and then insist that we operate on a pay-as-you-go principle from now on. Of course, shortly thereafter, you exempt your government-run health program costs from this rule. You are great with smoke and mirrors, Barack. You are the ultimate flim-flam man.

You are a corrupt man. You appoint tax cheats and disreputable people to positions of power. You promise no lobbyists in your administration, yet no other administration had close to the number you now have.

You fire people who uncover very serious issues of impropriety by organizations run by individuals who are close friends of yours. You had your Justice Department cancel a criminal suit against goons, representing your friends ACORN and the Black Panthers, involving voter intimidation tactics at election polls.

You are dishonest and lie when it serves your purposes. Including examples above, you ridiculed John McCain's idea of taxing employer-funded health insurance premiums, promising never to follow such a policy during your administration.

Change your mind, Obama? You promised no tax increases for individuals making under $250,000. What do you call proposals like getting rid of tax-excludable programs like Health Savings Accounts and Flexible Spending Accounts?

Millions of middle and low income individuals participate in these programs. What do you call new taxes proposed on soda and beer? I guess only the rich drink these.

You are proposing one of the large increases in corporate taxes in history. Who do you think ends up paying for these increased costs of doing business? I think these mentioned items also fall under the topic of incompetence. And I thought we could never get a leader less competent than Jimmy Carter. I was wrong.

How about your lying to the American Medical Association? You specifically said, "I'll be honest, there are countries where a single-payer system works pretty well." Why couldn't your press secretary name just one when pressed for an example?

Why did your main stream media stooges, especially The Washington Post, The New York Times and the Los Angeles Times, specifically leave that quote out of their news articles, but quote everything said before and after that part of your speech perfectly?

You continually show disrespect for and trample on our Constitution, especially when it bars you from enacting your most radical ideas.

There is hope however. Sixty-six percent of the voters from age 18 to 30 voted for you while only 32 percent voted for McCain. Voters 30 and above, on the other hand, favored you by a margin of only 50 percent to 49 percent.

Do you think you can fool the younger voting bloc twice Barack? I don't think so, especially when they see the impact of your socialist agenda on their lives. Maybe we aren't going to have to wait another 31/2 years for "change."

Too Much Government Is a Problem

Last Saturday, I attended a second local TEA Party. This one was held at Losie's on Oneonta's Southside.

Once again I was impressed with the organization of the event and the probably 200 normal, patriotic, good Americans who simply wanted to say they have had enough of too much government.

This event was about three times larger than the one held in Milford earlier this year, and it seems the thousands of similar gatherings across the United States experienced the same kind of growth. Atlanta had over 12,000 attendees.

No one can say that this was a nationally coordinated Republican Party event. The media and the left will try, but they are simply lying. They are afraid this movement will continue growing.

Rather, it was an event where ordinary people - Republicans, Democrats, and Independents - simply wanted to express their feelings and frustrations about the direction in which our government and our politicians are going.

Thank you to those who put in the necessary hours to make the event happen and the many people who took the time to attend. It was certainly a success. Congratulations Tim and Jim.

There are certainly many actions our politicians have in progress that should make ordinary Americans very nervous and angry.

As we have all seen just this last week, House members acted very irresponsibly by ignoring the majority of their constituents' feelings and passing the Waxman-Markey Cap-and –Trade Bill. This bill and its related amendment, 1,000 and 300 plus pages respectively, are ones they hadn't even read before voting on it.

It was exactly the same situation with the economic stimulus package passed earlier this year. No one read it before it was voted on. As a result of that fiasco, we are discovering every day more and more pork hidden in it.

Can anyone tell me how this is responsible representation? I think not. This is the kind of action you can expect to have happen when the Democrats are in charge, especially when you have radical left-wing leadership in both houses and the White House.

I was one of the probably few news junkies who actually watched the Cap-and- Trade Bill vote occur. The House membership is made up of 253 Democrats and 178 Republicans. The final vote looked to be very close when the count was 219 for the bill and 212 against. Nothing could be further from the truth. With 12 Democrats left to vote out of a total of 253, with only minutes left, only 8 had voted against the bill. When the final tally was taken 44 Dems had voted against it.

What courage! What conviction! Instead of basing their vote on conviction of principle, they had to wait first to see if the bill had a chance of failing or not before they timidly switched their votes to against the measure, apparently to appease their constituents and save their elected seats.

Why should a person be allowed to switch his or her vote after casting it? I hope the people whom these congresspersons represent are able to see right through this act of shallow political maneuvering, and especially remember their behavior November 2010.

We now have a bill going to the Senate that would be a disaster for our economy. The Congressional Budget Office estimates that the poorest 20 percent of families could experience their annual energy costs to increase by $700 while other families could experience increases of up to $2,200 annually.

These estimates are only for 2012, the year when the bill's provisions kick in. Families, especially low income families, are already stretched to the limit! Where's the sympathy, Barack? Pay attention to the working class. You are not a community activist anymore. You've got to grow up.

Did I also mention that it is estimated that we will lose approximately $400 billion a year in gross domestic product? How about the estimate of 1.1 million NET jobs lost each year?

No Barack, we can't count saved jobs that the Department of Labor has already
stated can't be measured.

Oh yes, I almost forgot. Since China and India aren't in any way required to restrict their carbon output levels, this bill's passage will result in a decrease of a tiny 0.1 degree Fahrenheit by 2050 instead of doing nothing. This was testimony by a research climatologist by the name of Paul Knappenberger.

So there you go libs. You are soon going to have to defend the policies of this incompetent, inexperienced, unqualified, man-child that you elected to be your leader.
And to make matters worse, you aren't going to be able to blame the Bush/Cheney administration for all this anymore. People will just laugh at you. I can't wait to hear what you have to say.

One of the hard parts of traveling is finding the time to write my column. I have to admit, I'm a news junkie, and USA Today and some of the local papers just don't cut it.

I was talking to our Tennessee real estate broker and asked him where I could find some New York papers and he just laughed. I wasn't expecting that response, and it made me think twice about relocating in Winchester.

Anyway, this column will touch on a variety of topics. First up, the Senate confirmation hearings for Sonia Sotomayor.

Everyone knows she will be confirmed. The script went exactly as planned. Sonia ran away from the tough questions, was evasive on the others, and the senators strutted and preened for the cameras.

I was looking forward to seeing Al Franken look foolish, and I wasn't disappointed. The failed host of the failed liberal talk station, Air America Radio, had a deep intellectual discussion with the judge about Perry Mason. Way to go Al. Way to go Minnesota.

Finally, there was Arlen Specter. What an embarrassment! He stuttered, stammered and was pretty much incoherent during his time of questioning. I'm so glad he finally, officially, switched parties.

The top five oldest senators are Democrats, with the young Arlen No. 5 at 79. Now, the age is ok, but don't these guys have anything else to do besides acting foolishly?

Robert Byrd, the undistinguished senator from West Virginia and past Kleagle and Exalted Cyclops (where do these clowns come up with these titles?) of the KKK, leads everyone in age, 91, and incompetence.

Even scarier is the fact that as president pro tempore of the Senate, he is third in line of presidential succession. That makes an all-star succession lineup of Biden, Pelosi and Byrd, in that order, to replace Obama if anything happens to him.

Anyway, Sonia will be confirmed, and I hope she will be less left-of-center than David Souter was. If there is anything positive to result from these proceedings, I guess that's the best I can come up with.

Now, when are the worshipers of Barack "The Pied Piper" Obama going to admit they made a mistake? All I want his followers to do is question his lies, distortions and dangerous policies.

You simply cannot justify his "cap and trade" boondoggle where the increased taxes are going to fall directly on the 95 percent of working families he promised would not see a penny in new taxes under his reign.

In addition to further increasing unemployment and significantly decreasing economic output, he is placing an annual burden of between $700 and $2,200 on these families.

How can you justify the $787 billion stimulus bill that is stimulating nothing but the special interests that supported him? $400 billion of the package was classified as pure pork, $200 billion went to special interests, and only 7.7 percent has been expended.

Remember how important it was to rush this bill through Congress? People, the economy will recover from the recession as it has with all previous ones. If anything, the stimulus package is seriously slowing this from happening.

How can you fans justify the socialized health care proposal that is going to further bankrupt the country with its $1.5 trillion cost (Congressional Budget Office)? He is trying desperately to get this farce through Congress before the 2010 congressional campaigns begin, hoping that people will forget how their congressperson voted. Not gonna happen.

And finally, please explain to me your silence relating to Obama's$3.6 trillion
fiscal 2010 budget that will result in an unheard of $1.26 trillion deficit.
You libs and Dems have got to stop following this failure like lemmings following each other off the cliff. You can't act like parrots and keep repeating "it's Bush's fault" over and over again.
Sorry guys, people with common sense don't buy that blather anymore. Just because Barack keeps repeating this mantra doesn't mean you have to behave like zombies and follow along.
I want to thank all those who responded to my column of four weeks ago. It was the most popular column since I began writing. As usual, I got some crazies who responded, but they were by far the minority (121 to 6).

I even had one delusional fellow who simply made up his own facts. His best one was that Barack still had a 70 percent approval rating! I think his research is limited to the White House press releases. All the independent polls have Barack with a 51 percent to 57 percent approval rating, and slipping daily.

Thank heavens for the independent voters. They will (if they haven't already)
see the light.

It's hard to follow what is happening in the U.S. being here in Romania, but it is quite easy to see that politicians are having a heck of a time trying to sell the idea of "Obamacare" to their constituents.

They have no idea what is even in the bill since they haven't read it. Whenever asked a specific question, they mumble something incoherent and try to move to another topic as quickly as possible.

Many of those people who have read it say we should be scared of what the bill includes. And these same politicians are going to vote on something representing one- sixth of our economy and affecting nearly every U.S. citizen? It might have worked with the cap and trade bamboozle, but not this time.

Obama himself is in full campaign mode, armed with his teleprompter, charm and rhetorical excesses, and telling everyone that opponents of the bill are lying and using scare tactics to defeat his proposal.

Excuse me, Barack. What is a pathological liar doing calling other people liars? Your image comes to mind when that old saying, "you can tell he's lying whenever his lips are moving" is used.

Scare tactics being unfairly used? Excuse me once again, Barack. You have used scare tactics (the Chicken Little, sky-is-falling strategy) to get legislation passed ever since you entered office.

Sorry, Obama, you're like the little shepherd boy who cried wolf once too often. More and more people every day are simply beginning to ignore you. It's too bad you didn't show your true colors while you were still running for office. The country wouldn't be in anywhere near the perilous position you have put us in.

Ok Barack, lead by example.   Will you be the first to sign up for your
government run (don't even bother to try to label it anything else) health care plan?

Will you promise not to receive special treatment and allow your loved ones to jump to the front of the line in an emergency? If not, explain to me why your loved ones are any more important than mine? How about you Kennedy, Kerry, Byrd, Dodd, Pelosi? I pose the same question to all of you. We all know you'll "think about it" or ignore the question altogether. We know your answer and your actions will be poles apart.

It might be time for normal citizens to take off their gloves and get serious. I don't really care how big some people want our government to become. Neither do I care how much of a nanny state some want. There are certain lines a government should not step over. One of those lines is determining who gets medical treatment and who doesn't.

Another is having them put a value on our economic worth. And the final line is allowing politicians and bureaucrats determine who will live and who will die.

Does the government really think that I, and millions of others like me, will stand idly by and allow you to prevent my wife or my sons from receiving a medicine or a procedure that exists and that would prolong their lives? It just isn't going to happen.

There most certainly will be serious consequences as a result. Do some of you people want to have your parents, grandparents, people who have lived a long and honest, law-abiding life, be told that they aren't worth the cost of being kept alive? Think about it from a personal perspective before you answer.

Personally, I would consider it to be the same as an attack on the lives of my loved ones. How would you expect me, or others to respond?

I think it is time for these elitist politicians, on both sides of the aisle, to realize that we citizens (and not illegal aliens) are important more than just at re-election time.

We are the most important people in their political careers all of the time. They were elected to speak and act on our behalf, not to think they know better than we do about what is best or be swayed (paid?) by special interests when they go against what the majority of their constituents want.

Be very careful Mr. Politician, Mr. Bureaucrat, Mr. Obama. There are political consequences.

Taxes OK If They Are Used Well

Radu Cristea is a very good Romanian friend from Cluj-Napoca and has been indispensable in the work I am doing there. It would have been almost impossible for me to have accomplished anything without his advice and unselfish assistance.

Radu is a successful entrepreneur and small businessman and has his finger on the pulse of everyday Romanian life

I asked him to write something for me that reflects his opinion on taxes and public health care in his country. After making massive cuts to his original article, this is what he came up with. I hope you enjoy it.

I'm not upset for paying taxes. I don't have a problem that taxation is so high for small businesses – even though small and medium sized companies are the engine that moves the economy forward.

I mean, after all, we do need a strong national revenue. If a company is taxed, it pays a part of its income or profits to the government so the government can pay for public services such as education, health care, military and police.

Paying all these taxes would not bother me at all if the money would go to the right places, where it's needed the most. However, finding out about overpriced acquisitions for government contracts delivered to certain politicians through companies owned by their wives, sons or relatives deeply disturbs me.

Seeing the poor quality of the centralized health care system and the low remuneration that doctors get also deeply disturbs me. I see the government wasting money like crazy, and this drives me nuts.

Now, as I said, the government collects taxes and then distributes the funds to all public services, including health care. The Romanian health care system has been in existence since 1700, and it has had many an unsung hero since. During the 1828 plague in Bucharest, 21 out of 26 died of plague whilst administering treatment for the disease.

Today, I can frankly say that the health care system is ill, very ill, and will probably die soon unless urgent measures are taken. Despite the high taxation, health care is dangerously underfunded, which causes problems.

Hospitals owe money to medical suppliers and make partial payment to laboratories so they can survive. The Romanian Association of Medical Product Suppliers even threatens to cut deliveries to several hospitals in the country. Despite the suppliers' sympathy for the problems of the Romanian health system, they are ready to turn off the switch.

On a personal level, even though I'm entitled, as a taxpayer, to free medical care, I would still have my wife give birth in a private clinic and gladly pay for that. It's not that the doctors in the state's health care system aren't great professionals. It is just that health care is generally poor by European standards.

Underpaid doctors have the tendency to either accept or even request certain financial benefits from their patients. For example, my friend who is eight-months pregnant has already made an appointment to give birth at a private clinic, but not before checking out a regular, government-funded hospital.

She found that in the state hospital she would have to bring a lot of things – including aspirin and a piece of cloth that the doctors would use to wipe the baby right after birth.

Besides this and the poor look of the hospital, she also found out that she should grease the squeaky wheels of the system by giving 500 Euros to the doctor and another 200 or so to the nurses that would deliver her child into the world.

Why the bribe? So they can take better care of her and the baby.

Now, on the other hand, the fee at the private clinic she is going to is 1,000 Euros. The clinic looks much nicer and has better equipment. The staff is great, and all she needs to bring are just clothes for the newborn baby. She will be paying the private clinic's fee because it's the better choice.

Could you imagine for a second how frustrating this is? I mean you pay for medical care with your taxes all your life; but when you need to benefit from that money, you find out that you need to pull more money out of your pocket just to be treated normally.

Centralized health care doesn't work. In a private health care system, you have
choices you can make on your own money.

When you pay revenue to the government and it decides how the funds are distributed to health care, you have no control over your money. You can't make decisions on how that money is being spent.

Despite my belief that everyone should have access to health care, I do believe that private, independent health care is the best.

I had to wait to write this column until Obama's ego was assuaged by giving yet another prime time campaign speech. He wanted bipartisanship yet continually scolded Republicans and conservatives.

Yes, Joe Wilson was right, Obama doesn't let facts get in the way, and he has no problem telling untruths in order to advance what he wants. We should be used to this by now.

Yes, in many ways he is enjoyable to watch. He has all the moves down pat. He is a great reader of the teleprompter, he does have charisma, and he still thinks these skills are going to get him anything he wants.

Fortunately, ordinary people who got fooled once are starting to see right through him. Just take a look at his plunging approval ratings and his soaring disapproval scores. But yet he plods on. As is his typical style, great rhetoric but no substance.

But, almost everyone, except for Obama, the main stream media (who are becoming more irrelevant each day), and the liberal left wing of the Democrat Party realizes that a change of such magnitude should be taken slowly, cautiously, and in phases.

He has pretty much used up his political capital and should have thought of this before he wasted it on his failed stimulus bill and his soon-to-fail cap- and-trade legislation.

The Republicans have a lot of good advice for you, but you haven't been bothered to listen to them at all since last April or May. Please define bipartisanship for me once more Barack. Here's some advice for you.

Baby steps, Barack, baby steps. An outline first and then I'll expand.

1.	Tort reform. I know you are in the front pocket of those ambulance chasing malpractice trial lawyers, but you have to give more than lip service to it. You don't think it is a little laughable to appoint your Health and Human Services secretary to run trial tests, on a small scale, in several states when for many years she was the director of the Kansas Trial Lawyers Association? Only you could not see the irony in that. Also, start to show our medical professionals the respect they deserve. They are not a commodity but dedicated individuals who you consistently accuse of lining their pockets with profits from unnecessary tests and procedures. You know that is simply not true Barack, and I am going to hammer you hard on that one in a later column.

2.	Medicare and Medicaid waste and fraud. Why don't you prove that the government is up to taking care of this problem before you try to convince us that the government can be a beacon of efficiency on a much grander scale? I can't wait to see how you are going to get $544 billion of savings out of this program. You never seem to be able or willing to tell us the specifics.

3.	Stop lying about the number of uninsured. You know that 46 or 47 million individuals involuntarily without insurance coverage is blatantly not true. Why do you need 1000 plus pages of legalese to cover the more accurate figure of 10 to 15 million truly uninsured? Darn those facts, huh, Barack?

4.	Open up competition on a national level so that there is more free- market activity between many more insurance companies, rather than the monopoly of two or three companies in each state. I guess your experience with ACORN and your radical associations didn't teach you much about free market capitalism.

5.	Stop lying about not funding illegal aliens or abortions. If this was true, as you say it is, why did your radical Democrat leadership disallow very plain, clear cut amendments to make this certain?

6.	Stop lying about a single-payer system that is not government run. This is what you have preferred all along and have called for it repeatedly, even well before you campaigned. Your bait and switch, smoke and mirror tricks aren't going to hide this one.

7.	Finally, there are plenty of ways to use our tax code to provide deductions and credits so that it will be easier and less costly for individuals to provide for their own insurance coverage IF they want it.

So Barack, it looks like I'm going to have a lot of fun these next few columns. I promise I will only use facts to back myself up.

I thought at one time Jimmy Carter was going down in history as the worst president ever and that you were simply going to be "Carter lite." I think I got it wrong. Jimmy is going to end up as "Barack lite." For the sake of the country let's hope your history is limited to 4 years.

In my last column I listed many ways that would allow Congress to move slowly, cautiously, and responsibly in trying to implement some kind of health care reform. I'll try to use the next one or two columns to expand on those possibilities.

First, nothing gets off the ground unless Congress and Obama make a serious attempt at medical malpractice tort reform. We are talking about billions of dollars saved annually and very easy to implement.

However, nothing happens until Obama and the radical leftist leadership in Congress decide to stop playing politics and start leading. Please do what is best for the country rather than what is best for your party, special interests, trial attorneys, who are presently pulling your strings.

What does Obama do? On one hand he gives tort reform a few lines in his reading to a joint session of Congress and, of all things, he wants this area to proceed slowly. On the other hand, he has demanded a speedy, successful conclusion to his monstrous, irresponsible, and expensive health care reform proposal he is presently trying to shove down our throats. His shallow rhetoric is starting to be recognized by people for what it really is: empty and untruthful.

And then, on top of everything, he announces he is going to appoint his Health and Human Services Secretary Kathleen Sebelius to head the demonstration projects involving limited tort reform in certain states. Conveniently, Kathleen was, for many years, the director of the Kansas Trial Lawyers Association! Barack, Kathleen, you don't need to run any trial tests. You have two states who have successfully implemented reform. Texas, who had a 30 percent drop in medical malpractice insurance premiums, and California, which had a 40 percent reduction. Both states, which were facing serious shortages in medical professionals, both primary care physicians and certain specialists, had doctors rushing back to these states.

The costs and consequences of doing nothing are huge! A study done in 2005 by the Joint Economic Committee of the U.S. Congress showed 80 percent of all medical liability claims filed aren't associated with injuries as a result of physician negligence. Of all claims made 61 percent are dismissed, 32 percent are settled without a trial (both involving large costs), 6 percent of claims result in a verdict for the defense and only 1 percent result in a verdict for the plaintiff.

This settlement percentage sounds good except that physicians have to incur very large legal fees just to defend themselves. Their costs average $17,000 for dismissed cases, $40,000 for settled cases, and even $86,000, just to mount a successful defense. And these costs don't reflect the costs of their lost revenues, significant time away from their practices, permanent damages to their reputation and the resulting adversarial relationships with their patients (understandably so).

Who pays for these malpractice premiums? Health care providers logically have to pass them on to insured individuals. How would you like to spend eight or more years after your undergraduate college experience and be burdened with probably well over $200,000 in college loans and facing annual malpractice premiums of between
$100,000 and $500,000 a year before even considering all the other extensive costs of starting and running your practice of medicine?

The committee estimated that costs of malpractice premiums passed on averaged about $87 per insured and $350 annually for a family of four. Reductions of these amounts to individuals' insurance just might make a difference in being able to afford health insurance.

If that doesn't impress you, add to that the costs of defensive medicine (additional tests and procedures called for to avoid litigation rather than being necessary for the patient), which are between three and six times greater than the above malpractice insurance costs being passed on. You certainly cannot blame a physician for protecting him/herself from such career ending risks.

Other consequences of doing nothing about tort reform? How about doctors retiring early, relocating to doctor friendly states or simply discontinuing their practices? How about individuals reconsidering their decision to even enter the medical field? There is already a serious shortage of qualified health professionals, and out of control malpractice costs along with defensive medicine practices will only aggravate the present situation. Research shows those hurt most by the skyrocketing costs of malpractice premiums are low income individuals, women, and those living in rural areas.

So Barack, be a leader for once and get out of your campaign mode. You wanted the medical profession to give you $300 billion in savings to put towards your plan over the next decade. Five to ten times this amount can be saved through responsible medical malpractice tort reform and all the related indirect costs associated with it.

Things are looking up for the conservative side of the Republican Party. No one could have predicted the overwhelming success of the two TEA parties held earlier this year. And then to top that success we had the overwhelming turnout for the March on Washington September 12.

The estimates from responsible sources numbered the crowd in Washington to be between 1.5 and 2 million people. As Bob Parks, a conservative Republican, said "It had to be around two million people because we never saw the end of the march. The Park Service likes it whenever conservatives gather at the Washington Mall because, unlike their ideological counterparts, they were orderly and there was no litter to be seen afterwards." It really doesn't matter how the White house, Nancy Pelosi or Harry Reid pooh-poohed the gatherings. They are becoming more and more insignificant by the day. But they are scared.

All you have to do is look at the wealth of facts on our side. Conservative TV is growing more dominant by the day. The latest survey had Fox News drawing a larger audience than MSNBC and CNN combined.

Conservative newspapers are also getting stronger and aren't having the same
advertising dollar problems as their liberal, main stream competition.

The Pew Research Center found that 63 percent of those surveyed find the information in the main stream media is often inaccurate, only 29 percent agree that "the media usually get the facts right," and only 26 percent agree that news sources, the main stream media, even make an attempt to keep their reporting politically unbiased.

Conservative radio talk show hosts are also dominating and growing stronger. Can anyone name a liberal talk show host that is economically viable? Check out the top ten hosts before you even try.

And how about conservative authors? Every new book written by a conservative shoots to the top of the best seller list. I bet the NY Times and its best seller list loves that.

Sarah Palin's book has sold over 1.5 million copies and it hasn't even been printed yet! Who do the liberals have? Michael Moore of course. Check out the success of his books and movies, in spite of all the awards Hollywood gives him.

We conservatives do have to be careful about the danger of letting our excitement and enthusiasm burn us out before the 2010 and 2012 election periods. These are watershed events that we, and our country, can't afford to lose.

Actually we don't have to do much at all. The liberal leftist leadership in Congress, along with the man-child in the White House just keep shooting themselves in the foot. It's like watching a Keystone Kops episode, except the bumbling ineptness and incompetence are going to seriously harm this country. Let's hope the damage isn't permanent.

Just look at the cap and trade legislation that will add between $1,000 and
$2,000 to the average family in new energy costs (taxes).

Another failure is the $787 billion stimulus package that Barack said must be passed or else unemployment would exceed 8 percent. Since we are at an unemployment rate that will soon surpass 10 percent and seriously impede an economic recovery, maybe our representatives should have read the bill before voting for it. The only things stimulated were Democrat special interest groups and pork projects. It has failed miserably and now Obama wants a second stimulus package passed!

Cash for clunkers? It was supposed to save the environment by getting CO_2 spewing vehicles off the highway. One estimate is that the program will save 0.04 percent of CO_2 emissions. This is the equivalent of two days emissions over the next decade.

Also, 59 percent of the cars purchased through the program were foreign made. All this for a cost of "only" $1.4 billion to us taxpayers. And the list of failures goes on and on.

So we must start a list of the promises broken and failed programs and not let the voters forget as election time nears. The liberals will once again talk like conservatives because they know that's the only chance they have of getting re-elected. We have to hold them accountable for their previous actions. We must call them on their voting history, not their promises.

We simply have to calmly present the data to common sense thinking Americans and independent voters. We have the truth on our side. The only things the liberal leftist crowd have on their side (to their detriment), is their loudness and their emotional, frenzied, in-your-face outbursts.

They will only get louder as our momentum builds, and it is time for our side to not sit around and take it anymore. It is time for us to be heard also. We can't let these ideologues get away with lying any longer.

Others More Deserving of Nobel Peace Prize

Albert Schweitzer, The Dalai Lama, Andrei Sakharov, Anwar Sadat, Menachim Begin, Martin Luther King, Mother Teresa, Lech Walesa, and Eli Wiesel. These, along with many other deserving individuals, were the type of persons who used to win the Nobel Peace Prize.

Now look what that selection committee has become. Even before this month, it had lost all credibility. Yassar Arafat, who won in 1993, was a signal of problems to come.

For years most of the Western world described him as the world's No. 1 terrorist. He was also the corrupt leader of the political faction of Fatah right up to his death.

Laughingly, in 2002 they gave the award to Jimmy Carter simply for speaking out against George Bush. Mohamed ElBaradei followed in 2005.

Then the most ridiculously shallow and politically motivated selection (to that date) took place in 2007. Al Gore, another person rewarded for simply being a President Bush hater (and sore loser), won the prize. The Committee had to come up with some reason for their decision, so he was rewarded for making a very nice PowerPoint presentation about poor polar bears floating on icebergs and the global warming myth.

Just when I thought the Nobel Committee couldn't make itself look more foolish and non-credible, it did just that. By selecting Obama as this year's winner, it made itself look idiotic, and in turn Obama has made himself look the same for accepting it.

So many past winners have done so much more and have risked and even sacrificed their lives in their pursuit of a better and more peaceful world. What has Obama done? Absolutely nothing! He is full of rhetoric and empty of substance. His selection was a joke. You have to remember the nomination deadline was February first, a mere 11 days after he had taken office!

Columnist Kevin McCullough said it best. "Obama is getting used by the international elitists who have hatred in their heart for an America that is both strong and good. He is getting played like a puppy who is having a treat given to him for sitting still."

The left was as harsh, if not more so, than the right. Michael Russnow, who even campaigned for Obama, wrote on the Huffington Post, "Whatever happened to awarding for deeds actually done?" The Washington Post: "It's an odd Nobel Peace Prize that almost makes you embarrassed for the honoree."

Liberal bastions like the Huffington Post, The Daily Kos, the Washington Post and The Times of London pretty much said that "Obama has only hot air to show for his efforts at world peace." NPR's Juan Williams said it was utter foolishness. And on and on went the left's comments.

Who was Irena Sendlerowa (1910-2008)? She has quite a story that I am copying verbatim from an Internet download, and yes, checked out for authenticity.

"During WWII, Irena received permission from the Nazis to work in the Warsaw ghetto as a plumbing/sewer specialist. She had an ulterior motive.

Being German, she knew the Nazis' plans for the Jews and smuggled infants out in the bottom of the large tool box she carried. Larger children were placed in a burlap sack in the back of her truck. Also in the back was a dog that she had trained to bark each time the Nazi guards allowed her out of the ghetto and back in.

The soldiers, of course, wanted nothing to do with the dog, and its barking covered any noise made by the infants and small children. Irena managed to smuggle out approximately 2,500 children before she was finally caught. When she was captured, the Nazis beat her severely, breaking both her arms and her legs.

'Irena kept a record of the names of all the children she smuggled out of that Warsaw ghetto and kept them in a glass jar buried under a tree in her back yard. After the war, she tried to locate any parents who may have survived so she might reunite the child with its family. Most, of course, did not survive the Holocaust, and the vast majority of the surviving children were placed in foster homes or adopted."

I forgot to mention that Irena Sendlerowa was nominated for the 2007 Nobel Peace Prize. She lost to Al Gore.

Check out the accomplishments of Denis Mukwege, Sima Samar, Ghazi bin Muhammad, Greg Mortenson, Piedad Cordoba, and Wei Jingsheng. These are just six of the 2009 nominees whom the Committee felt had a lesser impact on world peace than Barack.

My last question. Obama said he would give the entire amount to a charity.

Do you think that charity might be ACORN? Think we will ever know?

Be a true leader Barack. Give the award back to someone much more deserving.

Right-Wing Will Regain Advantage

It's hard to believe that this column represents four years of writing for The Daily Star. That's more than one hundred columns! I think I'll try for one more year so that I can get through the 2010 elections and celebrate all the election victories that will put the conservatives back in power, hopefully in both houses.

All that conservatives have to do is just let Harry, Nancy and Barack continue to show how inept and incompetent they are in leading (?) this great country. Hopefully, we will be able to kick them out of office while we can still call our country great.

The public is starting to wise up to the fact that they made a terrible mistake these last two elections, and I have every confidence in this same electorate to see through the lies that will be spun once again this coming campaign season.

Finally, the voters are seeing what happens when the liberal left is in charge. We conservatives are going to have to take caution, not allowing the Republicans a second chance at controlling Congress unless they do a much better job than they did the last time. They drifted away from the conservative principles and made the federal government larger and more intrusive rather than smaller, and were very irresponsible fiscally.

We really are at the point where we don't have to worry about the ideologically radical, left leaning liberals. They are becoming a smaller minority as time passes. They are simply loud, arrogant, emotional, and non-fact oriented, and the public is beginning to realize this.

Just look at a Gallup Poll taken the week of November 9. It is unbelievable how quickly people are running away from the left, especially the independents. As the Gallup Poll interpreter said: "Over the course of the year, independents' preference for the Republican candidate in their districts has grown from a 1-point advantage in July to the current 22 point positive gap."

At the beginning of the year, the country was still right of center. Forty percent called themselves conservatives, 40 percent called themselves independent and only 20 percent labeled themselves liberal. I would love to see what the percentages are now.

So, real Republicans just have to hang in there, and pretty soon our ideas will be listened to once again. You would have to be a liberal with your head stuck in the sand to have not heard the Republicans' alternative ideas regarding, cap and trade, health care, and the economy. It's too bad they are locked out of all the discussions going on behind closed doors.

And in addition to Obama failing miserably on the domestic front, he is making us the laughing stock of the world. He can't stand up to countries like North Korea, Iran and Russia. He dithers and won't make a decision regarding Afghanistan, thinking what about is best for him politically rather than taking the advice of our professional military leaders.

He is making us more and more dependent on countries like China and those in the oil-rich Middle East, and no one takes him seriously anymore. He does have time, however, to travel around the world rather than focus on the very serious problems we have at home.

Let's see. His major accomplishments to date have been to travel with Oprah to unsuccessfully beg for the Olympics to be held in Chicago, and I'm sure he'll have time to tear himself away from all our pressing problems to humbly accept some fraudulent peace prize.

And then there is a Copenhagen conference coming up to discuss, what do they call it now? Let's see, once it was man-made global cooling. then, when the facts proved them wrong they had to change it to man-made global warming, and once again, when they couldn't sell that one, they now use the politically correct term of climate change.

There is so much more to talk about, but I guess it will have to wait until the next column. It should be about the Fort Hood terrorist murders, the Barack Obama/Eric Holder debacle regarding trying terrorists as mere criminals, the politically correct crowd and the ridiculous notion of Islamophobia. Now I said it should be about these topics, but with Barack at the helm, I never know for sure.

Off the subject, a friend recently sent me an article about a Texas A & M University contest calling for an appropriate definition of the term "Political Correctness."
Here's the winning definition: "Political correctness is a doctrine, fostered by a delusional, illogical minority, and rabidly promoted by an unscrupulous mainstream media, which holds forth the proposition that it is entirely possible to........" (I can't finish it.)

Lastly, I'll leave you with this oxymoron: Islam; the religion of peace.

Global Warming Is A Hoax

Finally, the truth is beginning to be uncovered regarding man-made global warming "research." Sixty-one megabytes of confidential files from the University of East Anglia's Climate Research Unit were released onto the internet that exposed the lack of integrity and professionalism and the petty vindictiveness of the climate "scientists" who have been promoting the warming hoax for many years.

The scary part is that the information from this "research institution" has been relied on heavily for climate model-building and has been cited extensively in governmental and United Nations reports, which in turn have been used to establish harmful government policy.

Included in this material were over 1,000 e-mails and 72 documents that are very damaging to the global warming cabal. Here are quotes from a few of them:

"I can't see either of these papers (anti-global warming research findings) being in the next IPCC report. Kevin and I will keep them out somehow, even if we have to redefine what peer-review literature is!"

"Can you delete any e-mails you may have had with Keith re AR4?"

"The fact is that we can't account for the lack of warming at the moment and it

is a travesty we can't."

"I'm getting hassled by a couple of people to release the CPU temperature station data. Don't any of you three tell anybody that the UK has a Freedom of Information Act!"

Here's the best one: "I've just completed Mike's Nature trick of adding in the real temps to each series for the last 20 years (i.e. from 1981 onwards) and from 1961 for Keith's to hide the decline."

I have to quote one of the most disgusting ones. It actually gloats over the death of John Daly, who was one of the original climate-change doubters and founder of the "Still Waiting For Greenhouse" website. The creator of the e-mail commented: "In an odd way this is cheering news." It really doesn't get worse than that.

The need to reduce carbon dioxide emissions has been a solution in search of a problem for many, many years. Remember, this is the same crowd that said this was supposed to be the answer to global cooling in the 1970s and 1980s. Can anyone tell me why these pretenders should be given any credibility this time?

This should give everyone some insight to the predictive accuracy of the "science" being done by these "specialists." They are simply opportunists who, to receive money from the grant funding gravy train, will say anything their sponsors want them to say.

Even the global warming alarmists are taken aback by these recent revelations. George Monbiot of the Guardian concedes that these releases "could scarcely be more damaging," and then went on to say, "I am dismayed and deeply shaken by them."

But there are some who willingly ignore these revelations. Thomas Crowly, professor of geosciences at the University of Edinburgh, said, "These leaked files reflect badly on the people who are so desperate to discredit global warming." I wonder how much grant money he's taken to remain blind to debate.

I think most common sense people should give more weight to what a more prestigious mind, Robert Lindzen, a professor of meteorology at the Massachusetts Institute of Technology, had to say in an article he wrote for the Wall Street Journal on November 30. He claims, and backs it up, that the science of climate change is far from settled and the over-confident "predictions of catastrophe are unwarranted."

What has been uncovered is unfathomable. As Aynsley Kellow, professor and expert reviewer for a United Nations global warming report puts it, "There is evidence of a willingness to manipulate raw data to suit predetermined results, a resistance to any notion of transparency, an active resistance to freedom of information requests (critical original data input that were willfully destroyed after such requests were made) or quite reasonable requests from scientists to have a look at the data so that it can be verified." Fraud and collusion is a better way to describe these actions.

I want to see what will happen next. Hopefully, this scandal effectively kills the absurd "cap and trade" bill coming before the Senate. Also, I hope this show in Copenhagen proves to be the farce it really is.

The question is now whether or not the main stream media has the integrity to
report this news. So far that doesn't seem to be the case.

If all these research efforts do turn out to be bogus, will honest men of science speak out against the lowliest of "scientists" who have cheated to produce a predetermined result?

And lastly, why don't all you climate "experts" work on a model that will accurately predict next week's weather? You can't even do this successfully yet.

The more information being disclosed from the cache of global warming documents, the more the proof of the hoax perpetrated by unscrupulous research scientists and their claim of man-made global warming.

Stewart Hayward of the Weekly Standard describes them as follows: "Rather than being disinterested investigators after the truth, they're advocates for a preconceived conclusion about the issues at hand."

I see it worse than that. They are simply, criminally behaving, data manipulating, suppressors of honest dissent, unprofessional political hacks willing to say or "find" anything their grant giving suppliers are looking for.

Unfortunately, honest scientists, of whom there are many, will suffer the stigma of public mistrust created by these peers.

Bottom line: Don't listen to these charlatans and others who lazily bought into Armageddon-like claims. Fortunately, common sense individuals are forming their own conclusions. A CNN/Opinion Poll showed that only 45 percent of Americans consider global warming (say nothing of being man-made) to be a proven fact. This is down from 54 percent last year and before the incriminating documents came out!

Here's a good example how easily lies are put forth as truth until they have to be retracted. Al Gore, speaking at the climate conference, suggested that the Arctic Ocean might be ice free as early as 2014.

Afterwards he told the press: "It is hard to capture the astonishment that the experts in the science of ice felt when they heard this." I can imagine Al Gore, self- proclaimed inventor of the Internet, failed attorney, and living proof that money, not brains, gets you into the U.S. Senate - actually thinking he has something worthy of scientific data that would "astonish" these experts.

But poor Al blundered and had to retract his statements the very next day. He had cited new computer models from a Dr. Wieslev Maslowski that showed the entire ice cap would be gone in 4 years. Unfortunately for Al, Dr. Maslowski heard his talk also and came out with a statement saying: "Mr. Gore is wrong. I would never try to estimate a likelihood as exact as this."

Oops Al, another "Inconvenient Truth?" He is a perfect example of these unethical, immoral radicals who are trying to shove this nonsense down our throats, at a huge cost and much lowered standard of living to us. Did your news source print Gore's original claim and then did not print his retraction?

Scientific consensus? Settled science? I think not, even though that's what the environmental radicals want us to believe. The president's climate czar, Carol Browner, leads the "science is settled" group.

Even after the discovery of the incriminating documents she stated: "I'm sticking with the 2,500 scientists. These people have been studying this issue for a very long time."
Unfortunately, as Michelle Malkin points out, "last year more than 31,000 scientists – including 9,021 Ph.D.s – signed a petition sponsored by the Oregon Institute of Science and Medicine rejecting claims of human-caused global warming." I guess that is simply another inconvenient truth, huh Carol? There are thousands more very reputable experts in the field who say the same thing.

I can't fit in all the facts that I wanted to, so I want to recommend some excellent reading for open-minded individuals. The first is "Unstoppable Global Warming: Every 1,500 Years" by Fred Singer and Dennis Avery. The book includes essays by those scientists who are not part of the group claiming to be the "entire scientific community." Another great book is "Meltdown: The Predictable Distortion of Global Warming By Scientists, Politicians, and the Media," by Patrick Michaels. The book presents tons of scientific evidence that debunks Al Gore's sensationalism and fear mongering.

Lastly please Google "The Weekly Standard," click on "recent issues" and scroll down to a featured article titled "Scientists Behaving Badly" by Steven F. Hayward (December 14). It will be well worth your time to read it.
I know the closed-minded types won't bother with any of the suggested readings. I'm not even making the attempt to reach them.

Finally, to illustrate the hypocritical nature of the extreme left, let me include a quote from your esteemed leader. He was teleprompting to us about lifting the ban on government-funded human embryonic stem-cell research in March of 2009: "Promoting science isn't just about providing resources—it's about protecting free and open inquiry. It's about letting scientists like those who are here today do their jobs, free from manipulation or coercion, and listening to what they tell us, even when it's inconvenient—especially when it's inconvenient. It's about ensuring that scientific data is never distorted or concealed to serve a political agenda—and that we make scientific decisions based on facts, not ideology." Right Barack, unless it's your ideology.

Conservatives Must Organize To Win In 2010

It's hard to believe that it is 2010 already and November 2, Election Day, is less
than 10 months away.

That is how long the liberal Democrats will be in power, and I hope their careless, failed policies will not cause the country irreparable damage before we can do something about them.

We conservatives have to be activists for the next 10 months. This is not the time to run out of energy. There was a poll taken the beginning of 2009 that showed the country to be made up of 40 percent conservatives, 40 percent independents, and only 20 percent liberals. Remember, that was when most people were being charmed by Barack and company, and I am certain there are millions who now see the light and won't allow themselves to be duped again.

When I say be activists, I'm not talking the way the liberals do it with cute signs,
sayings and chants. All we have to do is talk to as many of the independents as possible.

Also, not all liberals are lost. Of the 20 percent liberals I think there are only 5 to 10 percent who are totally close-minded and beyond hope. We shouldn't waste any of our time and energy on them. Actually they will probably help us by continuing to be ranting and raving Bush haters, and most people will see that their spewing is all emotionally charged and devoid of facts.

This is what we have to capitalize on. We simply have to continue to point out the facts. Obama and the Democrat leadership are doing everything they possibly can to make our job easier.

They continue to behave like the Keystone Kops and keep shooting themselves in the foot. They seem to be out of touch with reality. It is truly unbelievable how they continue to march to the drums of their radical leftist leadership and ignore the wishes of their very own constituents and what is good for their country.

The only reason they believe they can do this is they think they can switch faces during campaign times and pretend to be moderates or conservative as they have done in every past election. They know that if they run as a liberal, they have no chance of being elected or re-elected.

The perfect example is Barack Obama. If he ran on the agenda he is now promoting, the election would have been over before the last voting offices closed, and Barack would be looking for a job.

This time, we conservatives have to call liberal candidates on every lie or distortion they try to slip by the electorate. I think people will see through them this time, and we have to make sure the candidates are judged based on their past performance rather than the fake promises they will make to get re-elected.

I really don't care if they are a Republican or Democrat conservative. If they have a conservative track record and are willing to stand up to their leadership, then that is the candidate who should get our support.

Also, their arrogance is going to bury them this time. Obama was on Oprah a while back, and when asked to grade his performance thus far, he actually gave himself a B+! Talk about grade inflation!

He is continuing to destroy the economy, making us less safe from terrorism, spending recklessly and aimlessly, worsening the unemployment picture, promoting a guaranteed to fail national health program, and on and on and on.

It's funny the public hasn't seen him the same way he does. The latest Gallup poll has him at a 47 percent approval rating and that figure continues to spiral downward.

Both Democrats and Republicans are becoming more dissatisfied with his incompetence. One poll has his approval rating as low as 44 percent. That is a solid "F" in my grade book. See why I don't let my students grade themselves?

Congress is certainly not exempt from negative approval ratings. Polls had it rated at 21 percent as late as November 2009. Disturbing, for the liberals anyway, is that, as in Obama's case, the trend is downward. I'm sure they would like to grade themselves also.

So our responsibilities are pretty much set for us. We have to encourage others to speak out and support their efforts when they do. We have to write letters to the editor, stay informed and work hard for the conservative nominees.

The TEA parties, which have been a huge success, must continue to grow. We have an obligation to support the organizers with our time and money this time and not let them do all the work.

Yes Barack, hope and change is coming. It's a year late and not what you expected.

Romania Provides Learning Experiences

Being in Romania this last January has prevented me from keeping up with the political process back home. I can't wait to research and write about the Massachusetts Senate election and see how the liberals spin that one.

Until then, I asked Radu Cristea, my good friend and the person most responsible for making the J-term trip so successful for the students, to write a little about his and our experiences. This trip would not have been possible without his involvement. Here he is:

Romania is a country of preconceptions for a lot of people. Some only heard of it because of Transylvania and its bloodthirsty Dracula; others because of communism and its dictator, Nicolae Ceausescu.

There is so much more to it, as the 25 students from Hartwick College, accompanied by their professor and soccer coach, discovered in the three weeks of the J-term trip they took.

This well-prepared trip could not have taken place 25 years ago. Behind the iron curtain, personally, I would've been forbidden to even talk to foreigners – Americans especially. I probably would have had to ask for approval months in advance to get an "official" translator and to fill endless pages of reports regarding my time spent with them.

This is not the case today. Things changed dramatically in the past 20 years after we put an end to the decades-long rule of Ceausescu, who took power in 1965, and his Securitate police state that became increasingly oppressive and Draconian through the 1980s.

The students who spent three weeks in the heart of Transylvania were able to experience the changes that took place here and had a huge impact on the economy, banking system, health care and so on.

Most of them came here without knowing a thing about Romania, with no
expectations, but they're leaving this country with so many pleasant memories.

Their chance to interact with a different culture, mentality, even language,
benefited both the Hartwick students and the Romanian friends they've made.

We all know how governments are the worst administrators of funds. This is nothing new; it's been like that since the Roman times, and the same goes for the Romanian government. It has been spending millions on commercials and advertising for Romania. To quantify how many tourists those commercials brought is almost impossible.

What Hartwick College Professor Sears and Coach Matt Verni did for Romania, bringing these students here, has a huge impact. They all loved this place. Some of them want to extend their stay, others want to return in the near future, but all of them will tell their friends and families what a great place this is.

This is the kind of advertising we need – personal experiences. And these students had plenty of those. They've gotten the chance to get in touch with the history of the country, to talk to businessmen, bankers, doctors, entrepreneurs, lawyers, politicians, economists and to tour businesses and a factory.

During the lectures they took part in, they've had the chance to ask questions,
to interact with the speakers, better understanding how things are done here.

Some of the things they've learned about our past shocked them and made them appreciate what they have today. Being able, in the past, to purchase only half a loaf of bread, 11 eggs per person per month or one pound of pork per month, were things that were hard for them to relate to.

Having only one channel on TV broadcasting for two hours a day and just communist propaganda surprised these students.
They met college students and talked to them about things that people their age are interested in, finding out similarities but differences as well in the way they study in school or spend their free time.

They took trips in the countryside and other cities, experiencing the local cuisine and traditions. They simply loved the place, and people here liked them a lot. They felt welcomed and safe; they were well-behaved and proudly represented their school and country.
Today, I can tell for sure that Romania won the hearts of these 25 young people, and they will remember this country for the rest of their lives.

It's Time to Take Control from Liberals

Although I am a firm advocate for Cluj-Napoca, Romania, it is still good to be home. It's hard to be in Cluj during January on crutches with lots of slippery cobblestone streets, and very few elevators. It's also hard to keep up with the political happenings in the U.S. except by computer, which I had problems with at times.

A digression please. One enjoyable event was when I was walking (hopping) down the street, and a picture in one of the Romanian newspapers really made my day. It was a picture of Janet Napolitano, our highly unqualified secretary of Homeland Security, actually sleeping during the State of The Union teleprompter reading. It goes to show you what the Romanians think of our state of readiness regarding terrorism.

Back to the column. I really wanted to follow the Brown/Coakley Massachusetts Senate race, but since Romania is 7 hours ahead, I had to wait until the morning to find out the results.

And it was certainly worth the wait: A sort-of conservative upsetting the anointed liberal for the most liberal seat in the most liberal state in the U.S. That makes three major victories in a row for conservative candidates going against incumbent liberals' seats. And the best is yet to come.

Of course, Obama's arrogance still doesn't allow him to admit that these victories have nothing to do with his failing policies. Remember, Barack stumped for all three of his chosen candidates. I guess he believed that his mere presence would carry the day.

I just hope he keeps supporting all of the liberal candidates and showing up at all the Democratic seats up for grabs, which are pretty much all of them. If it can be done in Massachusetts, it can be done anywhere. I'll bet the liberal candidates will secretly ask him not to show up.

Grass roots movements, primarily led by TEA Party Patriots, are making the difference. 2009 was the year of expression of common sense by regular Americans, and 2010 has to be the year of action in order to take the country back from these radicals. And it is going to happen in November. Now is not the time to run out of steam.

We have to carry this mission to a successful conclusion. We have to have the energy of ACORN, but with ethics.

You know the liberals are afraid of the TEA Party movement. They have been resorting to name-calling almost from the beginning. As the movement keeps growing, the name calling worsens.

Harry Reid calls us "evil-mongers." Nancy Pelosi calls us "un-American." Instead of recognizing us as the grass roots movement it is, she cleverly came up with the term "Astroturf movement." She hasn't used it again since people started laughing at her.

We've been called rednecks, racists, fascists and anything else they can think of. I guess my question is if we are considered such a radical, right-wing insignificant fringe element, why are they spending so much time demeaning us? The answer? They're scared…. really scared.

The good thing is this strategy is pushing previously non-politically oriented people, as well as all those who were duped by the lies from Obama, to be involved. Cities where rallies are held have gone from numbering in the hundreds to now numbering in the thousands. People involved number in the millions.

We must all make a very serious effort to discuss the issues with independents every chance we get, write letters to the editor, get involved in conservative candidates' campaigns, and shout down the loud-mouthed liberals who only use emotion as a weapon since they can't be fact based.

We can't let up now. There is too much at stake for the country, our children and grandchildren. There is only a little more than eight months to get this done. We have to treat it like a marathon and not a sprint and have energy left right up to Election Day.

Please, if you haven't attended a TEA Party rally, make an effort to do so. More than one would be great. You will find the participants to be peaceful, patriotic, everyday individuals who care a lot about their country. The events are well organized and professionally done. You'll have a very pleasant day and come away feeling good. You will see the nonsense being spread by the left has been nothing but lies.

Lastly, make sure you thank the people who set up the event. They have been putting in amazing amounts of their time, effort and, especially, financial resources to keep this movement moving and growing. They are the real patriots. We owe them a huge debt of gratitude.

Conservatism Is On A Roll; Still Work to Be Done

From all the recent events and their successful outcomes, it seems like conservatism is on a roll. However, now is certainly not the time to become complacent. There is a lot of work to be done over the next 8 months.

The Republican Party is about to be given a second chance at governing, and they can't screw it up like they did last time. I hope this time we will have the appropriately strong conservative voices in Congress (and the White House in 2012) to make sure conservative principles are carried out.

With the primaries and the campaigns coming up, you can be sure the Democrats, especially the liberals, will be doing their best to run away from their past records and instead make wonderful promises, telling everyone they have finally heard the message. This also applies to the Republicans-in-name-only candidates. Don't believe a word they are saying. They are simply desperate to hang on to their jobs and really don't care too much about us or the country.

Lying worked last time, and they think it will work again. They knew they had to look like a conservative to get elected, even though they had no intention of governing as a conservative. Just look at all the lies and promises Barack made during his campaign. It sure worked for him. It worked so well, he still is using this strategy.

Uh, Barack, it's not working any more. Just look at your plummeting approval rating which is well below 50 percent. Even the peanut farmer had a higher approval rating for the same time period.

It is time for conservatives to become activists. We have to tell people every chance we get to not listen to candidates' promises but rather judge them solely on their track record. Nothing else matters. If we had done this with Obama he would still be a relatively insignificant senator from Illinois, albeit the most liberal Senator in the Democrat Party. He would be back going to his "church" to hear Jeremiah Wright preach hatred and would still be hanging around his left wing radical friends like Saul Alinsky. Maybe he would even have time to spend a weekend or two every now and then for ACORN, counseling people how to get away with illegal behavior.

Back to our responsibilities as activists. We have to especially talk to young people of voting age who were duped the first time around with Obama. I don't think they had any idea their future was going to be so heavily mortgaged to the point where they will not have as good a standard of living as their parents now have.

These are the people who should be invited to the TEA parties so that they can see for themselves the liberals have totally mischaracterized these events, probably out of ignorance or fear, since most have never attended one.

We also have to be willing to stand up and shout down the liberals when they misstate the truth. Granted, they are loud, but they are relatively few in number and their arguments are pretty much based on emotion and lacking substance.

We have to make sure that we work tirelessly for conservative candidates, regardless from which party they come. Schumer and Gillibrand could be vulnerable this time, and it is inexcusable for any voter to say they didn't vote because their vote doesn't count, or the weather was too bad to go out, or they didn't have a ride.

Lastly, make sure you attend at least one, preferably more, TEA parties this season. Make sure to take one or more open-minded friends with you. They will be favorably impressed. I know there will be events in Oneonta, Sidney and Norwich, and if organizers will send me the dates, I will be happy to list them in my column. This offer holds for any other TEA Party event I don't know about. We all know how difficult it is to get appropriate coverage in the mainstream media.

Next time (unless Barack gives me something to write about) I'll try to make a list of what a true conservative candidate should look like. My observations might be different from other conservatives, but I know we will agree on the basic core values.

I never realized it until recently that my column printed on The Daily Star web site had a place where comments could be made immediately below it. I want to offer a very belated thank you for all the kind comments I have received from readers. I also get quite a laugh at those who are not quite so kind but at least I know I got their blood pressure elevated. Both types of feedback keep me writing.

Losses Loom for Left-Wing Lemmings

Just a little while ago the left's beloved leader, Barack Obama, said, "Everything there is to say about health care has been said, and just about everybody has said it." Oh, do I wish you would take your own advice and simply shut up, then. Maybe, in addition to this tactic, you should also listen.

The public is against the present health bill proposal by a three to one margin but you still don't listen. The Republicans have come up with plenty of common sense alternative proposals and you don't listen.

Only your subservient mainstream media and your delusional left wing followers hang on your every word. The best term to describe these mindless followers would be lemmings.

The Encarta Dictionary would define the term as a subarctic rodent, but a more apt description is the definition of a lemming as a doomed conformist. "A member of a large group of people who blindly follow one another on a course of action that will lead to destruction for all of them." You can't get a more perfect description than that.

Nevertheless, all their leader needs is a microphone, a teleprompter, the mainstream media and a selected group of followers, and he is so caught up in his own self-grandeur that he is oblivious to everything else.

On second thought, maybe we should just let him rant away. The 2010 elections will prevent this radical and the leftist, secular leaders in both the Senate and the House from causing any more damage.

There are many House Democrat seats that are vulnerable, some estimate as many as 60. If the Republicans can gain 40 we can finally say good bye to Nancy "I can't blink" Pelosi permanently.

The same holds true with the Senate. Poor old Harry Reid might be gone not only as Senate leader but also as a senator. Who says Christmas doesn't come early sometimes? And in two more years, 2012, people will begin to forget who this Obama character was anyway.

And this is where the Tea Party participants have a say. Only candidates with conservative credentials should and will be promoted. The left can rant and rave and call us every name in the book but all we have to do is continue to gain strength and not falter from now up to Election Day. And believe me, as they get more and more scared the worse the rantings will become.

When independent minded people come and experience one or more of the planned events they will see how wrong the lefty radicals are.

And speaking of rantings, one has only to look at the feedback under the electronic version of my column on The Daily Star website. All it took is a few brave souled individuals to provide feedback and support, and the crazies came bounding out from everywhere.

I want to thank those individuals who have written in on my behalf, and if you could only see the number of positive e-mails I get, you would certainly be relieved, knowing that you are the true majority.

One final question. First let me say that I know many attorneys, and, with the exception of one or two, I have found them all to be ethical and honest individuals. I respect every one of them.

But I still have to ask, who the heck writes these bills coming out of Congress? I thought the law was supposed to be written so that it was understandable to the reasonable man. Just go online and see if a reasonable man can even begin to read, much less comprehend these laws.

We have the latest Senate version of the health care bill that is 2,074 pages. This comes after a House version of 1,990 pages and an earlier Senate version that was 1,502 pages. No one in either house has even bothered to read what they contained but still voted for them. Is this responsible behavior?

We are talking about the government takeover of one-sixth of the nation's economy! Maxine Waters was made to look like an idiot when she was asked about certain portions of the bill, and she tried to bluff her way through with an answer before finally admitting she hadn't read any of it. The same experience was repeated with other Democrats.

I don't know, but there are two much more important documents that provide guidelines as to how to live that are much clearer and much shorter.

The most important, my NIV version of the Bible, has only 1,635 pages. Also, I usually carry around a pocket sized version of the Constitution with all the amendments, including a copy of the Declaration of Independence. That booklet is only 58 pages with each page less than a 3x5 card. After these two works, we don't need any more laws.

Attend Tea Parties To Find Truth

What happened on March 21st was the ultimate of big government arrogance. Congress passed a health bill that a large majority of Americans didn't want. Democrats were bought, threatened and bribed to sell their principles to the devil. They felt they had a choice between being scared of Pelosi, Reid and Obama, or facing the wrath of their constituents. Boy, did they make the wrong choice.

Watch the attempts the Dems make, spinning how they voted. This law is just one of many nightmarish examples of what happens and will happen again when radical liberals seize control of power.

Speaking of spinning, I was watching a newscast where a Democrat congressman was trying to explain away a recent poll where Pelosi's favorable rating was 11 percent and Harry Reid's was 8 percent. The politician actually said the reason that these numbers were so low was because they took so long to get the bill passed!

There was a letter to the editor a while back that displayed either ignorance or the lowest level of behavior by attempting to intentionally distort and demean the Tea Party movement. After a letter like this it is even more important than ever for independent thinking individuals to attend a Tea Party event and see for yourself what this movement is really all about.

The left will stoop to any level in attempting to distort the facts. I attended three events last year and hope to attend more this year. There were no loaded guns, no words of racism, nor any of the other things the writer claimed to have experienced. The good, honest people I was with would not have tolerated such things and would have asked such individuals to leave.

I think the writer was confusing herself, instead remembering the vulgar
activity that took place when her kind protested President Bush's policies.
Also erroneous was the statement made about the number of attendees at the thousands of rallies across the country last year. All one has to do is go to the Internet and see for himself the postings that reported the cities where the rallies took place and the respective attendees.

Also, when pictures taken by independent sources, such as those taken at the Washington D.C. event, scare the liberals, what do they do? They simply say the pictures are doctored. Is that the best that these individuals can come up with when exposed? We conservatives have to start fighting back when these vicious smears are attempted. And that is exactly what good, honest, Americans are finally doing.

But this is what the radical left does best....lie. You can be assured that this summer they will attempt to plant some of their own at the upcoming rallies, pretending to be Tea Party members and try to make the movement look bad. And the media will play right along.

Also you can be assured that the above writer will, as well as many others of her ilk, claim to have attended such a rally but never really did.

Remember all those people who claimed to have been at the original Woodstock festival? It was later said that if all the people who actually claimed to have attended actually had, the crowds would have been six times larger than actually were there. The same was true about all the people who claimed to have been at the game when Hank Aaron hit his last home run. There would have had to have been seven stadiums to hold these "attendees."

Why do libs do the same thing about the Tea Parties? It seems that they feel the need to lie in order to give their statements credibility. It's beyond me why they do this.

Let them spew on. All we conservative Americans have to do is move forward with purpose and determination and we will take this country back in November. We have to make these radical liberals powerless and insignificant for the sake of our
country's future.

218 days to go. Stay strong, stay focused, stay united and this November the Democrat Party will go down in history as a past embarrassment of this country. After seeing the agenda they have planned and the harm they have caused this country, they can never be allowed to lead again.

Tea Party events that I know about:

Saturday, April 24th from 1 to 4pm at River Valley Ford, which is about half way between Oneonta and Otego on Route 7.

Saturday, July 3rd beginning at 10am in Sidney and going on all day. I'll give directions at a later date.

I know there is an active group in Norwich, and if a verifiable member will send me a schedule of its future events I will be happy to post the information here.

I'm getting motivated. The Tea Party season is heating up, and all the events that I know of are predicting three to four times the attendance from last year. I'm bringing 10 people myself; last year I brought one.

But just as predicted, the liberal, secular left is already planning to do everything they can, using every sleazy trick in the book, to make Tea Party events look bad.

There is actually a website that provides various strategies to disrupt these events. Some of the tactics include misspelling signs, making vulgar or racially oriented signs, and shouting vulgar chants. Remember the woman who wrote a letter to the editor two weeks ago? All her claims seemed to be suspiciously similar to what the web site suggested doing.
All they are trying to do is attract media attention, and the main stream media will be happy to oblige.

My advice would be to hold these protest events on private property if at all possible. That way these clowns can be asked or told to leave. Also, make sure that you and others are right there when they are being interviewed by unprofessional, leftist reporters looking for a good story. We have to let them know that these people are in no way part of the decent people who are trying to take this country back and have it become a morally, constitutionally based country once again.

Last week I was attending a Hartwick College lacrosse match and asked a friend if he was going to any of the Tea Party events. I was disappointed when he said he was an independent and didn't want to be part of anything as radical as these groups. Sadly, when asked, he said that he had not been to one. This meant that he received his information from only biased, leftist sources, or what the main stream media told him to think.

I had to point out to him that 46 percent of all Tea Party members were either Democrats or Independents. Sadly, this too fell on deaf ears.

This example shows why you should attend one of these events and see for yourself what and who are involved. You will come away very favorably impressed and see that the other side is painting demeaning and erroneous pictures of Tea Party members and their cause.

I am not asking you to fall in love with the alternative news sources I am mentioning below but please listen to them at least two or three times each to get a good idea of the substance they provide.

Talk show hosts should include Glen Beck, Laura Ingraham, Mark Levin, the dreaded Rush Limbaugh and Sean Hannity. They all have very good websites to peruse, also. Sean Hannity is on his "Conservative Victory Tour" and has so far been to Minneapolis, Detroit, and New Orleans. In each case they were sellouts and the crowds of typical, average Americans were fired up. He will be in many more cities in the near future.

Listen to Fox News starting at 5 p.m. at least a few times. You'll hear factual information that you won't hear in the main stream media. You will soon see why Fox News is rated No. 1 in cable news and has more listeners than CNBC, MSNBC, and CNN combined!

Try reading the New York Post editorial and columnist section, The Washington times, The Wall Street Journal Editorial section and NewsMax.com. Of course you should already be reading "On The Right Side."

Columnists to read are Charles Krauthammer, Thomas Sowell, Michael Barone, Larry Elder. Michelle Malkin, and Dick Morris, just to mention a few, taken from a list of more than 100.

All I'm asking is to please not let the mainstream media and liberals spoon feed you only the information they want you to read or hear. Make your own opinion after you have given both sides a fair chance.

There are two important Tea Party rallies coming up that I hope you can attend. The first one is in Norwich on Thursday from 11 a.m. to 6 p.m. It will be at the East Side Park across from the Chenango County Courthouse. Call Gilda Ward at either 607-764-8303 or 607-244-5528 if you need more details.

Another good one will be held Saturday, April 24, from 1 to 4 p.m. at River Valley Ford, which is located halfway between Oneonta and Otego on Route 7. Contact Tim Shorer at 607-435-1623 if you need additional information. There will be some good speakers at each event.

Also, please remember that the costs to hold these events are pretty substantial and are being borne by only a few people. If at all possible, try to kick in $4,
$10 or more to help these individuals out.

Last Saturday, while attending a Local Tea party rally, my worst fears were confirmed. As I approached the site I could feel the hate generated by the music being played and the people trying to trick me by smiling and conversing, just trying to lure me into their trap.

Sure enough, as I was directed to my parking spot, the parking attendants also knew the trouble I was getting myself into. Their smiles and their pointing and their comments such as "welcome" and "glad you could make it" even made me more certain that I was being led to my demise.

As I got out of my car and approached the frenzied crowd (they wanted to appear calm on the outside but I knew it was simply a ruse to fool me) I could feel the anger among them. There they were, sitting in their lawn chairs or standing and talking to each other, smiling and laughing and just waiting for me to turn my back so they could hit me over the head with their signs.

And talking about their signs! I couldn't believe the hateful, radical statements that were printed on them. They quoted such radicals as Thomas Jefferson, Ben Franklin, and John Adams, among others, and tried to get me to react by saying "smaller government," "less taxes," "no Obamacare" and on and on.

I knew then that I should leave but I was afraid that I would get back to my car and find the windows smashed and my tires slashed, so I stayed near the front where I knew I could rush to the highway and flag down a passing motorist if I had to flee for my life.

The speakers were also in on the act. They pretended to be patriotic and talked about topics such as the Constitution, the Second Amendment, a less intrusive government, but I could see right through them. I knew that underneath their jackets they had pro-Obama, Reid and Pelosi re-election buttons. It's a good thing the media warned me about all of this ahead of time.

And guns! They were everywhere! Well, no, I can't say I saw any, but I knew they had to be there, hidden under everyone's shirts or in their pocketbooks. I'm so glad I was warned by the press ahead of time.

I take it back, the NRA was there and raffling off what appeared to be a collector's item. I couldn't believe the organizers allowed that organization to participate! After all, they do express support of the Second Amendment and provide programs such as hunter safety education for youth. Just the sight of that unloaded rifle sitting there almost made me faint of fright. You can bet I steered clear of that tent.

Ok libs, you can breathe again. No, you don't have a new convert. I just had to point out the ridiculousness of your statements when you write to the editor. But you should be worried about the growth of the Tea Party movement. We are for real; we are a danger to your socialist agenda, and will keep growing in spite of your feeble attempts to label, insult, or demean us. As a matter of fact you might deserve the credit for causing us to grow as fast as we have been.

From the first rally last year in Milford that had about 50 people attending, to the second one that year held in Oneonta attracting 250 people, to the one (of many more rallies this year) held last Saturday drawing over 1,300 participants, it is obvious we won't be running out of steam or be intimidated by you elitist radicals.

Yes, we do stand for a lot of things. Only a blind liberal or a person preferring to keep his or her head in the sand thinks we are the party of no. We are for a smaller, less intrusive government, a strong defense, secure borders, and lower taxes. We happen to believe in the Constitution and the rule of law. We happen to be true patriots rather than like those who pretend to be but still let their country slide down the slippery socialist slope.

And yes, there is a grain of truth when one says we are simply against everything. We are against everything that your leader, Barack Obama, that bastard child of Marxism, stands for. But in less than two years he will go the way of his predecessors.

After the 2010 elections you will find us to be more demanding and more of something you liberals should fear.

Congratulations go out to Arizona Gov. Jan Brewer and the state's legislature
for having a backbone and passing a tough new law dealing with illegal immigration.

What else was Arizona to do? It simply passed a law that mirrored an existing federal law that makes it a federal offense to be in the country illegally. It is now a state violation also. The federal law was to protect citizens. Unfortunately, Obama chooses to not honor (again) the oath he took and favors illegals as potential voters over the lives and well-being of his lawful constituents.

If Obama and his minions had the integrity to secure the border and enforce already existing immigration laws, Arizona wouldn't have had to take the action it did. It's as simple as that.

What is Arizona to do Barack? Their economy is going bankrupt and is experiencing 9.4 percent unemployment. The cost to educate the illegal aliens' children has to be bankrolled by hard working taxpayers.

Hospitals have to close because they simply can't afford providing free health care to illegals while being unable to provide services to citizens (which include legal immigrants). Gangs are running rampant, illegal drugs are flowing across the border, and Arizonans (including law enforcement individuals) are being murdered.

Got any ideas, Barack? I'll bet the teleprompter doesn't have any suggestions, either. Is this your idea of spreading the wealth and providing social justice for all?

Meanwhile, don't listen to the loud, arrogant protesters. Seventy percent of Arizona citizens (including minorities) support the law, and a new Rasmussen poll shows 60 percent of Americans also support the bill. The same poll shows that 56 percent of Americans believe that federal government policies actually encourage illegal immigration and 83 percent of Americans are angry, not at the illegal aliens, but at the federal government over illegal immigration.

Now what does the law actually say? If you actually read it you will see that police officers may only question a person's immigration status after they have already made a lawful contact (some other violation committed) or have "reasonable suspicion" and "may not solely consider race, color, or national origin" to believe that the person is in the country illegally.

The activists think they are going to have a field day with this, but the Supreme Court in 1968 ruled that the Fourth Amendment prohibiting unreasonable searches and seizures is not violated if a police officer stops a suspect and searches him without probable cause to arrest if the police officer has a reasonable suspicion that the person has committed, is committing, or is getting ready to commit a crime. Darn, libs! Laws always get in the way of your emotional overreactions, don't they?

You might also want to check the 10th Amendment, which states "The powers not delegated to the United States by the Constitution, nor prohibited by it to the States, are reserved to the States respectively, or to the people. Shoot Barack! There's that darned document that is always getting in your way.

As was to be expected, the professional activists came out in droves. Give them a sign, a slogan to chant, a camera to demonstrate in front of and they're ready to go. Speaking of chants, they actually came up with the recycled oldie "power to the people." Maybe they should have checked out the polls I mentioned earlier before they used that one.

And this is really special. Before they had done any research on the bill itself they were calling for a boycott of all things Arizona. There were actually airheads calling for a boycott of Arizona Iced Tea. Great idea, except that it is brewed in New York.

These are probably some of the same people who voted for Obama because he could read a teleprompter really well, had charisma, could strike a great pose of him looking regally off into the distance, and promise everything to everyone. Try research next time.

Maybe we 70 percent of Americans should take some action ourselves. I'm going to try to take a trip down to Arizona as soon as I can. We all should. The state has plenty to offer. Scottsdale, Phoenix, Tucson, the Grand Canyon, lots of old Wild West history, and on and on.
How about a boycott of our own? San Francisco wants to restrict city employee travel to Arizona. I think maybe people should boycott California wines for the immediate future.

Even better news. Georgia is considering a similar law (480,000 illegal aliens, sixth in the nation) as are other states. Never forget the power we patriotic Americans have over these radical secularists.

Important! More good people are organizing a Delaware County Tea Party. It is being held Saturday, May 22, from 3 to 6 p.m. at West 38 Restaurant, West Street, Walton, NY. Call 865-6003 or 865-5657 for more info.

Change Is Happening, But Not the Change That Liberals Want

Change is happening but not the change Obama intended. From the New Jersey and Virginia governorship wins, the Massachusetts Senate upset, Dodd resigning to avoid embarrassment and possible prosecution, Arlen Spector rejected by his own party, Rand

Paul defeating the Republican backed candidate, to Senator Blanche Lincoln forced into a runoff with 56 percent of Arkansas voters voting against her, the tidal wave is just getting started.

Thank you Barack, for campaigning for both Spector and Lincoln. Please campaign for more of your chosen ones this coming fall.

The results thus far are just the tip of the iceberg. More good news is yet to come. Democrats Reid, Gillibrand, Boxer, Bennett, Murray and Feingold are also vulnerable. Some political pundits are predicting a 40 to 70 seat swing in the House and possibly a Republican majority in the Senate.

There are only 161 days left until Election Day, and we conservatives, patriots, and Tea Party members can't let up now. The Tea Party movement is growing daily and there is now a rally scheduled in Walton on June 19 (I want to thank Patricia Breakey and The Daily Star for the balanced coverage the group received). Call Maureen O'Connell at 865-6003 or Susan McNeill at 865-5657 to see if you can help out in any way.

We have to keep our momentum going, build on our enthusiasm, and maintain our stamina. Yes, we know there will be further attacks and insults by the left, so we have to be sure to support each other and make sure our conservative voices continue to be heard.

We are winning, and more and more independent voters are supporting us every day. The left has been used to getting in other people's faces, being loud, arrogant, insulting, and emotionally empty of fact, with no consequence. Those days are over, people.

And by support, I mean when conservatives run for federal, state, or local positions, including town and village boards and school boards, they are often in the minority. When asked by them, we have to attend those meetings, stand with them, and encourage them to stick to their principles.

Yes, lots of incumbents of both parties have to be thrown out. However, conservatives can't afford to form a third party. We must use the Republican Party and make it become the party of conservative ideas once again.

I would like to say support the most conservative candidate, regardless of party affiliation, but I can no longer do that. Democrat Party members, who claimed to be fiscally conservative, turned tail and voted for Obama's health care fiasco, supporting the ultra liberal party Democrat leadership rather than what the majority of Americans desired. Also, the socially conservative pro-life Democrats in the House, sacrificed their principles and voted for the bill, using the empty excuse that Obama, the most liberal, anti-life person to come out of the Senate, would issue an executive order banning federally funded abortions.

That's not why they voted for the bill. It was an attempt to save face after showing they could be bought, very cheaply it seems.

The last straw came when the President of Mexico, Felipe Calderon, came and addressed both houses of Congress and insulted our country repeatedly. The Democrats frequently supported his condemnation of the Arizona law by repeatedly cheering and giving him standing ovations.

Now please tell me why incumbents will toe the party line instead of supporting their constituents and their country? First, the bill is not the least bit racist, and in fact prevents abuse by prohibiting police to act based on "race, color, or national origin." Liberals must be blind or simply can't read.

Columnist Debra Saunders said it well by stating, "What a spectacle. Senators and House members were cheering a foreign leader for bashing an Arizona law intended to bolster the federal immigration law passed by – who else? – senators and house members."

It was a very good column, and you should go on line and read it in its entirety. Liberals, you now have another strong conservative woman to demonize. You will fail as completely as you did with Sarah Palin.

Remember, Democrat candidates will go out of their way to lie about their conservative credentials. They have a great role model to follow in Barack Obama. Don't fall for it again. Judge them solely on their past actions and voting records, not their promises. The same holds true for Republican candidates; it is their actions, not their promises, that mean anything.

This is a four-year test of our resolve. This year we completely change the out of control, unbridled growth of our government and get rid of as many liberal, lobby loving, socialist leaning incumbents as possible. We must stop Obama's agenda in its tracks. In 2012, we get rid of Obama.

It's time to mention several topics, rather than just one, in my column this week.

First of all, please mark your calendars for two important dates. There are two Tea Party rallies being held in Walton this month at Robinson's Auction Barn from 9am to noon. The dates are June 12th and June 19th. Please make every attempt to participate and give this new group our strong support.

Another observation: The last few times I have been driving down Main Street in Oneonta, I noticed something different but couldn't put my finger on it. A good friend, W. S., nailed it for me. He said it was the absence of the anti-war sign wavers that used to be present every week, and he was right. Where did they go?

I consider myself pretty well-read, but I must have missed the fact that the wars in Afghanistan and Iraq were over. I double checked and sure enough they were still going full blast, especially in Afghanistan.

As a matter of fact, Obama, following the successful Bush doctrine, actually sent more troops to Afghanistan. At the time I wondered why the number of protesters didn't increase dramatically when he did this.

The only reason I can come up with is that these individuals really didn't care
about the wars, or our brave troops, at all. They were simply the same old, unoriginal Bush haters who saw their numbers dwindling and their hero, Barak Obama, failing. This is a perfect example of what you get when people like these put politics first and sacrifice their principles.

Third, the same friend pointed out to me the fact that the congressional health- care bill HR3590 requires that health insurance premiums paid by employers be shown on individuals' W-2s by 2011. He called our U.S. Congressman to find out if this was in fact true and whether the premiums would be taxable.

As is probably typical with almost all of our representatives, he didn't know initially. To his credit he eventually sent my friend a letter with what he found out. Yes it is a requirement, but no, not all plans will be taxed, just the "Cadillac plans."

Unfortunately, he didn't define what a "Cadillac plan" was. Also, he said that the levels were inflation adjusted, but since medical costs are increasing faster than the rate of inflation, that only means that more and more plans, and taxpayers, will be subject to this new tax.

Maybe someone can tell me why the insurance premiums paid have to be included on an individual's W-2 to begin with. If you really believe that it is an innocent requirement and the premiums will never be taxed, then you will probably be foolish enough to vote for Obama all over again.

Finally, don't you wish we had a leader with a backbone like Israel's Prime Minister Benjamin Netanyahu? He actually puts the safety and security of his own countrymen over world opinion. Obama just wants everyone, especially the bad guys, to like us.

Someone want to tell me where the reasoning is incorrect? Israel and Egypt formed the blockade in 2007 when Hamas took control of Gaza from the rival Fatah party after Israel unilaterally withdrew. The blockade is simply to prevent weapons from being smuggled in by sea. The ships are then told to dock at a nearby Israeli port and trucks will transport the humanitarian aid to Gaza. Just last November a ship bound for Gaza was seized after 200 tons of weapons were discovered.

The terms of this blockade were well known by all since it was instituted. The blockade itself was legal according to international law. Three cheers for Israel for putting the safety of its citizens first and foremost.

Here's an idea. Why don't all these anti-Semite, Palestinian sympathizers take themselves and their families and relocate in the towns and villages near Gaza. Let them put their children at risk of the hundreds, if not thousands, of rockets that have been fired upon these areas.

It's just like those idealistic Americans who went to Iraq to chain themselves to hospitals and schools so that American bombers wouldn't bomb these facilities (knowing full well that our Air Force wouldn't do that anyway). When Hussein instead wanted them to be located around military facilities, they put their tails between their legs and scurried home to safety. Once again, so much for principles.

And where has the mainstream media been defending Israel actions? As usual, AWOL. As columnist Joel Mowbry said: "Much like the narrative of Israel's 'peace- loving' enemies, the story of the mainstream media's downfall is pretty straightforward.

As the news titans have continued to disregard the truth, the general public has likewise
decided to disregard them."

Ignore Liberals on Rallies, Palin Stories

I want to congratulate Maureen O'Connell and Sue MacNeill for making the first Walton Tea Party rally a huge success. Even with the inclement weather more than 100 people were in attendance. This was the case even though the date was misprinted in the paper.

There will be a huge rally this July 3 in Sidney, starting at 10am. It is being organized by Steve Anderson and there will be speakers, music, food from Brook's BBQ, and fireworks in the evening. This one is going to be impressive. Call Steve at 607-563- 2554 for directions and information.

The liberals are trying their best to downplay the impact of these rallies, but our numbers are growing by leaps and bounds. If you are truly an Independent, and an independent thinker, please, don't listen to these liberal lies. Come to one or more rallies and see for yourself the excitement and grass roots attitudes of the people attending. You will be favorably impressed.

If you want to see the lengths these secular progressives will go to smear a person's good name please, please read Sarah Palin's book "Going Rogue." You will see why the last thing you should do is listen to these morally deficient individuals and why you should have a great deal of respect for this very strong woman.

Remember, I am writing this column for conservatives and those independents that have an open mind. Just to show you how careful you have to be in guarding against liberal lies is the tired old, continuing accusation of the famous Palin misquote, "I can see Russia from my back porch." It started out to be just another smear started by the radical liberals but it is amazing how many people were too lazy to actually research it as to its truth.

The fact is that the quote came from Tina Fey, a Sarah Palin imposter performing on "Saturday Night Live." It was not said by Sarah Palin herself! Is this an example of where you people are too lazy and rely on SNL or the talking heads to get your information? Do you lazily let them form all your opinions?

Okay, if you still want to believe she said that, I have another task for you if you are ambitious enough to make the effort. Get a road atlas and look up the map for Alaska. Now locate Wasilla. I'll even give you a hint, it's near Anchorage. Then check out the mileage scale. You should find that the distance from Wasilla (I really don't know where her back porch is) to the Russian coast is more than 800 miles. Need I say more? Have you ever heard of something called a figure of speech?

This reminds me of a joke that is very apropos. Two liberals were sitting on their back porch in upstate New York one evening, looking up at the full moon. One liberal had a furrowed brow that made the other one ask what the problem was. The first liberal said, "I was just wondering, which do you think is farther away, the moon or Florida?" The second liberal looked at him in wonderment and replied, "Duh, that's easy, you can see the moon can't you?"

So just remember, the next time you hear a person repeat that earlier phrase and attribute it to Sarah Palin, you are probably talking to one of those liberals on the porch. Just smile and walk away.....quickly.

Oh yes, now their latest smear is where they are claiming Sarah Palin has had breast implants. Libs, do you really want to admit to being in favor of the people who behave like this, or support the character of people who use smear tactics like this? Your silence says you accept these tactics.

Now, as for you womens' groups, self-proclaimed feminists, etc. Do you actually stand on principles, or are you merely political hypocrites when groups attack women as viciously as this? I don't need to hear your words; your actions will speak volumes for you. The ball's in your court now. What are you going to do?

You can now tell the election season is upon us. U.S. Sens. Gillibrand and Schumer, as well as Reps. Arcuri, and Murphy are all of a sudden remembering that they are supposed to be representing New York and no longer (temporarily) lap dogs for Harry Reid and Nancy Pelosi.

All of a sudden they are telling all of us how hard they have been working for us and making brand new promises to show us just that. What fakes they are! They are really into the Washington power scene and want to stay there. They actually think our memories are so short that we will forgive them and re-elect them to another term. Let's all vigorously support their conservative opponents.

Humble Man Will Make Good Opponent For Gillibrand

Last Saturday I was able to go to a meet-and-greet for David Malpass, an individual running against Kirstin Gillibrand for a New York Senate seat. I was very impressed.
He is a humble man with humble beginnings and is a true fiscal conservative with very strong conservative credentials.

He was a respected member in both the Reagan and Bush Sr. administrations.

He writes on a regular basis for Forbes Magazine and The Wall Street Journal.

He has 10 common-sense strategies for reducing federal spending, which he promises to advocate for from day one of his Senate term.

Just a few of those pledges: He promises to fight for no more earmarks, no new entitlements and no more bailouts. He pledges to limit the size of the national debt, defund the new health care law and use excess TARP (Troubled Assets Relief Program) money to reduce the national debt.

He will not vote for any funds to implement a VAT or IMF bailouts and will not vote for any new spending without matching cuts. (I think it should be $3 in cuts for every $1 of new spending.) These pledges and more can be found on his website, www.davidmalpasseforsenatecom.

It would be well worth your while to take a serious look at this individual. His credentials are for real. Gillibrand is very weak in comparison and very vulnerable. She had to be appointed to her seat and has only a 27 percent approval rating, according to one poll.

Also, look what happened when you voted for a person without looking further
than his reading and oratorical skills...a disaster.

Remember, liberals will once again try to lie their way into office since they know they have to appear to be like conservative or they have no chance of being elected. It looks like this same philosophy is going to work for the latest Supreme Court nominee.

The sad part was that there was no one there to cover the Malpass event. It seems a little unfair that Gillibrand, Schumer and Murphy get all the coverage they do by making their late-term promises and then call this news. It is simply free campaign coverage and nothing more. It is very unfair to their opponents. I guarantee you that the above three Democrats will be receiving coverage, much more than their opponents, from now to Election Day. Keep track and see if I'm right.

Now, on to some more incompetence by Barack Obama. He sure talks tough, doesn't he? He famously said earlier that he is looking to look for some rear ends to kick. Well, bend over Barack, yours is the one that needs it the most. This liberal leader has to be the cheapest holder of the office to buy in our history.

He has been bought and paid for by the labor unions. You can almost see the puppet strings attached.

It's now been learned, only 70 days into the oil spill, that 27 countries and six international organizations offered their assistance from the beginning. The reason they haven't been able to act is because of a law known as the Jones Act that dates back to 1920. It is simply a union protectionist law that prohibits foreign boats from operating within U.S. waters without American crews.

Because of this law, he has said thanks, but no thanks, to offers until this last week. Other presidents, including President George W. Bush, have waived the act temporarily, but immediately, when there has been a disaster. This was done when Hurricane Katrina hit New Orleans. It's called leadership, Barack. It's what grownups with experience, competence, less arrogance and better judgment do in a crisis. Your inaction will cost billions of dollars and you have no one else to blame but yourself.

Under Barack's leadership the Coast Guard stopped 16 crude-sucking ships from collecting oil until it could be guaranteed that "there were fire extinguishers and life vests aboard,"

Also, as of last week, it was reported that although there are 2,000 skimmers in the United States alone, only 20 are being used. Admiral Thad Allen, when asked about why this is the case, said we might need then for an oil spill. Way to go Admiral, I think that is what we have now.

Obama likes to compare the oil spill disaster to the events of 9/11. Can you imagine how this guy would have reacted in a 9/11-type disaster? As columnist John Hawkins aptly writes, "I guess we're lucky Obama wasn't president when 9/11 happened or he'd probably still be trying to figure out who to bow to and where
Afghanistan is on a map, between games of golf."

Time for another photo-op, Barack. Get down to the gulf beaches, kneel and look serious, at least you're good at that. I also hear they have great golf courses nearby.

Libs, Stop Whining

I want to sincerely thank Chuck Pinkey for doing such a bang up job with the column while I was gone. I couldn't have chosen a more capable person and writer to temporarily take over the job. I am certainly his No. 1 fan. Thank you for going along with my choice, Sam Pollak.

As much as I love Romania and its people, I always realize how good it is to come back to such a great country. It helps me to realize anew all the great freedoms we have, yet take for granted. I can't understand why we have the whiners who are always finding fault with America. Why don't they ever show an appreciation for the generosity, in the form of time, money, and supplies, that the American people always come through with to help with any natural disaster, either foreign or domestic.

This disdain starts at the top with the present occupant in the White House. He goes around the world apologizing for us, tramples the Constitution, sides with a foreign government against his own constituents (Mexico vs Arizona), treats its allies like dirt, sympathizes with terrorist groups with an "it's Israel's fault for all the violence" attitude, and on and on.

I'll try to be nice and label Obama and his followers enigmas. He is causing our massive deficit and debt to spiral out of control and then blames George Bush for his comparably miniscule deficits. Obama spends so irresponsibly and then complains that if the Bush tax cuts stay in place they will add to the deficit by $700 billion (not true, but when has he or his followers ever let facts get in the way).

He appoints a consumer advocate, another czar who wouldn't make it through Senate hearings, and says she will make the big, bad banks write credit terms that the average person can understand, yet he promotes a 2,300 page health care proposal that no one, including himself, can understand or bother to even try to read.

As for his domestic policies and economic stimulus programs, can anyone point out anything working? I can hear the lefties scrambling for their word processors now, hardly able to type "It's George Bush's fault, its George Bush's fault," without mis-typing everything in their rabid, irrational anger.

Let me give them a few more worn-out lines they always use. They will never fail to bring up Bush and the Patriot Act. I say, thank you George Bush for its creation. The liberals can't point out one instance of misuse.

Also libs, don't forget the "blame Bush" excuse for the collapsing housing market, Freddie Mac and Fannie Mae fiasco, even though there was a CNN and Fox News report showing Bush and his Treasury Secretary repeatedly warning about the lack of appropriate oversight of the two above-mentioned mortgage giants.

I have a video (as of today it was still on YouTube) and a timeline clearly pointing this out. There they are, good old Barney Frank, Maxine Waters, and old Chris, "Mr. Countrywide Financial" Dodd himself, defending them to the bitter end. Open minded people, independents and conservatives can e-mail me for these two items. All you secular, leftist, liberals probably shouldn't even bother requesting them. The facts could slap you right in the face and you still wouldn't budge from your blind, irrational, loyalty to Obama.

One more humorous mantra of the deaf left is that the Republicans have no ideas of their own. Can anyone tell me when any of the conservatives' proposals have even been listened to? We have a lot of good, solid ideas but Obama won't even give them consideration. This arrogant attitude began from day one when he said in a meeting after getting frustrated, "Hey, we won, you lost, it's our turn now." Now there is a guy who really wanted to end partisan bickering, right?

Remember Conservatives, November 2, which is only 36 days away, is only the beginning. Hopefully we can regain enough seats to put the brakes on Barack's socialist agenda, but we have to keep working hard. It's a marathon rather than a sprint, so we have to make sure we don't get too excited and burn ourselves out.

We have to have a strong, unwavering, steady pace for the 2012 and 2014 elections. Our numbers are growing by leaps and bounds daily. Why else do you think the lefties are panicking and resorting to slander and demeaning phrases to describe us? They are simply scared of us and have nothing but emotion and fear on their side to fight back with.

We have to remain vigilant and remember what happened in two short years when we let our guard down. We certainly don't want a repeat of the Obama, Reid, Pelosi fiasco.

Only 21 days to go! I'm getting excited and nervous at the same time. On the one hand, I know there will be tremendous conservative gains in both houses of Congress. Every day, races that were either secure or semi-safe for Democrats are now either a tossup, solidly, or leaning Republican (most of the time a conservative Republican).

As a matter of fact, on Wednesday, for the first time, Republican candidates lead in the polls in 10 Senate races! That would have been unheard of only one month ago. You probably didn't know that. The press likes to be one-sided in its "reporting."

On the other hand, what worries me is that it is Halloween season and you can be sure that liberal Republicans and almost all of the Democrats will be putting on their conservative-type disguises, attempting to lie, deceive, and do whatever is necessary to put politics over principle to win or hold onto their seats.

Liberals know they have to walk and talk like a conservative and pretend to support conservative values in order to have any chance of winning an election.

Unfortunately this has worked for them in the past, and I worry that too many voters will actually believe all the sound bites (libs have resorted to some of the most blatantly false and misleading campaign ads, worse than ever before) and false promises (lies?) rather than judge the candidates by their records during their term(s) in office.

Just look at all the lies and fake promises their grand role model made during his campaign. Enough so that 68 percent of voters in the 18 to 25 age group and 69 percent of the voters in the 26 to 30 group swallowed all the lies in 2008. I can guarantee you that these groups won't fall for the lies again in this and the next election coming in 2012.

Just listen and watch all the Democrats scurry away from Pelosi, Reid and the grand deceiver of them all, Barack Obama. Boy oh boy, they are really huffing and puffing and declaring their independence from these radical leftists while their past shows them supporting all their leaders' failed policies for the last two years.

They can't run away from the fact that most were in favor of cap and trade, a much liberalized immigration policy, and they voted for the non-stimulating stimulus bill ($787 billion which took unemployment from under 8 percent to now well over 9.5 percent), the disastrous Obamacare health plan and other unpopular, foolish Obama proposals.

Talk about liberal candidates rebranding themselves. The only thing they can't hide are the hole marks left from the nose ring that Pelosi, Reid and Obama had them on a leash with, and they will willingly put this ring back on and be water boys once again soon after the election.

You can run, RINOs (Republicans in Name Only) and Democrats, but you can't hide any longer. The day of reckoning is upon you, and none of the big three will or can help you in your travails.

Obama's coat tails? Where are they? As a matter of fact where is the coat? Obama is simply bad news. Why do you think Democrat candidates are avoiding him like the plague and not asking him to campaign in their district? Every time he does their candidate loses.

It must be frustrating for Barack. All he ever really had going for him was his campaigning skills, and he doesn't even have these any more.

By the way, thanks to all of you who asked for a copy of the tape and timeline showing the Bush Administration's innocence with the home foreclosure disaster as they repeatedly warned Congress about Fannie and Freddie while Maxine Waters, Barney Frank and Chris Dodd staunchly defended them.

Predictably, not one request for these two items came from a lefty liberal. These people have only one thing going for them; they are ridiculously loud yet vacuous. Instead of even considering what the truth might be, they continue to harangue people with their lies, distortions, snobbery and condescension.

They could have easily asked to see the same proof other people asked to see, but instead they felt more comfortable with their heads in the sand, raising up once and a while (too often actually) to spout their nonsense. They also are about to become even more insignificant than they are already and they are afraid.

Keep moving forward conservatives. We and the country are winning and are On The Right Side.

It's hard to believe that there are only seven days left until the upcoming watershed election takes place. Only a month ago it was believed to be an uphill struggle just to capture 39 House seats and flush Nancy Pelosi. Now, poll after poll estimates that Democrats could lose between 80 to 102 seats. Also, the Senate is now in play where just a short time ago that was also considered an impossible event. Could it be possible to also unseat Harry Reid?

Every two years I have an election night get-together party at my home with a few friends, and some students who belong to the College Republican Club on campus. It was a rather depressing time back in 2008 but this time it's going to be entirely different. It is a good thing I have a late class on Wednesday as I'm going to savor every last moment this time.

But please don't become complacent yet. Keep on talking to as many people as you can between now and the Nov. 2.

What we have been doing so far is having impressive results as indicated in the first paragraph. It also helps that Obama is constantly shooting himself in the foot. His approval rating has dropped another 4 points in a recent Reuters-Ipsos poll, a new low, and this also happened over only a one month period. It simply shows that sane, logical people are starting to see through all the smoke and mirrors.

You should be ashamed of yourself if you don't make the effort and get out to vote this time. This election is too important for you not to. Even though it looks like it will be a landslide of epic proportions, if people just assume it will happen automatically and enough voters lazily decide to sit this one out, they could be sorely mistaken and all those hard fought efforts could be for nil. To all you conservatives and independents out there, please, please vote.

Obama has certainly lost his rock star status in two short years. Have you noticed that the cameras don't show the size of the groups he reads to anymore? It must be tough for his ego to handle. Yet he will always have a handful of delusional individuals who will be blindly loyal to him. They remind me of the teens and preteens, who screamed with delight when Elvis shook his hips or when the Beatles first came to America and these teenagers, screamed, swooned, and fainted.

There are actually people out there who think that he has accomplished many good things and that ObamaCare is really one of those things. They are still talking about the impossible to measure "saved jobs" or that his socialist agenda has actually softened the effects of the recession when just the opposite is true. We would have been in recovery long before this time if his incompetence wasn't allowed to create the policies he has pushed through Congress.

Also, you have people out there resorting to plain and simple lies. We now hear that there are all these secret billionaires out there that actually created, and are presently training, all the Tea Party members and their events. These people will never be reached and are best ignored. They do, however, push more and more independents to the conservative side of center.

I guess it is hard for them to explain away is why none of the Democrats in trouble are running on Obama's record or policies. Also, I wonder why the rock star or his right hand man hasn't been invited to campaign with these same incumbents who are in trouble. It's getting harder and harder to distinguish between Barack and the bumbling Joe Biden.

Maybe some of you ought to Google a few columns and see if you can explain away these facts. One of them is "Why Texas Has the Jobs," a Rich Lowry piece. If you want to read about how ObamaCare is already having disastrous results you should read Sally Pipes' column, "Killing our Choices." If you want to read about yet another Obama lie uncovered (by himself actually) read Jonah Goldberg's "A Shovel-Unready Prez."

As to the people with the ridiculous conspiracy theories and the same, old, tired lies of privatizing Social Security and the like, those individuals are too far gone. Just ignore them.

Only seven more days before we turn our attention to 2012. I'm looking
forward to a new challenge

Not a bad Tuesday. Not bad at all. Historic gains for conservatives and disastrous results for the liberals. Sure, there were some disappointments but all we have to do is come up with better candidates next time.

Now remember, the libs are certainly going to try to spin these election results positively so as to save face. This will be quite amusing to watch. They will probably focus on the Senate and call it a positive that we "only" gained 6 Senate seats. Before they gloat too loudly over that "victory," I think it would be best for them to remember that only a third of the Senate seats were up for election this year. In 2012, only 10 Republican seats will be on the slate with only one truly vulnerable. On the other hand, the Democrats have 23 seats up for re-election with at least 10 senators vulnerable. Anybody want to take bets on who wins the Senate next time?

And speaking of the Senate, even though the Republicans hold 46 seats, do you really think the senators coming up for re-election will continue to drink Obama's Kool- Aid? All we need is for five Democrats to see the light and realize what happened to a lot of their colleagues when they followed their Dear Leader and master ideologue. We might get more positive legislation passed than we thought possible after all.

Hey libs, do you still think this Tea Party thing is just an angry, racist, small fringe element and inconsequential? I hope you secular progressives keep thinking that way. We have been awakened; we easily have the numbers, and will no longer be the silent majority.

You Republicans have been given a second chance. Don't blow it this time. You say you realized the error of your ways, but you only have two years to prove it. If you lied to us to get elected then you will be flushed along with more liberals and Obama in two short years.

All you have to do is continue to listen to the voice of the people who put you in power, legislate accordingly, and you will see success similar to 2010 happen in 2012. You have been derisively labeled "the party of no," and it seems people are ok with that. Just be ethical, moral, and hold true to conservative principles, and the liberals won't get another chance to ruin the country.

As unbelievable as it seems, Obama still can't grasp the concept that this election rejected him. Instead of seeing his policies have been terrible failures, he still thinks the only problem was that people were too stupid to know what was really good for them and he only did a poor job in communicating. You can now add arrogance and a condescending attitude to his inexperience and incompetence. But that's ok Barack. Please just keep thinking that way and we will only have to put up with you for two more years.

Do you honestly think Obama will actually concede and let the Republicans in on the decision making? Even though the Republicans have had plenty of good, alternative ideas, they haven't even been allowed to be a part of the discussions. Barack isn't going to change his stripes, so all you can hope for is to block his socialist agenda, stopping him and his liberal cronies dead in their tracks. You know that anything the party recommends that comes close to a conservative agenda will be rejected and vetoed by the temporary occupant of the White House.

As shown by last week the people are fine with that. All we have to do is stop Obama from further ruining this country and in two years we can begin to move the country forward with a positive agenda.

And can you believe this Nancy Pelosi? She doesn't think all that happened to her party had a thing to do with her. She is actually going to run for the minority leadership position. If the House Democrats are going to allow her to continue to be their leader then they are dumber that I thought.

On the other hand it won't be a bad thing for us. You run, girl, and you Democrats run along right behind her. You still haven't learned from the painful results and you are going to be "shellacked" again. Don't forget to keep the Kool-Aid handy. However, you still have time to see the light and get "On The Right Side."

How Will GOP Deliver All Of Its Promised Cuts?

People are constantly coming up to me and saying, "Now that you conservatives have the reins, how are you going to come through with all the cuts you promised? It's easy to get elected by saying you're going to cut spending, shrink the federal government, and balance the budget, so let's hear the plan."

I sometimes wonder if these people are simply liberals who are being snide because they have just suffered embarrassing, historic losses (thank you Democrat congressmen for not learning anything and re-electing Pelosi as your Minority Leader) or rather people who really want to know how we are going to go about accomplishing these goals. Actually, I'm sure it is some of both.

I hope these individuals asking me this question are intelligent enough to realize that it is a process, a mind set, and it certainly isn't going to be accomplished overnight. It is also going to involve short-term pain. Pain always accompanies a healing process. Everyone has to share in the sacrifices.

Therein lies the problem. Give a liberal a dollar and then later ask for a dime back and he will squeal like a stuck piglet. All they want to do is climb back and continue suckling on the teat of the federal sow and think of a reason to ask for another dollar.

Another thing to emphasize is that Congress can't be trusted. Before there is even any talk of raising taxes (which really shouldn't be necessary), Congress must come through with the spending cuts. Remember when the Democrat controlled Congress promised President George H. W. Bush that if he would allow increased taxes Congress would match that with spending cuts? He made the mistake of trusting them.

The next thing to remember is that it was originally intended for most of the power to belong to the states. States should assume the responsibility for the well being of its citizens. The federal government should keep its nose out of about 90 percent of what it is doing and what the Constitution gives it no authority to do.

Lastly, the starting point is to go from a general strategy to specific actions. How about starting with no new spending, no new programs, no new bureaucracies, and no new government jobs.

Sorry Michelle, your new anti-obesity initiative shouldn't even see the light of day. How many times must one repeat that that is an example of a power that belongs to the individual states. Should I say it more slowly?

However, in this case common sense dictates that this particular responsibility falls on the parent.

There are a lot of good areas to explore. The libs love to take an idea and pooh-pooh it as not being a drop in the bucket. For example, when it is suggested to eliminate earmarks the libs will remind you that it will ONLY save $14 billion. You mention a federal program that no one has ever heard of and they say that will ONLY be a $5 billion savings.

Aren't they intelligent enough to realize that all these ONLY amounts start adding up to something big in pretty short order? You have to look at it as a process, a series of steps, and not just one huge leap. Remember how they use the same strategy of not deporting illegal aliens? They say it can never be done. There are just too many. When they ask how can it possibly be done, the answer is pretty simple.....one illegal at a time.

Then they bring up and try to impact peoples' emotions. They begin to talk about our responsibility to the poor. Any American knows that there has to be a safety net for the unfortunate, and it is most certainly our responsibility to care for these people. Don't forget to throw in the word "temporary," however.

You read all the time about third generation welfare recipients. These people have no concept of the word "work." How long is long enough? One year, two years, more? As I mentioned above, at some time the person has to be removed from the government teat and stand on his or her own two feet. If you want to see real poverty come with me to Romania, Bulgaria, Albania or any other third world country.

The next column will look at the U.S. Government Deficit Reduction Commission and their preliminary report. There are a lot of good ideas listed in this report. However, listen carefully. I can hear the squealing beginning already.

If We Cheat On Taxes, Will IRS Censure Us?

It's hard to believe that my previous column represented my 5th full year of writing for The Daily Star. That's around 120 columns (I missed a few times), 100,000 words, hundreds of supporters and a bunch of ticked off secular progressives.

It is impossible to run out of ideas, and there are a lot of topics I still want to write about but haven't yet had the chance. I must admit, however, that the submission deadline has been creeping up on me faster and faster, and I find myself procrastinating more and more.

But back to the latest news. This time it involves that crook Charlie Rangel, just the latest of a string of dishonest Democrats bringing embarrassment to their colleagues. He was just censured by his fellow House colleagues when in all actuality he should have been expelled from Congress and then prosecuted for all his brazenly intentional misdeeds that took place over many years.

Wouldn't it be nice if we could commit all kinds of ethical lapses and cheat on our taxes like Rangel did and only have to stand before an IRS panel and be chastised for a half hour or so? Also, after this "censure" we could go on and pretend nothing had happened while we suffered no further consequences.

My, what an actor Charlie has been over the last week or so. First he was all smiles and not worrying one bit about what was going to happen to him. After all, Nancy Pelosi, that old self-proclaimed swamp cleaner, was going to continue to ignore the facts for a little while longer. All his misdeeds were going on under her surgically perfected nose and she hadn't done a thing about it for the last four years so why should she start now?

She also stalled the ethics hearings on Rangel for over 60 days so that he would not be a distracting and embarrassing element during the then upcoming 2010 elections. After this, all of a sudden, the push was on to have the hearings take place as soon as possible before a Republican was appointed head of the ethics committee.

Alas, it was to no avail. He tried everything from talking about his heroism from 60 years ago (as a matter of fact, he kept bringing this up until people were beginning to get nauseous), then he kept shrugging it off as if it was no big deal. He tried the brazen approach when he chastised the committee for not giving him enough time to prepare (the investigation had been going on for over two years) and not giving his entire 60 year record the appropriate respect.

After the bluster strategy, he tried the whining approach and then even turned on the tears to see if that gained him any sympathy.

Maybe he finally quit because of the 4,200 pages of evidence the committee had. Maybe it was because the committee attorney presenting the case said there wasn't even the need to call any witnesses since the evidence was so damning.

Whatever the reason, the embarrassment should now switch to the House itself and its members. The evidence was so stacked against him the House should have been voting for expulsion rather than censure, but it circled the wagons around a colleague and only voted to censure him. Even then there were 79 representatives who voted to not even hit him with censure, even when the evidence so clearly proved his guilt. These people are going to have to be the next to be evicted from Congress in 2012. I'm sure some of them also served on the O.J. Simpson jury and voted not guilty.

We the people are going to have to continue to take matters into our own hands and take out the trash ourselves come election time. Charlie Rangel is an embarrassment to himself, his colleagues, and his country, and should be sitting in jail this very moment. Let's hope this still could happen.

Atheists' Numbers Doom Them To Irrelevance

Atheists are once again trying to bring attention to themselves by attempting to denigrate, insult or demean religions and, in particular, Christianity and therefore Christians.

This time it is a billboard advertising stunt in New Jersey; the billboard was placed there by some atheist activist group that calls itself American Atheists. Once again their attempt to put down Christianity will be doomed to irrelevance.

Polls show atheists to be 3 percent or less of the total population of the United States, a number that has remained about the same over past years. However, in a desperate attempt to make the number appear higher, the president of this organization now claims that there are many more "closet atheists." He goes so far to say that there are many who attend religious services during the holidays but don't believe in them. Kind of pathetic if you ask me.

Fortunately, the country is headed back on the right track to sanity. A few years ago only 20 percent of the nation's top companies dared to make any mention of Christmas in their stores. A great many were simply intimidated by the ACLU or similar organizations. The number mentioning Christmas has reversed itself and is now up to 80 percent and continuing to rise. It's also nice to see the Salvation Army bell ringers back in places where they were previously banned.

Why are atheists so afraid of Christianity that they feel they have to go out and aggressively attack it every year around this time? Why don't you instead proudly proclaim your "atheistic religion" and explain all the reasons and research that led you to your stance. Maybe you can't? Maybe your choice was made out of laziness and you didn't even give religion a chance? Are you going to give your children the right to choose?

Tell you what; why don't you pick a day, any day, call it Atheist Day, and spend the day celebrating your atheism. Get yourself an atheist tree, exchange atheist gifts and have a great atheist meal. Call all the other atheists you know (won't take long) or send them a card and exchange happy atheist wishes.

Since you believe that there is no being more supreme than yourself (a rather egocentric viewpoint), you can celebrate you by staring at yourself (or small groups staring at each other) in the mirror all day. Isn't this a better idea than going around and putting other religions down? At least you are doing something more positive for yourself if you follow my strategy for you.

We Christians are on the Right Side of this issue. Atheists have no real beliefs; they just want to tear down one more long standing tradition and belief. How can they claim that a baby in a manger, a Cross, a Christmas tree or some innocent Christmas songs cause them untold suffering and still keep a straight face? And then they tell the rest of us to be more sensitive to their feelings. Wrong atheists; you are the ones who need the sensitivity training sessions. Your claims of hurt and pain are bordering on the side of ridiculousness.

As has been shown over the past few years, Christians can make their feelings known by voting with their feet and their wallets. As much as the atheists hate to admit it, their impact is becoming smaller each year. Remember the movie "The Passion of The Christ"? It is now No. 15 of the top 1,000 grossing films of all time in the United States. On the other hand, Bill Maher and his classic film, "Religulous," is number....well, I can't find it on the list. As a matter of fact, I wonder if it even covered its costs. I think it was popular for about three weekends. Examples like this abound.

The same thing holds true for retailers. Whose business do they want? Do they want 3 percent of the population frequenting their stores or a much larger percentage? I think the answer is obvious when you look at all the establishments who realized they made a huge mistake a few years back and have since rethought their positions.

Even though I do push back hard against you atheists, I still hope you will rethink your position and change before it's too late. You are making the biggest mistake of your lives by not at least giving religion a serious try. In the meantime I wish you a Merry Christmas and I will be praying for you.

It's getting rather tiresome to hear the same old chanting from the left, the liberals, and the free spending politicians. "Tax the rich! Tax the rich! I've got a better mantra for you. How about "It's not my money"?

Aren't you a little ashamed of the self-demeaning characteristic of being jealous or envious of those people who have worked hard, sacrificed or had good fortune?

Are you also envious of people who have nicer homes, drive nicer cars, and take better vacations? It's time to focus more on yourself and stop being so bitter. I know lots of entrepreneurs who have sacrificed, taken risks and who have succeeded and yes, some who have failed. I, for one, look up to those individuals.

Sure, you can think of an example where it seems a person who is undeserving of the wealth he or she possesses. Take, for example, Paris Hilton. Sure, she is a bubblehead. She didn't even graduate from high school; she dropped out her junior year. Sure, she contributes nothing of any worth to society. But it still has nothing to do with you. She was just fortunate to be born with the right last name.

But for every Paris Hilton there are thousands of individuals who have worked hard and made sound choices to get where they are today, and yes, have probably accumulated a sizeable amount of wealth as a result. Good for them.

Who are you to decide how much that person should earn or how much you think they should be allowed to accumulate or inherit? Well, you say, "the rich can afford to pay more." That makes absolutely no sense whatsoever. Take Bill Gates for example. Yes, he is worth a lot but do any of you have any idea of the size of the industry he created, the number of jobs and the amount of wealth he is responsible for? I thought America was supposed to be the land of opportunity. Maybe Mr. Gates shouldn't pay any taxes at all. And look at all the good things he does for charity, education and other such causes.

Even though the statistics will fall on deaf, liberal, leftist ears, they are worth repeating. The top 1 percent are responsible for 38.2 percent of all personal income taxes paid (tax year 2008 statistics). The top 5 percent pay a total of 58.72 percent. Isn't that enough?

On the other hand the bottom 50 percent of AGI taxpayers pay only 2.7 percent of the total. Should they decide how much someone else should pay? They are getting all the freedoms, all the liberties, and all the opportunities available in this great country of ours and are paying a ridiculously small amount or nothing for these privileges. I'll say it again; stop being envious.

You don't think the federal government taking 35 percent of every dollar earned is enough? Come on, folks, get real, that's enough. As a matter of fact, it's way too much.

The problem is on the spending side of the equation. Hopefully, with the new Congress and the 2012 elections coming up in less than two years, we can put a stop to the spending hemorrhaging going on that the present administration and Congress is responsible for. For the next two years I will be proud to be the party of "no" if it means stopping the Obama socialist free spending, big government agenda dead in its tracks.

One more tiresome issue. I can take a second grader and tell him that tax rates are going to be the same this year as they were the previous year. He certainly wouldn't see that as a tax cut for the rich. And the libs say these "tax cuts" will create an additional $700 billion deficit in our budgets. Only the mind of a leftist liberal thinks this way. The problem is that the Democrat controlled congress has spent the money before the issue was resolved.

I wish I had enough space to talk about the equally ridiculous notion of taxing the rich, mean corporations. Who do you think ends up paying all the corporation taxes? You do.

It has been estimated that 22% of the price we pay for consumer products represents embedded taxes. Our corporate tax rates are already among the highest in the industrial world. Corporations aren't relocating overseas because of greed. The government's burdensome regulations, unions, and high tax rates are chasing them away. Come on libs, think before you speak. Get On The Right Side.

Obama's Tactics Won't Work A Second Time

Unfortunately I was in Romania when Obama made his State of The Union Speech. If I wanted to watch it live I would have had to stay up until 4 a.m. I certainly wasn't about to do that. Maybe for the Super Bowl but definitely not for Barack.

When I returned home I was feeling kind of guilty, so I watched a replay. It was exactly what I expected. Miraculously, he had become a reformed moderate and seemed to promise everyone his far left liberal days were over. It's the same tactic he took to get himself elected and I guess he thought it would work again. I thought maybe I was watching his first campaign speech for the 2012 elections.

Unfortunately, Barack (for you that is, not for the country) it's not going to work this time. Your soaring rhetoric and charismatic charm dazzled a lot of people the first time, but you have lost a lot of those prior supporters, simply because they have seen that you were untruthful about everything you were promising in 2008.

It worked the first time when you had people totally ignoring your past track record of being the Senate's most liberal senator, having no experience, abstaining on many Senate votes (what leadership), and no history that proved you had the competence to sit in the White House. How much of the youth vote do you think you're going to get this time after they have watched you on your foolish spending spree, which yielded no results but saddled them with an impossible-to-pay future debt burden?

I can't wait to hear you explain the $3 trillion additional debt you created in only your first two years, bringing the total up to $14 trillion, and most of this debt is owed to the Chinese. I seem to remember when you called the $8.3 trillion debt limit requested by President Bush "a sign of leadership failure."

How about the $1.4 trillion budget deficit you have saddled the country within just your first year. How about the failed trillion dollar stimulus bill to create jobs yet unemployment went from 7.8 percent to well over 9 percent (I think it peaked at 9.8 percent) with no sign of lessening? The only policies that have worked for you have been those that were a continuation of President Bush's policies. You remember him don't you? The guy you loved to blame all your failures on. Rational people are seeing through that strategy as well.

Let me teach you a lesson. Government doesn't create jobs, Barack, all governments create are bureaucracies.

No, Barack, your days are numbered. You have called in all your chits, and no one trusts you anymore.

You are so caught up with yourself that you don't even see yourself - or the Democrat leaders of Pelosi and Reid - to blame for the historic shellacking your party took this last November. The three of you gave the Republicans (mostly conservatives) 63 seats in the House of Representatives and six more Senate seats so your majority there went from filibuster-proof to now only 53 to 47.

Even better news is the 2012 elections will allow further gains in the House as conservatives find better candidates to run. The Senate picture is looking pretty rosy also. Of the 33 Senate seats coming up for election in 2012, 23 are Democrats and only 10 are Republican. It is estimated that only 8 of the Democrat seats are safe, and 12 are from states that went Republican in 2008. The other three are toss ups. Do you really think your slim majority in the Senate will hold up in as those vulnerable senators fight for their political lives?

So, Barack, your political career is coming to a rapid end. It does not matter what you say anymore or how well you say it since you have proven yourself to be dishonest. Remember all the times you or your minions have called the Republicans enemies who "should be punished" and arrogantly told them to passively sit in the back? How about when you said they (the Republicans) bring a knife to a fight and you'll bring a gun? What civility Barack; what bipartisanship.

But we conservatives can't afford to rest. We have plenty of facts of his failures to keep reminding centrists and independents that they didn't get what they thought they were getting and not to make the same mistake again. I can assure you that there are vast numbers of individuals who are having voter remorse.

Yes, I became very distrustful and suspicious very early on in his speech. I think it was when his lips started moving.

Riding Into The Sunset While On The Right Side

It's time. After almost 5½ years and 130-plus columns I am going to call it a career. I had originally considered doing this sooner, but there was no way I was going to miss the fun of the 2010 elections. It's only fair to let someone else enjoy writing the column for the 2012 celebration.

I would never have imagined that I would get the huge number of supporters and new friends that I have over the last five years. This little local newspaper has an unbelievable reach.

I have received feedback from all 50 states and four foreign countries. Several columns appeared on Lucianne.com; one on illegal aliens was read on national radio, and most enjoyable was when my column was reprinted (without permission) on the website of Mr. atheist, Darwin lover, secular progressive, himself, Richard Dawkins.

Because of that posting, I was able to antagonize a very large number of Dawkins disciples. Just go to his website, type "Sears" in the search window and have a bunch of laughs. His disciples seem to be very unstable people.

I remember when I first bounced the idea of "retiring" off Daily Star Editor Sam Pollak. It was back in August when I mentioned the idea, and he talked me out of it by saying, "Look at it this way, there are a lot of liberals you haven't ticked off yet."

It was a convincing response since it had been a lot of fun causing liberals such apparent angst. My, how they rant and rave. I wonder if they punch the walls and kick their pets around. I know they dislike immensely what I have to say, but they keep on reading, now don't they? There have been about ten regulars who have provided about 90 percent of the negative feedback.

I have to sincerely thank Sam for giving me the opportunity to write the column. I remember the first time he called me with the offer. I wasn't sure if I wanted to do it.

The first person I went to was my brother, who told me I would be crazy not to accept the offer. He was right, but it is rather pathetic that there are individuals who have gotten angry with my family members and relatives simply because of me. Again, very pathetic people.

I hope Sam doesn't regret his decision to recruit me, but he is a man whose word can be totally counted on. I remember early on when he told me he didn't agree with me 99 percent (maybe it was 100 percent) of the time, but he would staunchly defend my right to say what I felt was important.

He never once went back on his word. He is an honorable man and a friend I know I can count on. I do have to apologize for the number of angry phone calls and letters he must have received because of me.

Conservatives everywhere should write to Sam and thank him for trying to bring balance to the newspaper. I don't think people appreciate or realize the efforts he has made to bring more balance to The Daily Star.

Lastly, I couldn't be happier that Sam, in his wisdom, selected Chuck Pinkey as my replacement. I have known Chuck for about 1½ years, but I have been enjoying his classified ad section mini-columns for a number of years. I have found him to be a very honorable man, a rock-solid conservative who will not be intimidated by anyone (especially a liberal), and a good friend. I would have never met Chuck had it not been for this column. The baton has been passed to a very capable person.

But please don't take Chuck for granted. I know from experience that support in the form of phone calls, e-mails, and giving feedback in person will be greatly appreciated by him. Remember, he is stepping up to the responsibility of carrying the banner of conservatism publically, and he will certainly receive lots of abuse.

I am leaving with mixed emotions. I know I will miss writing the column but at the same time will appreciate all the free time I will now have. Just remember, fellow conservatives, facts and logic are on our side. The left has nothing to fight back with other than emotions. We will be successful in taking back our country but only if we continue to stay involved and stick together.

Part of the fun of writing my columns is the feedback I received. Although 98 percent of the feedback is positive and supportive, I do get some that are pretty vicious. I have had some e-mails run 4 to 5 pages in length and pretty much are simply rabid rantings. Let me give you some examples:

My columns on atheism made it to the web site of Mr. Atheist himself, Richard Dawkins. I received a lot of responses from those people and some were pretty nasty (predictably, they were all unsigned):

"Tell me Mr. Sears, was the ocelot, depicted on this card, presented by God (1) Clapping his hands, (2) Willing it, or (3) Another means? You have nothing."

"F*** YOU! Stop writing articles attacking atheists and go celebrate your stupid f***ing holiday. I am the kind of atheist that works tirelessly to demote your bull**** worldview because I know that you won't stop your hate mongering until there are none of us left.
I am your enemy and I am better than you because I see right through you.
I don't want you to think that I am just sending you an e-mail. I want you to fear your
religion and you aren't going to stop me. I'm coming"

"....there is really no reason to expect that an Accounting professor would be versed in religious history but, I would think that somewhere along your educational path you would have been exposed to the absurdities of religion, in general, and Christianity in particular."

"Congratulations on making yourself look like an educated dolt. I'm glad you are only a
professor of accounting, and not of something that people actually care about."

"Sir, you are the egocentric, not to mention arrogant, one in this scenario. It frightens me that your email comes from an educational institution. If you don't know the difference between fact and belief, perhaps you should cease to be lazy."

"When you have something intelligent to say, please do so. In the meantime, you are welcome to keep your dime store psychology to yourself."

"You are a sad pathetic person – stick to accounting."

"Psycho! This is truthfully THE most ridiculous article I have ever read. Quit spreading
your disinformation."

Enough from atheists. Here are some from other columns:

"You may be a professor but you are a very ignorant person to use the terms 'Environmental Crazies.' Your stupid grinning face is an eyesore in The Daily Star."

"I hope you don't get paid for your articles in The Daily Star because they suck just as much as you do. And you are teaching our youth at a private school, haha what a joke. Stop being an ass and start embracing change you moron!"

"I wonder how long it will be before you are impeached as a columnist after all the older stubborn closet confederates that soak up your brand of nonsense die off. A very robotic group of readers and listeners."

"….but remember that in the polls he put John McCain to shame. People all across this country voted 3 to 1 for Obama."

I had to remind him that the final vote was 53% to 46% and that 3 to 1 would be 75% to 25%. I told him that that was the problem with liberals. They were all emotion and no facts. When they do use facts they distort them in their favor. This person really didn't want to hear this and proceeded to go off the deep end.

"Buzz off prick. They should remove your section. It's stupid and it's only your view….Why don't you go back to Texas and kiss Bush's ass and thank him for us for what he put this country thru the last eight years…….Why don't you take that stimulus check you received and stick it up your candy ***"

He still wasn't done. "three words to say to you F*** YOU A******. Republican faggot"

"Here's MY solution to the problem….(and Very ecologically friendly)….PLANT A BUSH….6 feet down, where the sun NEVER shines….your ignorance is ONLY outweighed by your arrogance….but that tends to be the Republican way….and you carry that mantle of mental inability SO well!!!"

"Hilarious. The idiot conservative who mindlessly prattles off discredited nonsense about Hillary Clinton says someone ELSE can't think for himself. What a joke. Just like you are. And you are, as I said, nothing but a liar."

"So I suggest that you stick to what you know best: spread sheets and ledgers and leave the political analysis and commentary to your better-educated colleagues who may be able to discern the difference between the truth and threadbare right-wing propaganda."

See why I loved writing this column?